Money

Know More, Make More, Give More.

ROB MOORE

JOHN
MURRAY
LEARNING

First published in Great Britain in 2017 by Hodder & Stoughton. An Hachette
UK Company.
This edition published in Great Britain in 2018 by John Murray Learning.
Copyright © Rob Moore 2018
The right of Rob Moore to be identified as the Author of the Work has been asserted by
him in accordance with the Copyright, Designs and Patents Act 1988.
Database right Hodder & Stoughton (makers)
British Library Cataloguing in Publication Data: a catalogue record for this title is available
from the British Library.
Library of Congress Catalog Card Number: on file.
Trade Paperback: 978 1 473 64132 7
Paperback: 978 1 473 64133 4
eBook: 978 1 473 64134 1

5

The publisher has used its best endeavours to ensure that any website addresses referred to
in this book are correct and active at the time of going to press. However, the publisher and
the author have no responsibility for the websites and can make no guarantee that a site
will remain live or that the content will remain relevant, decent or appropriate.
The publisher has made every effort to mark as such all words which it believes to be
trademarks. The publisher should also like to make it clear that the presence of a word in
the book, whether marked or unmarked, in no way affects its legal status as a trademark.
Every reasonable effort has been made by the publisher to trace the copyright holders
of material in this book. Any errors or omissions should be notified in writing to the
publisher, who will endeavour to rectify the situation for any reprints and future editions.
Typeset by Cenveo® Publisher Services.
Printed and bound in Great Britain by Clays Ltd, Elcograf S.p.A.
John Murray Learning policy is to use papers that are natural, renewable and recyclable
products and made from wood grown in sustainable forests. The logging and manufacturing
processes are expected to conform to the environmental regulations of the country of origin.
Carmelite House
50 Victoria Embankment
London EC4Y 0DZ
www.hodder.co.uk

Contents

Money

For everyone who wants to make, grow and give more money. For everyone who wants to know the story, psychology and history of money, and the positive counter arguments to the mass negativity around money. For everyone who knows that you don't have to be evil to make money, you don't have to feel guilty to make money, and you don't have to be greedy to make money. For everyone who wants to learn, earn and love money, do things that matter with money, and use money to make a difference to others. This book is for you.

If it wasn't for you

If you're anything like me, you probably just want to dive into the nuts and bolts, and you don't want to read long Oscar speech-style thank yous.

So let's keep it short: thanks to Suneep, my amazing researcher, agent and friend, for his contributions to *Money*. To Heidi, my editor and proofreader, for her attention to detail while painstakingly editing the manuscript. Thanks to my publishers for listing the book for sale before it was written to force me to write it fast. Thanks to Mark Homer, my supportive and analytical business partner, who taught me how to manage money properly and learn the true meaning of 'tight-arse'. Thanks to Gemma, the love of my life, for giving me freedom and love, and helping me spend my money. To my beautiful kids who challenge me to grow and are so expensive that I have to be filthy rich just to keep them in school. To my teams at my companies who inspire me every day, and the Progressive, Unlimited Success and Disruptive Entrepreneur communities for your votes and suggestions in researching *Money*.

And thank you. Yes, you. You're committed, focused, inspired and you want to be better. You are willing to learn and grow and I'm very grateful to you for that, and for allowing me to be part of your amazing journey. And of course, you love money!

Rob Moore
The Disruptive Entrepreneur
https://www.facebook.com/robmooreprogressive
http://bit.ly/disentpodcast
https://twitter.com/robprogressive
https://www.instagram.com/robmooreprogressive/

SECTION I

Introduction

Thank you for having the faith in me to help you on your journey to money. I congratulate you for investing in yourself wisely. You are your best asset and pay yourself the best interest and return.

As a thank you I have some special gifts for you, very valuable and leverage-able – you'll find them at the end of the book. I am certain you will be one of the smaller percentage who reads this book from start to finish. After all, those who don't read have no advantage over those who can't read.

I

So you own a Ferrari?

The thing I remember most about growing up with my dad was how big the old brown £10 notes were that he held in his huge hands and kept in his back pocket. He'd always have a big bunch of them, folded in half with the Queen's head always facing in the same direction. He'd pay for everything in cash. He always liked getting a deal or discount, and he used to take me with him when he'd buy his new pubs, hotels and restaurants, and the fixtures, fittings and stock. He'd let me get a wholesale box of flumps when we went to the cash and carry, and I'd eat about 300 of them on the way home, looking up to my dad who I admired and wanted to be just like. Then I'd feel sick … but not because of the money!

My dad taught me to work and earn money from around the age of four. My first job was 'bottling up' at the pub, where I'd go down into the cellar, which was like a hidden cave – cold, damp and deep underground. I'd carry up the crates, barely able to see over them, with all the bottles that needed replacing on the shelf and in the fridge. He taught me how to get the maximum number of bottles crammed into the crate and to do it in the shortest possible time – I could replace most of the stock at 6am on a Saturday morning, after a packed-out Friday night, in around half an hour. Dad would pay me 50p and I could do this on Saturday and Sunday, as Mum wouldn't allow it on schooldays. I'd take the pound I'd earned over the weekend, probably around £956,000 now with inflation, to the local pound store and buy a framed picture of a car. They had all my favourites – Lamborghini Countach, Corvette, Ferrari Testa Rossa, Porsche 911, the old Mercedes Gullwing and more. I yearned for these pictures, and one by one bought them all and hung them on my bedroom wall. Back to the relevance of this in a moment. Dad also let my sister and me hoover and clean the bar. The carpet in the pub was brown and garishly patterned, and the great benefit of this was that if you dropped coins on it you couldn't see them easily. It's almost like my dad planned this, being from Yorkshire, and it was the perfect flycatcher for £1 coins dropped by the punters. Early on weekend mornings we'd get up, sing 'hunt for money, hunt for money', and find a nice little pouch of coins that we were allowed to keep. Dad used to say that wherever money was lying around I'd find it 'like a fly-to-shiiiite'. (That's a northern England 'uddersfield accent, in case you're wondering.)

As I grew up this desire to earn money grew too. The benefit of being brought up in pubs and hotels was that it forced both independence and enterprise at a very young age. We would often be left alone in the flats above the premises, and I loved the freedom this gave us. We had to fend for ourselves, and by the time I went to secondary school I'd learned to cook, clean, wash and iron, and bareknuckle fistfight my sister, amongst other valuable life skills. In my early teens I put a business proposal to my mum saying that if she wanted to 'leverage' the ironing out to me (I don't think I used the word leverage then), then I would do a large item for 20p, and pants and smalls for 10p. She accepted my proposal and I had my second start-up. I ironed my way through my teens while watching *Headbangers Ball* on MTV. Once I passed my driving test, dad used to send me shopping for pub essentials, and let me keep the change. I'd save it all and count it regularly.

Let's fast-forward about seven years to me aged 24. I'd been to university; I'd had a great time but had drunk away all my own and my parents' money. I had all these dreams and grand ideas, but Dad had fallen very ill, so my plans to take on the world were put on ice for a few months so I could come and help out back at my parents' pub in Peterborough. Four years later I was still there, and had amassed some debt – considerable personal, bad, deep debt. The mess I'd got myself into (more details of this later) came to a head when I was out with a friend one summer morning, likely with a filthy hangover, and a Ferrari F430 Spider drove past. The driver had the roof down, his tunes blaring and his nose in the air. Now, to that date, the car that I'd coveted more than any other was the Ferrari F430 Spider. It was like all the memories and emotions and desires through my childhood had been designed into that beautiful car: elegant lines, raspy exhaust, of course in 'rosso' red. As the car flew past I could see and feel all these images and emotions and desires in slow motion, and I turned to my friend and barked harshly:

'See that twat, he's a drug dealer.'

And then we went on our way to the pub.

And right there is a single sentence, the comment I made that day, that shows the absolute low point I had reached in terms of my attitude towards, and beliefs around, money, manifested in debt, bitterness and judgment. Once an open-minded, limitless child and then teenager, taught to value, earn and respect money, with big dreams to turn ideas into cash, I had changed into an envious, defeatist neghead with a confused relationship with money and more maxed-out credit cards than you could fit in Bill Gates's wallet, who stereotyped people by their possessions.

And what's worse is I didn't even know the guy driving the Ferrari.

That statement summed up in seven words everything that was wrong with me, about money. Though I didn't know it at the time, those seven words summed up everything that was wrong with the media, about money. Those seven words summed up the huge gulf between the wealthy and the poor, more in mindset than in skillset. And the strange irony continued when, between the ages of 30 and 31, I became a millionaire, and the first Ferrari I bought was that exact same F430 Spider in 'rosso' red. Now, before you judge me for good or bad, like I judged that Ferrari owner (though he could have rented it for the day), stay with me as we go on a journey from good upbringing around money to spiralling debt and bitterness and back again to sustained wealth.

My story is very much woven into yours. I've been poor and I've been rich, and you've been at least one of those two. I've made money and lost money, as have you. I started with no money, and that is the same for all of us once we pop out of the womb. I've had all the negative beliefs around money any other first-world-poor person (see the next chapter for more on this) has had, or still has, and I face the same challenges and opportunities as anyone else who is fortunate enough to have been raised in a land of opportunity such as the UK, the US or any other developed, first-world country.

When I judged in one instant the man who was driving (ironically) the car of my dreams, I was in that exact moment projecting onto him my personal, individual perceptions, beliefs and attitudes. This had nothing to do with him. I didn't know him, but I thought I knew people just like him. Now he could have been a future version of me who worked for and earned his money, dreams and Ferraris. He could have been a drug dealer. He could have been test-driving the car. He could have been hiring it for the day. He could have been a dentist, therapist or philanthropist. He could have been the salesman giving it a run in before a test drive with someone like me (now). But that's all irrelevant because there are all types of Ferrari drivers, and you can't stereotype them like I shamefully did. I will share all my personal negative beliefs about people with money that I had for 25 years (that were merely a manifestation of myself) later. I will also share every single belief that I've come across in educating over half a million people in wealth, and it is likely that you will relate to some of them. Maybe this is what has drawn you to this book? When I was 'first-world poor', I could not prove what Ferrari drivers were really like because I didn't know any. Now I know many, and indeed am one myself, though if you know me you'll know I crash them as easily as I drive them (more on that later).

2

First-world poor

An important distinction when discussing money, wealth and poverty is differentiating between 'first-world' poor and 'third-world' poor. I am truly lucky to have been born into a family that could afford running water and didn't have to walk 30 miles for it. I am truly lucky to have vaccinations and sanitization, a good healthcare system, a good policing system and a (mostly fair) capitalist free market society. I am lucky to have safety, ownership of my possessions and access to the world wide web of information and leverage of the Internet. How ungrateful would I be to blame and complain with this amazing opportunity and luck to be born into a good family, society and government? How shameful would it be to moan about a lack of opportunity? Many times in my poorer days I blamed or complained about these things, as I'm sure you have too. This type of behaviour repels wealth.

It is not true that we are all born equal. In the third world and even areas of the developed world, people are born into extreme poverty through no fault or choice of their own. They are pre-destined to be without basic human amenities and without the educational tools to access the free information online that we all enjoy in the first-world. Everyone else, however – you, me and most people we know – are born with equal and abundant opportunities. In addition to security and amenities, the Internet is virtually free and provides access to a limitless amount of information that we can use for self-improvement, as long as we have Wi-Fi. Moving through this book, the 'poor' will be referenced often, and this reference is towards the 'first-world' poor.

Those of us fortunate enough to have access to limitless opportunity could and should help those in the third world have their own fair share of opportunity, and we can help them if we choose to. We can become vastly wealthy and use this wealth to serve others in equal balance to serving ourselves. This book will cover that important part: the responsibility of how you can use money for good when you have it. But first you've got to make enough. So heed this advice from one who knows:

> If you are born poor it's not your mistake,
> but if you die poor it's your mistake.

Bill Gates

3

The land of the free market and opportunity

In the developed world and capitalist societies, you have what I consider to be an effective monetary system that creates fair (perfect) competition and freedom to set up your own enterprise, in conditions that support profit and growth. Of course Marxists will challenge this view, but I challenge back for even the most devout socialist to stick with me here. Most people complain that times are hard, the 'system' isn't fair, the time isn't right or the risk is too high. They cite taxes, greedy corporations and tycoons and other external factors as the reason they can't set up their own enterprise or make more money.

The free market, which we enjoy and I am grateful to have been raised in, is an economic system in which prices are determined by unrestricted competition between privately owned businesses. Buyers and sellers are enabled and incentivized, and can make the deals they want without any interference, except by the forces of demand and supply, and fair regulation. Businesses need and enjoy a free market so there are no restrictions or clawbacks on the profits they can make. The idea is that prices will self-regulate in line with supply and demand, increasing or decreasing in line with the current need.

The free market and the free price system make goods from around the world available to consumers and to you. Without the free market, you may not be able to access consumables or commodities, or you may be paying £97 for a pint of milk if there were unfair competition, unfair markets, monopolies, dictatorships or other non-free market conditions.

The free market gives the largest possible scope and opportunity to entrepreneurs, who risk time, capital and loss of secure earnings from a job to allocate resources to sell to and satisfy the future desires of the mass of consumers. The free market creates fair competition, which serves the consumer as efficiently as possible. Savings and investment can then be reinvested to develop capital goods and increase the productivity and wages of workers, thereby increasing their standard of living. The free competitive market also rewards and stimulates technological innovation, as the innovator is allowed a head start in satisfying consumer wants and needs by having more demand than supply. It then allows competition, which balances fairness, as profits and prices reduce to balance self-interest and service to the consumer (free markets, perfect competition and other monetary and economic concepts will be detailed in Section 4).

This is not anywhere near the case in the third world, or in dictatorships, communist societies, countries with a less-evolved government or in formal employment (where your boss can also be a dictator like I'm sure I've been accused of in the past!). This is my longwinded way of saying that we are fortunate enough to live in a land and society of immense opportunity, so let's all stop bitching and complaining and get out there. Create great products and services with fair profit margins that serve the pursuit of wealth and give great value to customers, clients and consumers. And sell shed loads of them.

4

What is *Money*?

In *Money*, we present a new concept, belief system and philosophy around money. The wealthiest people throughout history all have three things in common in the way that they have amassed vast and lasting wealth. One of those is an understanding of what money really is (and isn't). They are able to transcend any feelings of guilt or shame, or beliefs from their culture, religion or upbringing that they have towards money. They are able to rise above the hysteria and gain true understanding of the nature and meaning of money. One of the aims of this book is for you to gain this clarity of purpose too. Because once you really know what money is — a secret held by only a select few over the centuries — you too can amass money and wealth that could go from a minus number to having the same digits as a telephone number.

This book will give you a real, accurate and deep understanding of what money is, its purpose and history, as well as the system behind it, the natural and economic laws that govern it, how it flows and operates and how to leverage that knowledge to *make* more, *grow* more and *give* more. You will discover the balance of spiritual *and* material, the balance of attraction *and* action.

The *Money* philosophy provides a mindset, skillset and emotion overhaul and reprogramming. It is a monetary philosophy and a way of life to help you live to your highest purpose and vision, using money as the fuel and as a force for good, claiming your fair share and creating a lasting difference and legacy.

We all have deeply ingrained beliefs about money, impressed upon us by our surroundings as we grow up; these have shaped our worldview of money and wealth, and how much we have or lack, perceive or receive. This book will bust all the myths, lies, exaggerations, distortions, hidden secrets, agendas and one-sided falsehoods, and give counter-arguments to all the beliefs you may have held onto that could have (or actually have) held you back from more wealth and money.

Money is a book that states a positive claim to the great benefits personally and globally for *making* more, *growing* more and *giving* more. *Money* is a positively biased book on the benefits of wealth, and a book that counter-argues the media-driven one-sided view that money and wealth are bad and unfair: with proof and real-world application for start-ups, scale-ups and cock-ups (like I was in 2005).

If you are looking for a 'get-rich-in-five-minutes-super-quick' guide, then you are in the wrong place. If you are looking for a transient scheme or scam, that makes money at the top of the pyramid but doesn't last, then don't waste your time with this book. This book isn't called: *Money: Beg It, Borrow It, Steal It.* Though maybe I should trademark that?!

But if you are looking for a guide to 'get-rich-in-the-quickest-and-most-realistic-timeframe', then this book can help you. If you are looking for vast and lasting wealth and money that is sustainable, scalable and realistically attainable, then you have the right book and I am grateful that we have found each other.

Contrary to popular belief, you can be happy and make money. You can make money and be a great person, parent and partner. You can make money and make a difference. In fact, there is a chapter dedicated to exactly that, and this book will show you how to make one hell of a profit and still go to heaven;-)

5

What you can expect from *Money*

In this book, we will suggest and prove that you can simultaneously make money and make a difference, that you can serve others best by serving your own needs too, and that you can (and should) balance selfishness and selflessness for scalable and sustainable wealth. You really can have not just a love affair with money but a lifelong harmonious marriage of money and happiness.

This is not another self-help book about chants, affirmations, incantations and tapping, but a balanced view on how you can leverage the spiritual and material, embracing both attraction *and* action. It is not another hard-core textbook about economic theory from 1906 (there are smarter economists out there than me). It's an overview of the most relevant economic and financial concepts and laws that govern the world we live in, and how to leverage them for maximum sustained profit and contribution.

It is not a book that complains about the economy, the booms, busts and crashes, the self-prophesized cures to the cyclical problems, because it seems a delusion to me to search for a utopic equilibrium and think we can stay there. But this book will show how there is disequilibrium and ever-moving 'in-and-out-and-in-and-out' swings in any economy, any time over history and in the future, as proven as far as records date back. To me it is futile to attempt to change what cannot be changed, but it is agile and worthwhile to follow economic and universal laws to help you, me and as many people as we can to leverage existing systems for local and global wealth. You don't try to change the waves – you adjust the set of your sail.

In this book we present a mouldable money model that enables you to monetize and scale any passion or profession in its existing form, as economic and social landscapes evolve. You can expect to control and balance business and work, family and kids, passions and making a difference with giving back, on your terms, without sacrifice or decades of delayed gratification. You can do what you love and love what you do, merge your passion with your profession and your vocation with your vacation, while making one hell of a profit and one hell of a difference too.

Anyone who knows me knows I don't hold back. Someone has got to say what everyone wants to say, and really thinks, but doesn't and daren't and won't say, about money. If colourful language offends you, blunt directness and candour upset you and challenging convention makes you uncomfortable, you have been fairly warned.

If you were looking for a short book and a nice easy read, with no actions to take and no changes to make, then you just took the wrong pill. Buckle up. Hold on tight. It's going to be one hell of a ride, but I'm with you all the way.

The 'Disruptive Entrepreneur'

In this section we get to grips with the *Money* philosophy and look at how it will give you the time and freedom to do what you want, where you want, when you want, with whom you want, and how you can use it to help and share with others too.

6

A disruption in finance

In the fields of business, technology and money, we could be living through a time in which, in Darwinian terms, the fittest survive. Over recent years there has been a seismic shift towards less cash and more speed-of-light transactions through devices and chips. We are moving fast through an information age into what is likely to become a technology age, if it isn't already. The industrial age is well behind us. Anyone still relying on manufacturing or manual labour work for freedom, wealth and early retirement is vulnerable, overworked and underpaid. They got left behind years ago.

This technological age is fast – so very fast. Moore's Law (Gordon Moore's – not mine) indicates that the processing power of computers is going to double every two years. Gordon Moore, co-founder of Intel, observed that the number of transistors per square inch on integrated circuits had doubled every year since the integrated circuit was invented. This has a compound effect that gathers considerable momentum the longer it continues. In fact, Moore's Law has continued unabated for 50 years, with an overall advance of a factor of roughly 2^{31}, or 2 billion. This significantly affects money because it speeds up the flow, increases the number of forms and platforms and creates significant leverage (much of which will be detailed later in this book).

The world's fastest billionaires

Almost in the blink of an eye, global interconnectivity and disruptive monetary systems have enabled early adopters, innovators and entrepreneurs to gain massive wealth in shorter than ever timeframes. If you look at the fastest billionaires list, nine of the top ten according to The Hustle are post-1987.[1] The slowest of all, surprisingly, was

Bill Gates, who was also the oldest. Of the top ten, seven were online leveraging the Internet, including Jeff Bezos of Amazon, Mark Zuckerberg *and* Sean Parker of Facebook, the founders of eBay, Groupon and of course Google.

A money epidemic?

You can exchange money anywhere in the world, at the speed of light, from a small device you hold in your palm. In the future these transactions and exchanges will be through virtual reality, artificial intelligence, the Internet of Things, wearables, contactless, subcutaneous chips and weird and wonderful means we haven't yet dreamed up. All you need is Wi-Fi.

You can also start up a shop or business with no need for staff, inventory or stock, virtually no overheads, and on someone else's server or cloud. You can access a billion customers or followers for free across the globe as quickly as you can log on. You can leverage social and marketing platforms and media fast and for free. You can grow multi-million and billion pound enterprises aggregating other people's ownership, stock and responsibility. Alibaba.com, the world's largest e-commerce platform, holds no stock. AirBnB owns no hotels. Uber owns no cars. Facebook creates no content. Netflix owns no cinemas. Clever, hey?

Money for nothing

Social platforms that have made zero actual sales have floated for billions. Twitter's IPO (initial public offering) sold $14.2 billion of stock and there was no revenue model. Facebook raised $104 billion in its 2012 IPO before they added Facebook ads to their platform. These companies are selling 'ethereal promises' and 'future sales' for billions. Set up by teenagers living in sweaty student digs, coders and hackers are the new celebrity rich. Anyone can post a video and get millions of views if they have a strong enough opinion. And they can generate tens of thousands of pounds in ad revenue or sponsorship for videos, social media accounts and podcasts.

Our social and private lives are now in the public domain. We can get anything we want at the touch of a button. The gulf between the old and the new is widening further and further. Embrace the new technology age, or get left behind at an alarming and ever-increasing rate as the speed of technology compounds.

Moore's Law of acceleration has upsides and downsides. Embrace and leverage technology innovations and disrupt convention, and you will get the highest margins, growth and scale. But continually miss the boat and you will end up clinging to antiquated models in the hope that someone will come and save you. And so it is with money.

Paynuphobia

There's a lot of fear around the future of money. New research from PayYourWay.org.uk, the Payments Council's consumer education campaign, estimates that 26 per cent of people avoid using the latest payment methods due to security concerns.[2] These people even have a phobia named after them – 'paynuphobes'. More interesting is that only 25 per cent of people are scared of spiders. I think it is accurate to say that many people struggle to deal with change.

When contactless cards were introduced, a study by Ingenico found that just 13 per cent of consumers had ever owned a contactless-enabled debit or credit card, while just 5 per cent made a payment using one of these cards. It also found that 61 per cent of Brits are wary of using contactless cards as they do not feel they have been sufficiently informed about the technology. Forty-one percent said they didn't even know about it.[3]

This is all largely irrelevant now, as almost all of us take these payment methods for granted. You could argue there was a much more seismic shift going from cash, cheque and paper payments to early online payments than now when all the current digital currencies and payment methods are simply leveraging the Internet. The Internet was the biggest game changer, and that shift happened in 1990, which feels like 973 years ago now. So come on, embrace it my friend.

A cashless society?

There are also growing fears about a cashless society. My fear runs deeper: that I won't be able to bribe my five-year-old future-world number-one golfer son with real paper money any more.

People do fear that cash will be taken away and currency rendered worthless, all so that governments can control the flow and therefore increase taxes. I can't yet comment if this fear is well-founded, but let's join the dance between the authorities and the entrepreneurs and innovators for a moment.

According to the Payments Council, The Federal Reserve estimates that there will be $616.9 billion in cashless transactions in 2016.[4] That's up from around $60 billion in 2010. In Sweden, about 59 per cent of all consumer transactions are already cashless, and hard currency makes up just 2 per cent of the economy. In the UK in 2014, the proportion of cash payments made by consumers, businesses and financial organizations combined dropped to under half for the first time, to 48 per cent. Denmark, Sweden and Finland are the countries closest to a fully cashless society. The UK and the US would have to undergo some policy changes, but you can see the momentum shifting fast. Countries like Germany, Italy and Greece either don't have the infrastructure or culturally they accept these advancements more slowly. In Germany the word for 'debt' and 'guilt' are the same. I can imagine similar challenges and resistance that must have come about when moving from barter to coins and coins to paper and then the removal of the gold standard. So just how different is this?

We should be truly grateful for these amazing advances, count our blessings and fortunes, and engage with them. The story of money is simply repeating history in a different, more advanced and faster form. Disruption is the new order. The only constant is change.

In many countries or demographics across the developing world, the most vulnerable in a cashless society are the elderly, the non-digital savvy and the poor. This is a skills and training issue much more than it is a tech issue. For people who are homeless, there are fundamental problems about proof of status that go beyond mere up-skilling. Having no fixed abode renders establishing credit impossible and managing a bank account incredibly difficult. It's not like people who are homeless are going to start accepting crypto-currencies from passing strangers. While a lack of cash doesn't make one homeless, it has the potential to widen the gap between rags and riches. You have an amazing opportunity to embrace this disruption in money and make more, grow more and give more. This lag in the developing world also offers entrepreneurs huge growth areas and opportunities to solve bigger and more meaningful problems.

Disruption to the banking system?

Peer-to-peer or market-place lending platforms which connect borrowers and savers, such as Zopa, Funding Circle or Ratesetter, have changed the lending and access-to-capital landscape. The opportunity for growth on these platforms is phenomenal because they make borrowing and lending money faster, easier and more accessible to more people. They bring the crowd together. They increase convenience. They disrupt mature and more monopolistic industries. You should by now be spotting some commonalities in these disruptions that you can leverage in your own enterprise, ideas and income.

The Liberum AltFi Volume Index, which tracks peer-to-peer lending, puts cumulative lending in the UK at £4.3 billion. Not bad for a sector that is only celebrating its tenth anniversary.[5] You can access millions of individual lenders with individualized risk profiles, regulated and risk-reduced by crowd platforms, or lend your money though an app on your phone. You can have an idea for a business, take a few minutes to set up a Kickstarter campaign and then fund your start-up with all-or-nothing funding, which de-risks the lending environment. Nearly half of all Kickstarter campaigns have been successfully funded since inception. These didn't exist a decade ago. Just a little longer ago than that and you had to put on a suit, have a handkerchief to wipe the sweat off your face and go and beg to the bank manager.

Electronic and 'crypto-currencies'

Recent technology that's changing the game of money and the speed of movement is electronic currency. The best-known example is Bitcoin, a 'crypto-currency' that is digital or virtual in nature, based on cryptography. The concept has grown because it is difficult to counterfeit, and data can be 'hidden in plain sight'. It is organic in nature and is not issued by any central authority. This renders it (theoretically) immune to government or corporate interference or manipulation.

As currency becomes personal and not institutional, the landscape has potential for huge change and disruption. Transaction ease and speed are obvious, and this speed and leverage reduce overheads and so can challenge bank margins. Trade cost reduction results in increased trading and speed. Increased trade brings about increased economic growth, and the potential for economic growth in a future of frictionless money transfer is vast. Banks act as a friction on money because they control it, slow it down and add transactional costs, all of which can be removed by crypto-currencies.

If some people are concerned that cashless societies give control and power to governments and central authorities, then the authorities themselves have the fear and risk of money laundering and tax evasion through these same entities. The very platforms that give us online and data security have the power to hack us and steal our identities. The disruptive qualities of these innovations by nature make them volatile and, as we will discuss later, for money to operate in *any* form or function there has to be trust. Trust comes with proof and time. How close are we really to a completely digital financial world? Closer than you may think…

Subcutaneous chips and bio-hacking

The disruption has only just started, both in this book and in the world at large. At a bio-hacking company in Sweden, RFID (radio-frequency identification) chips, about the size of a grain of rice, are being implanted in people's hands. At first they will operate doors and photocopiers, then they will allow payment at the café, and then what? Many people in technology believe there is no doubt that more sophisticated chips will soon replace wearable technology such as fitness bands or payment devices, and that we will soon get used to being 'augmented'.

The future-future, now

In my podcast 'The Disruptive Entrepreneur' I interviewed Kevin Kelly, founding editor of *Wired* magazine, noted participant in cyber-culture and author of many futuristic books including *The Inevitable*[6], which examines the deep trends of the next 20 years. The two main future trends that Kelly feels are coming (and are here) are AI (Artificial Intelligence) and VR (Virtual Reality). I learned a lot interviewing Kevin, and while already keenly interested in how the future affects and drives business, enterprise and money, this sent me wild with excitement and a hunger to learn as much as I could. I feel the more you learn about the future (and future now), the more you can positively affect your own future. Anything that serves humanity can be turned into vast wealth and money, because money serves humanity. A block of flats has recently been 3D printed, as has a man's ribcage and sternum; drug warlords have created drones that can pack 1000 kilos of drugs; and you can buy a fridge with a brain.[7]

AI, VR and IoT

Artificial Intelligence is intelligence exhibited by machines that is developed through computer systems. Anything electrical can in theory gain intelligence – even your car can have a brain! A future where every electronic device has AI and tracks data, behaviour and is able to make decisions is not far away at all. Your fridge will be doing it, as will your wearable or even your subcutaneous chip. Your phone already is 'smart', and knows more about you than you might wish to believe. And if you move early and fast enough, as a disruptive entrepreneur, you will find a way to get money flowing through all of these very fast. Money loves speed. The IoT (Internet of Things) will mean that every electronic device will be able to access the Internet, which means it can plug in to all shared data across the web, likening it eerily to Skynet, the AI 'neural-network' in the *Terminator* films.

Back to reality

Change brings huge opportunity, and money loves change, especially when the change increases in speed. In Darwinian terms, it is not the strongest of the species that survives, nor the most intelligent, but the ones who are most responsive to change in the environment. Engage with change and disruption in finance and money. If many people fear change then this adds to the opportunity for you, as the competition is reduced.

The one fact around the evolution of money is that the speed of flow (velocity) has continually increased. It used to flow at the speed of an animal, then it flowed at the speed of machinery, then at the speed of telecommunications, then at the speed of light. In the future it may be able to flow simultaneously and this is very exciting! (See Chapter 44 for more on this idea.) As the speed of money increases, the speed at which it moves from those who value it least to those who value it most increases, as does the speed at which it flows from the poor to the rich. The opportunity for you to create more enterprise, economy and wealth increases. Time is the most precious commodity we have and anything that preserves it will bring wealth, riches and money your way.

As humans evolve so will the nature of money, as it is a representation and service to humanity and evolution. As we have evolved as a species we have become more complex, 'hyper-niched' beings, serving more and more specific functions and purposes. When there were just two, Adam and Eve perhaps, the purpose was to procreate and survive. There was no concern for becoming a celebrity on Instagram or a repairer of iPhone screens. Then the next generation kept the human race surviving through incest and a few tools and the use of fire, with a similar basic, primal purpose, slightly more specialized than their parents. Fast-forward to now and we are more evolved and complex than ever, and this is reflected in everything that we have manifested to serve us as a species.

Hyper-specialism

Do you remember when you wanted to buy a car a decade or two ago – maybe a sports car or saloon car, or you preferred a specific manufacturer? My dad loved Jags. There was an XJ6, XJ8 or XJS. He deliberated over the '6 or the '8. I think there were about six colours. Today you go into a Mercedes dealership and there are a staggering number of different models, engines and colours.

This hyper-niching has continued to compound and accelerate, just like the size of the population, the specialism of our trades and services, and the amount of money that has been printed and put into the economy.

Opportunity in disruption and evolving specialism

Money, wealth and enterprise are a manifested service towards our evolution and a reflection of our species and nature. Hyper-niching creates more abundant opportunity to serve people more specifically to their individual needs, and they will pay more money for that, and use your product or service more frequently to keep their ever-increasingly specific desires met. Later in this book, I will give many examples of this, current and future, and show you how you can monetize virtually anything now compared to a few short years ago.

Don't fear evolution and disruption – embrace it and invest in it. Disruption creates early-adopter opportunities, as our needs become ever more specific and more complex. If you adapt to and engage with this accelerating, specializing evolution, and the continual disruption in finance that reflects hyper-specialism, you become more relevant to the evolution of the species and so you will make more money.

Anything that disrupts the control of money will reduce fees and increase the ease. Banks and corporations have held a large portion of money for many decades and now this is being disrupted. We are in the early stages of a mass redirection of the flow of money, from banks to private investors and entrepreneurs. Trust in banks and institutions has significantly reduced, and money flows from distrust to trust.

Private wealth is the new bank

Private wealth inter-connected is the new fund. Crowdfunding and peer-to-peer lending are fast growing finance innovations, which are reducing bank margins, capital reserves and power. The playing field between the conglomerate and supercorporation and the private investor and entrepreneur is levelling. This book is going to teach you all about how you can redirect the flow of money more in your direction to get your share of wealth in this Darwinian financial climate, while adding value to others.

SECTION 3

Major money myths

There are many common myths that people have around money that hold them back. You may be able to relate to one or more? In this section we will pick off each common one-sided money myth, in the hope that you can look at any beliefs you've held or been raised to hold that haven't served you or others, and discover ways to set yourself free to scale, serve and sustain more money.

7

Money doesn't make you happy?

They say that money doesn't make you happy, don't they?

Fuckin' does. Not in the last decade have I ever heard a millionaire or billionaire say that their money doesn't make them happy, and I have met more than enough to get an accurate data set. Never have I heard a wealthy person say, 'Rob, please please please take all my money away; it is making me sooo unhappy.'

I'd suggest that only (first-world) poor people say that. It's a culturally influenced soundbite that millions make their reality. And what evidence do poor people have about money not making you happy, if they don't have any, or put a low value on money? That's like children who say they don't like food they haven't tried.

In a survey undertaken by the University of Michigan research department, three of the findings regarding money were:

1 What do people worry most about – money
2 What makes people the happiest – money
3 What makes people the unhappiest – money.[1]

Of course it is true that money in isolation, with none of the things it provides, doesn't make you happy. But all other things being equal, you have the ability to leverage money for increased happiness, and you have the ability to do more of the things that make you happy. I've had (less than) no money and I've had money, and I can tell you categorically which brings more happiness. If all other things in my life were equal, good or bad, and I had a Ferrari, I would be happier than if I had a rusty brown B reg Nova banger.

The 'money doesn't make you happy' argument is globally misunderstood because the assumption is that people are using purely money in the pursuit of happiness, and not those things in life that are free (that actually cost money).

The myth of 'the best things in life are free'

Sure, the best things in life are free: love, time spent with your kids, seeing them grow up and make great memories together. Experiencing nature, beauty, art, music, giving, long health; insert the things you love, that are free, right here. To experience more of these you need passive income from assets to free up the time to do them. Or someone to fund you and pay all your overheads to liberate you to have all these 'best things in life are free' experiences. Imagine trying to enjoy all of these 'best things in life are free' moments with the weight of debt and stress at work and 80 hours a week in the office.

The un-relatedness of money and happiness

Money and happiness are not the same entity. They are mutually exclusive, separate concepts, which means you can be any one of the following combinations: 1. Rich and unhappy 2. Poor and unhappy 3. Rich and happy 4. Poor and happy.

Here's a shocking thought: why not have money *and* happiness? Money creates happiness because it pays for you to do the things that make you happy, more often and more easily. Money is a vehicle that gives you more of the free things in life that are often referred to as the best. If you want more happiness, work on happiness. If you want more money, work on money. Do not rely on one for the other, other than to allow yourself to become happier and happier the more money you make, grow and give. Surround yourself with all the opulence that money can bring, because as you will learn later, that is what the wealthiest people in history have done. It is not just about gratuitous spending, but gratuitous creation of economy and velocity of money.

8

The 'rich getting richer' argument

You hear many people debating, 'Why do the rich get richer and the poor get poorer?' Many people get disgruntled about this and demand a redress of the balance through higher taxation, setting up unions, and greatly increased philanthropy.

There are simple economic laws that explain why the rich tend to get richer. These economic fundamentals bust many of the myths about the rich and poor divide, certainly in the first world. And guess what? The wealthy know and leverage these, and the poor don't and are leveraged by them.

Common sense?

Common sense suggests that something tends to move more easily in the direction it is already going than if it changes direction. You could call this momentum, or compounding, or simple common sense. Newton's first law of physics is this:

'An object at rest stays at rest and an object in motion stays in motion, with the same speed and in the same direction unless acted upon by an unbalanced force.'

Of course you're likely looking for a deeper argument than the rich get richer than 'because they are already rich', and the poor get poorer because 'they are already poor', but let's not dismiss something for its simplicity. If you are moving in the direction of wealth and money, even if you haven't attained the levels you desire yet, keep going. Keep on keeping on. You will get there.

Balanced economics

In any monetary system (containing a finite, but huge, amount of 'money' at any given moment in time) all expenditure must equal all receipts. This means that all spending equals all money received.

People don't burn money (unless they are The KLF, the British band who set fire to a million pounds of their own money) and even if they did, that money would be out of the system and all existing money in the system would balance between expenditure and receipt. Even when more money is printed, that new money in the system, like all the existing money, balances where all expenditure equals all receipts.

Therefore, of that finite (but huge) amount of money in circulation at any one time: it distributes exactly from those who 'spend' the most (expenditure) to those who sell or receive the most (receipts). If there is an inequality of balance, which there always is because products and services are not of equal value and humans value money differently, then money moves more freely and in higher amounts from those who value and focus on expenditure higher than receipt to those who value and focus on receipt higher than expenditure.

In other words, money moves from those who value it least (or value expenditure more than receipt), to those who value it most by saving, investing, compounding (or value receipt more than expenditure). Money moves from consumers to producers.

No matter how many times you may try to use power, rule, unions, regulations or governments to more equally distribute money, it will always reset its 'balance'. So, if you want to redistribute wealth more towards you, don't ever get dragged into the victim mentality of a higher power or system, begging or expecting them to redistribute it for you. The capitalist system is unlikely to change in your lifetime, so it is a huge waste and opportunity cost of your time and energy to fight against it. Instead, learn about and focus on the management, mastery and rules of money, service, contribution, enterprise, momentum, compounding and velocity, and make it more important to you to understand and value money and wealth. And more will come your way. The more you learn, the more you earn.

Theoretical redistribution of wealth

It has often been suggested that there should be a redistribution of wealth, from those who have the most to those who have the least. Before we delve into this, there already is a redistribution format: it is called taxation. In most developed countries, taxation is geared towards being a higher percentage of income the more one earns. Sometimes this amounts to half or more of what the well-earning person has dedicated much of their life to bringing in. The less one earns, the less tax one pays in absolute *and* percentage terms. The more one earns, not only does the amount go up, but the percentage ratchets up too. The rich are already being penalized, and the poor are already being supported.

The main problem I see in theoretical wealth redistribution is that it doesn't stay with or serve those it is redistributed to. I'm certainly not against sharing wealth with those who need it more, in fact it is contribution that plays a big part in building wealth, as we shall discuss later. However, you can't manage more money until you learn how to manage what you already have, and the big abundant lack is in education as much as it is in (re)distribution.

Imagine if a wealthy person owns a betting shop. A gambler comes in and spends all his money, helping the owner make more money. The state increases taxes and redistributes much of the money back to the gambler. The gambler then goes back to the betting shop and makes more bets. The owner might have to increase his margins to compensate for the increased 'taxation'. This costs the gambler, who keeps gambling, more money. And so the cycle continues, but doesn't help or change anything other than perhaps the owner moves to another country if too much is taken from him, and the gambler spends more and has a bigger addiction.

Perhaps if the business owner was allowed to create fair profit, was given assistance, protection and tax breaks and incentives to start up, and there was fair competition so that prices self-regulated, then the system would work. Oh, wait a minute, that's called capitalism. And for the gambler, education and help on the addiction is likely to be far more effective than feeding the habit. While this might seem an extreme example, most people manage their money like a gambler, wasting it and only just keeping their heads above water. It is education that is needed, in our schools and society, on how to manage and master money, not redistribution and handouts that de-incentivize work and contribution.

Lottery redistribution

The National Endowment for Financial Education cites research estimating that 70 per cent of people who suddenly receive a large sum of money lose it within a few years. Forty-four percent of lottery winners had spent all of their winnings within five years of winning the lottery. Nine out of every ten lottery winners believe that their new family wealth will be gone by the third generation.[1] Again, you can't manage more money until you learn to manage what you already have. Interestingly, only 2 per cent of respondents said that they were less happy with life after winning the lottery, despite the data above suggesting a greater percentage can't handle it, lose it, or feel it will be lost soon enough. Who says money doesn't make you (more) happy?

So in fact, there actually is a seismic wealth redistribution right now: from the poor when they get large sums without knowing how to handle it, back to the rich.

Production vs consumption

Non-wealth, first-world poverty doesn't contribute. It doesn't create service, enterprise or economy, and doesn't care enough about humanity to give value to others. Poverty in this sense consumes more than it produces, and is more selfish than selfless.

To be wealthy is to give service, to produce for other people in physical (consumable) or ethereal (information) form. To be poor is to consume: wasting or spending money and time-consuming depreciables. The wealthy produce for the poor to consume, and so redistribute wealth towards themselves from the first-world poor. Vast wealth comes from vast production nationally, globally, and in high volumes, whereas poverty comes from a negative differential between production and consumption. Individuals, geography or governments could cause this.

The wealthy create enterprise and economy through jobs, value creation, increased flow and velocity of money, contributions to taxes, hope, belief and inspiration to others, service to vast numbers of people. The poor are dependent on these to survive. Virtually all global wealth is now private: 99 per cent according to Thomas Piketty in his book *Capital*.[2] This means that producers finance all state benefits that poor consumers consume. Because poverty consumes more than it produces, this has to be economically balanced by large-scale production, and because of the 80/20 principle, the 20 per cent will produce for the 80 per cent to consume, roughly speaking. And so this will compound in the direction it is already going – the rich getting richer and the poor getting poorer. It is hard to change the velocity of money once it has momentum, which explains why when starting a new vocation it can be hard to make money in the early years, yet those who've been doing it for decades seem to have vastly compounded wealth and passive income, more easily.

For redistribution of wealth to work, consumers would have to take responsibility to produce more than they consume. If you give a drug addict money, you know where much of that is likely to go. If you give any consumer more money without the responsibility and education to produce with it, it will be consumed in the same manner all previous money was consumed. If a producer receives more money, mostly through cashflow, increased profits or leveraged loans (rarely through gifts and subsidies), they will invest it to produce more. Of course you could call this greed, but you could also call this growth, evolution and supply and demand. Greed and growth are only differentiated by an individual's perception. As long as there is demand and a need for the human race to grow and evolve, producers will produce more and more and more, and consumers will keep consuming. The titans of wealth across the last 6000 years are the largest, most vast producers, as you will learn later in this book.

The question is: which will you choose to be, a producer or a consumer? Will you get sucked into debating the rights and wrongs of the rich and poor divide, or focus on service, solutions, scale and contribution, and enjoy your fair share of wealth?

9

There's not enough money

I used to buy a lot of designer clothes. My dad used to tell me that you can only wear one pair of shoes at any one time, but I needed at least ten pairs of Jeffery Wests in my life. The irony was that I couldn't afford them. When I worked at Mum and Dad's pub, I earned a small amount of weekly money; I'd get paid and go straight to my local designer clothes shop to spend it all on the latest brands. Even if they didn't fit that well, as long as they had the logo clearly on the front, I was parting with my hard-earned cash.

Thankfully, my fortunes changed and a few years later I was able to buy clothes I could afford, using spare capital or residual income from assets. I recall very clearly in the depth of the recession, popping in to see if there were any new lines in stock. The manager, a friend for over a decade, was slouched over the payment desk like those cartoon characters that have been run over. You'd have thought he'd have woken from his hibernation for some cash to fill his till, but instead when I said, 'Alright mate?', he just carried on typing on his Blackberry without even looking up in acknowledgement, and grunted. I said my usual line, 'How's business?', and he fired straight back with, 'Shit'.

I apologized on his behalf, and he looked right up at me with a stone cold stare and shouted 'No one's got any fucking money!'

In fact, according to Mervyn King, there's around £80 trillion in the world economy. The total value of stocks and bonds is between £150 trillion and £180 trillion, and he estimates £200 trillion or more for total global stock of marketing instruments plus loans.[1] Some sources say there has been in excess of $8.2 trillion of gold mined, though it is estimated that it is much more as mining gold predates records and it is hard to track data on illegal mining. If you look at the coinmarketcap.com top 100 capitalization figures of crypto-currencies, ranked 100 is currently Ethereum with total capitalization of $30 billion, second is Obits with more than $37 billion, and first is Bitcoin with nearly $38 billion.[2] While I was tempted to add the total 100 up, I didn't see it as a leveraged use of my time. The point is clear: there are virtually limitless, almost infinite amounts of money in the world economy, especially when you (a) add all these up, (b) consider that these are liquid and will continue to flow and move from person to person to person to person and (c) that factors like inflation and QE (quantitative easing) will drive an ever-increasing money supply.

There's more than enough money in the world economy for us all to be millionaires.

So it begs a very important question: Who's got your money?

And no, it's not me.

Your mindset

So, do you have a reality-based, abundance view and mindset of money: that it is everywhere and virtually limitless? Or do you have a scarcity, there's-not-enough-money mindset? Do you think that *the* economy controls *your* economy, or that *you* control *your* economy, regardless of *the* economy? Money is printed by machines made by man, and money serves humanity. All money in current, past and future physical form has come from the ethereal, in the form of an idea. You could call it spirit turning into matter. There are unlimited future products, services and ideas, and so there is unlimited future wealth and money. We will explore the material and spiritual equation, and the scarcity or abundance mentality, later.

There's a lot of money out there, the question is are you going to grab your fair share?

10

Making money is hard

If one person can make money, anyone can make money. Let's say for a moment that you believe in nature over nurture (which I don't entirely) and you believe there are some things that most people can't do, no matter how hard they try. This could be a slam-dunk, run the 100m in 10 seconds or whatever you consider to be an amazing feat of human genes and genius. Well, here's the great news about being great at making money: anyone can do it. You can be tall or short, strong or skinny, smart or slow. Pick any subject and you will find someone who is not superhuman making a living, or even a fortune, out of the most obscure hobby, pastime or vocation.

Making money is a learned system. There is a formula (I will reveal more on this later), which means you can literally learn how others make money, model the commonalities and own the traits of the greats. And once you are exposed to the systems and common-alities, as you will be when you've finished this book, then it really is quite easy. Your main challenge will be to not take on too many of them.

It is easier than ever to make money

Don't delude yourself that making money is hard. Imagine being a tech-geek teenager growing up in the 21st century. You can get Wi-FI anywhere, log in to your parents eBay account from their computer, laptop or iPad, list and sell their possessions without fees, collect the cash, transfer it to your PayPal account, then to your bank account, and then go and spend, save or invest it, all online if you wish through crowdfunding, or on your Hargreaves Lansdown app. You can raise finance you don't even have to give equity away on

Kickstarter. You can set up virtually any business you want online in five minutes flat, signing up to free web-hosting accounts, with no need for premises and long leases, no stock to hold and erode capital, no employees to manage or pay, no HR or sickness; then you can set up free social media accounts on LinkedIn, YouTube, Instagram, Facebook, Twitter, WhatsApp, Pinterest, shoot videos from your iPhone and immediately reach thousands or even millions of customers at the speed that light travels through fibre optics. You can do all of this from anywhere in the world, 24 hours a day, 365 days a year.

So why is it that so many people struggle to make money? Why do they spend their lives worrying about it, experiencing guilt and envy around it, and living with barely enough to be able to do more of what they love?

Why is it that most people have such a negative relationship with money? Why do they think it is evil, hard to make, dirty, un-spiritual, greedy and capitalist, and that if they have it they will be judged and lose all their friends? All these beliefs and their counter beliefs are coming up.

This book will take you through every facet of the learnable system that I know, from personal experience, mistakes-a-plenty, humble successes, research and from mentors and people who've inspired me and shown me the way. If someone can become vastly wealthy and have a love affair with money, then so can you. If anything is physically and humanly possible, you can do it too.

Success leaves clues of success. If you can learn to play chess from a grandmaster, you can learn to make money from a money master. The belief that you need to be born into wealth is everywhere, but as you'll discover, not only can you make money from a standing start, even if you are deep in debt, you can also own the traits of the greats by studying them and learning how to think and act as they do. And you can do it without being an evil bastard!

According to my research, there is no special, specific genetic code or chromosome within DNA for 'money master'. It is not genetically pre-ordained that you will have a net worth of £2.1 billion, or any amount of money, so the almost universal belief that wealth is born and not made must therefore be a myth.

When I was at junior school, often just wearing only my Y-fronts in PE because I always forgot my kit, we had to warm up by touching our toes. I could barely get past my knees, and my teacher used to shout in my ears, 'Don't bother Moore, you'll never get anywhere near your toes!'

Sorry to have subjected you to that scarring mental image, but the point is clear – it was projected on me by the opinion of another that I would never be able to do something. I took this belief to be true and convinced myself I had 'tight hamstrings' and was born inflexible. That was my story to myself. Tight hamstrings. But says who? Is that a physical, DNA fact? I was also very overweight then so I likely blamed that on 'big bones' and an 'over-active thyroid'. More stories said to myself to stay comfortable.

The first time I went to a martial arts class I held this belief that I was inflexible; I probably even told my instructor that I had 'tight hamstrings'. He told me to stretch twice a day and in around one year I would be able to do the splits. I doubted him, but sure enough I could do the box splits before I got my black belt, something I had been convinced by someone else I couldn't do and owned that belief. While doing the splits has nothing to do with money, unless you are Jackie Chan, it was a watershed moment for me that if I applied myself well I could do things others had convinced me I couldn't. And so it is with money.

Don't worry, I won't be asking you to 'wax on, wax off', but you can follow systems and mentors to remove your own limiting beliefs around money and reach financial targets you never believed you could reach. It's not that people can't make money; it's simply that they don't yet know how. Mostly it's not their fault; after all they don't know what they don't know. They haven't learned how to make money, or been exposed to the systems and processes, or they haven't made money important enough to them, yet. That can change right now. Those who've made money have honoured and studied it, served and solved for others, and observed the rules and laws of money. So the question isn't why is wealth so hard for so many, but why is it so easy for some?

Easy to do, easy not to do (RIP Jim Rohn)

I think I first heard Jim Rohn say that 'it is easy to do, and easy not to do'. It was an important lesson. It is easy to choose the pizza or salad in the moment. It is easy to save or spend the money in the moment. It is just as easy to love and make money as it is to work hard for a living earning just enough to pay the bills. You have to work hard at anything at the start to get ahead, whether it makes a lot of cash or not. You have to make sacrifices in anything that you do, whether it makes a lot of cash or not. It is just as easy making money doing what you love as it is making money doing something you hate. Of course you may not think that right now, but maybe that's because you don't know what you don't know, and perhaps society or your upbringing has conditioned you to believe that you can't, or it's hard, or some other myth that has become your current reality.

George Soros made $1 billion in one day on 16 September 1992. In 2011 he made $8 billion and Mark Zuckerberg $11 billion, and neither of these men had the 'billionaire' chromosome in their DNA. Still, it would likely be harder for these men to not make money than to make money. Christiano Ronaldo gets $303,900 per tweet, Wayne Rooney $94,000, and Kim Kardashian gets $10,000. As you will discover in Chapter 34, some people are making it only to give it away, and others can't give it away fast enough.

Money struggles? Why?

Money struggles are predictable. People struggle for money either because money, and things that relate to money, are not important enough to them, or they haven't yet found a way to link how making money and creating wealth will serve their highest values. I've not seen two people on the planet with the same values, and therefore you and everyone else is completely unique. If society or an individual labels one person a genius because they have mastered an area of great importance to them, then everyone must in fact be a genius. Every individual on the planet exhibits greatness in their areas of highest value and focus, and as we are all different we must all, therefore, be a genius at being ourselves. There is no one like us and we are the very best on the planet with our specific set of values. It is only society assigning labels and value to geniuses in certain areas that drives the few to be labelled a genius and the many to be labelled otherwise. A lack of wealth and money is therefore simply a non-conversion of your unique wealth and genius into cash form. Others have monetized their genius, and so can you. The first step is to allow yourself to receive it and accept it, both that you are a genius and that you can monetize it.

11

Greed, power and money – why should anyone have so much?

Greed and power are not a reality, nor are they absolute. Some would see bankers as greedy in the boom years before the recession, but bankers may see it differently. A poor person may feel it is greedy for someone with vast amounts of money to have so much, yet they may not know how many millions the rich give away to worthy causes. Some may perceive pushy salespeople as greedy, others may say that selling is caring. Robin Hood may have been perceived as greedy by the rich he took from, but not so by the poor he gave to.

Every person has every trait

Every person has the power and ability to be greedy. Every trait in others that you hate, you have in yourself too. And you've used it when your values have been challenged or you've stood up for something you believe in. You are a balanced, self-interested and humanity-interested individual serving a greater whole of humanity. You have greed and kindness in you, you have power and vulnerability in you, love and hate in you, and you will use these polarities in equal measure when it serves you and serves others to do so.

Greed is growth

Which authority draws the absolute line between greed and growth? Where does striving for the growth that is essential for humanity become evil greed? The reality is that there isn't one all-powerful authority on the fine line between greed and growth. Greed *is* growth, and there is a constant, fine, ever-changing balance between greed and growth. You have a perfect self-regulating feedback mechanism through your feelings and intuition, so you will know when growth is growth because you will be inspired, on fire, in flow and rewarded handsomely. You will know when you have pushed a little too much and growth has become greed, because your feelings will feed back through guilt, worry, shame and other emotions 'designed' to put you back into balance. Society will do its best to project its own meaning of greed onto you. In some cases it will be irrelevant and another's projection, and in other cases it will be useful feedback needed to balance you out. Wisdom and self-worth come from knowing the difference. Life gives to a giver and takes from a taker, so if growth is growth life will give you more, and if growth is greed life will take away and teach you the necessary lesson.

Are banks really greedy?

Society and the media love to accuse the banks of being greedy. All banks are greedy. All bankers are greedy. It was the banks and the bankers who caused the global crash and recession of 2008. Looking a bit beyond the mass-hypnotized hysteria, we will see that if it weren't for banks the following serious issues would arise in the management of your money:

1 You'd have to store it and insure it

Banks are very effective at storing, saving and insuring money. They can hold billions of any currency and protect it from loss, theft and you spending it! If there were no banks and it was common practice and knowledge that people stored money at home, you'd need a vault and serious security to deter thieves. You'd have to set up a separate insurance policy to protect your money, and yourself. Coupled with inflation you may find your money would cost 10 per cent to 15 per cent a year just to store.

2 You wouldn't earn interest on it

You can't pay yourself interest, unless you become a bank! While many moan about inflation and interest rates, they would moan more without banks. Who would pay the interest? You can't pay it out of your own money.

3 You would have to borrow from private lenders or loan sharks

How would you borrow money if there were no banks? Without banks the likely replacement would be individual opportunists looking to lend money at high rates and make big fast money. This is how lending worked before the banking system, and it was the Wild Wild West in most places. While not all private lenders could be called 'loan sharks' – there are many bridging lenders, business angels, dragons, private financiers, crowdfunders, who lend at very high rates of interest and penalties.

Banks use a huge pool of money 'loaned' to them by many people, known as depositors, and gain great leverage that individual lenders could never attain. They are more easily and tightly regulated, which serves the consumer (depositor).

Because private lenders and loan sharks are using their own money rather than a big pool of other people's money, they can't offer loans to as many people, nor as large a loan, and don't have the economies of scale. Private lenders are often a lender of last resort (LOLR), when people can't get finance from banks and, as such, are a higher risk. Higher interest needs to be charged to compensate for the risk of default on the loans, and the lower volume. These rates can be anywhere from 5 per cent a year to more than 2,000,000 per cent a year on payday or weekly loans. Private lenders don't have the scale, systems or networks for cheques, debit cards, credit cards or wire transfers. Loan sharks are unregulated and often operate against local laws. They don't have the ability or financial clout to collect on debts through the courts, and so must rely on other, less legal, more aggressive methods of enforcement.

Banks leverage vast amounts of other people's money, lending it out to grow economies through fractional reserve banking, and provide a wide variety of financial services, security and liquidity. Their scale enables them to take much lower margins than private lenders. They are tied together in networks, and have government sanction, support and regulation. The government or central bank will even become the LOLR in the event of a crisis, like in 2008.

4 Regulation and protection would be much harder (LOLR)

Loan sharks work with their own money, take more risks, have little or no leverage, have more to lose personally and provide lending services only. Most of their clients are high-risk, and their interest rates can be huge. They are often opposed by the government, and cannot use the government for debt collection or protection. Their collection methods can be unethical or illegal.

Government regulation, which subjects banks to certain requirements, restrictions and guidelines, is designed to create market transparency and trust. Due to the volume of money, control and networked nature of the banking system, protecting individuals' money and maintaining trust is imperative for the entire capital system. Banks are very keen on appearing reliable, regulated and trustworthy. They don't want the owners of the money to withdraw *en masse* due to lack of trust, known as a bank run, because it can break their business. As such, they tend to be conservative on the whole. Sure, the repackaging of repacked loans became unsustainable, but when you compare a bank to a loan shark, they are very safe, secure and omni-present. Only in extreme cases dotted sporadically throughout history do banks lose people's money.

5 The economy would grow much more slowly

Banks figured out long ago that very little of what they received in deposits was needed at any one time in reserves, and that all the credit and debit transactions could be reconciled daily, or in real time, without labour-intensive vast money movement and thousands or millions of individual transactions. This brought about opportunities to lend out some of the deposits and significantly reduce the transactional costs of all the money movement. Fractional reserve banking, and money moving digitally rather than physically, allowed banks to lend more than the deposits they held, at very low costs and very quickly. This enabled economies to grow very quickly, because it created more money flowing through the economy, and increased the velocity of money. Banks could make margins on lending money and the other additional services described in this chapter. This is how banks became so huge. Some banks have GDPs the size of countries. While the banks were certainly part of the global recession, they were an even bigger part of the periods of boom and growth of all the world economies. If you can lend out £10 for every £1 deposited, just think what that does to the size of an economy.

6 Support in a downturn would be much harder

It is easy to criticize banks, central banks and governments for the parts they play in recessions and crashes, but what about the protection, insurance and security they offer? If it weren't for interest rates being held superficially low for a very long time, quantitative easing (QE) and central banks acting as lender of last resort (LOLR), many more people would have gone bust and the recession would have been longer, deeper and harder.

7 Fees could be higher, money could move slower

Without the protection of regulation and intervention of governments, central banks and the courts, money lending would attract all manner of waifs and strays, fly-by-nights and people unqualified to lend and manage money. Transactions would carry much higher fees and interest and penalties due to the increased risk and lack of scale. More people would probably die too!

The people who control the world

Perception of who are the leading authorities and influencers in the world is shifting. Perhaps we thought presidents, prime ministers, politicians and policy makers wielded all the power to create change? Perhaps we viewed the huge corporations and central banks as wielding all the power? Yet new breeds of social-capitalists and philanthropreneurs seem to have vast influence and global-inspired leadership. My guess is that most people would not view Mark Zuckerberg, Elon Musk and Richard Branson as evil greedy corporate monsters. My guess is they wouldn't view Cheryl Sandberg or Melinda Gates or Oprah that way either. These people are making money and making a difference. They have tens of millions of fans and followers. They are using their influence to make positive change and contributions and to serve vast numbers of people. They are following the patterns of the commonalities of the wealthiest people throughout history, detailed later, and would not be perceived as greedy by most people. The typical stereotype of the greedy corporate suit-wearing banker is outdated. The big change-makers are breaking moulds and barriers and connecting the globe, solving meaningful problems.

You get to choose how you use money. Why not be inspired by the great change-makers who are clearly making money *and* making a difference. They are earning *and* contributing. If you view the Forbes list of '50 biggest philanthropists', you will see over $100 billion in total donations to philanthropic causes, enterprises and donations, just in the top 20.[1] And you will see not one of them is poor, and every single one a billionaire. Of course it is complete common sense that the more you are worth, the more you can contribute, so why do most on the planet not make the connection and assume the wealthiest people are also the greediest? In absolute monetary terms, the wealthiest people in the world give the most, create the most, increase the most GDP, and contribute to causes the most. You have to embrace making lots of money to give lots away. I don't know about you, but that sounds like the best option to me.

If you have a lot of money, someone else doesn't

Having shared wealth and money strategies with over 400,000 people, and still learning all the time, I'm continually surprised by the number of people who think and feel that if they make money it has to be at the expense of someone else. This subject needs deep exploration. People must somehow assume there is an ever-decreasing amount of money in the economy, or that people reluctantly hand money over and feel screwed in the process, or that the passing of money from one to the other is a win-lose equation. None of these is absolute reality, but rather is an imagined belief of an individual. Because your beliefs are real to you and drive your reality, if you believe that someone gets screwed over or loses something when money changes hands, you'll never sell anything for fear of being the very thing you despise. This would affect the very identity of who you are, and so you will resist it at all costs.

Non-monetary exchange

There is always an exchange when money moves from one to another. That exchange isn't just in the money changing hands, but in ideas, energy, inspiration, service, solution, expectation, information, knowledge, wisdom, time, debt, credit, goodwill; I could go on, but you get the picture. People do not lose or get screwed in a money exchange, they get a whole lot more. If the giver of money perceives they get equal to or more in one of the aforementioned forms for giving money, they will feel fair exchange and good value. That will self-perpetuate and grow. If the giver perceives they get less than in the amount exchanged, they will feel unfair exchange, or in more extreme cases, feel ripped off or screwed. So it is not the money exchange, it is the *non*-money exchange that creates the feeling of value or non-value. Give more value, get more money, more easily.

One cannot sustain unfair exchange. It is impossible because it is not in balance. There have been many instances, especially in the property world pre- and post-crash of 2008, where I've thought,

'They can't keep doing this forever'. That may be how high the sale prices and rents were, what companies were selling that didn't seem to have value, or the volume and quality of loans. I have been surprised how long they have sustained, but then they have fallen. It has, in fact, taught me that people or entities can go on longer than you think in unfair exchange, but when they fail or they get found out, it all falls apart quicker than you'd expect, like a house of cards.

Money is not 'lost' from one person and 'gained' by another when exchanged, it is that the non-money forms are created and exchanged. As you will learn, money is never lost. It does not disappear, it simply moves and morphs from ethereal to real, idea to action, physical to spiritual and spirit to matter. One person does not have 'more than their fair share', they have exactly their fair share through fair exchange. Money doesn't lie. One does not have more than their fair share and someone else less, money simply moves from those who value it least, to those who value it most, and those who contribute least to those who contribute most.

SECTION 4

What *is* Money?

What is money *really*? And what isn't it? In this section we look at the concepts and laws around money and how money works, including the governmental and societal rules and systems that underpin it, as well as alternatives and relevant history that you can leverage for profit, purpose and philanthropy. We strip back all the layers of distraction, illusion and confusion placed upon money by media, environment and upbringing, to uncover its real meaning, purpose and power.

12

Wealth and money

Many people associate wealth and its meaning with money as cash, surplus savings, investments, capital, houses and other material riches. Yet the word *wealth* comes from the old English words 'weal' (well-being) and 'th' (condition) which together mean 'the condition of well-being'. The original meaning of the word *wealth* is 'welfare, well-being', while other dictionary definitions describe *wealth* as meaning 'happiness' and 'prosperity in abundance of possessions or riches'.[1] The original, derivative meaning of *wealth* is therefore not related to money alone. A lot of people who aren't wealthy in the form of money state that wealth isn't all about money, and they are partly right. However, many of the other forms of wealth they refer to or desire need monetary wealth to fund them.

For the purpose of this book, let's call the non-wealthy those with a first-world poverty mindset and unhealthy bank balance, but with equal opportunities to become wealthy. There are many people across the world with virtually no material or monetary wealth, and little opportunity because of their third-world location and upbringing.

So, just as we addressed the delusion of 'money doesn't buy happiness', let's suspend the belief that 'you don't need money to be wealthy'. You do. It is a balanced part of a greater equation that also suggests 'the condition of well-being', welfare, happiness and 'prosperity in abundance of possessions or riches'.

The real definition of wealth?

So perhaps a new, holistic and more accurate definition of wealth combines *both* the spiritual and material, financial and emotional: wealth is well-being and prosperity in the form of money, caring and service of yourself and others.

Everyone is wealthy

Everyone is actually wealthy; it's just that people's wealth takes unique and individual forms. Everyone is wealthy, or 'well' in the form of their highest values and what they've made most important in their lives. Everyone is uniquely abundant and a genius in being themselves, where they have zero competition. A relatively small percentage of people have converted their wealth into significant cash, physical assets, capital, or focused on cash as their 'wealth'. Still, 1 per cent of 7 billion is still 70 million. What or who says you can't be one of the 1 per cent? However, most people have their wealth 'stored' in an alternative form, with the latent potential to convert it into cash. For many, it stays latent and dies with them.

Your wealth might be latent in the form of your relationships, network, hobbies, sports, areas of specialized knowledge or technical skill, the way you've raised your children, your ability to lead and inspire, how you make people laugh, knowledge at pub quizzes, computer game skills, or wherever you hold highest value, are inspired by and have therefore continually focused on.

Earl Woods, Richard Williams and Rose Kennedy all had their wealth in raising successful children. Tiger Woods became the world's best golfer, both Serena and Venus Williams became world number one in tennis and JFK, Robert and Ted were three successful children of the nine that Rose raised.

What you work on, works. *Where focus goes, energy flows and results grow.* Your challenge, once you become consciously aware of your value, is to add the wealth formula to it and figure out how to monetize your uniqueness and convert one form of wealth into monetary wealth. In 1923 it probably seemed unlikely that a young boy's passion for drawing could be turned into a $52.4 billion a year company in 2015, but that's exactly what Walt Disney built. Joe Wicks turned his passion for working out and dieting into 15-minute workout plans and meals. Now a number one bestseller in the UK, the kitchen table entrepreneur is turning over £1 million per month, from what started out as a hobby in an already oversaturated fitness and workout industry.

It's not your (their) fault

The reason most people don't have monetary wealth isn't because they can't, or it's hard, or there's not enough, or it's evil, or it was their parent's fault. It's because they haven't, don't or won't (yet). They simply haven't learned how to convert their unique form of individual non-physical wealth into cash, *yet*. Or they haven't connected how having physical wealth and money can help serve their highest values and vision. We will show you how you can do, have and be both. The Post-it® Note was an accident. An untapped idea hidden in plain sight that now generates £1 billion annual revenue. All from small sticky bits of paper!

Millions of millionaires

There are millions of people across the planet who have become millionaires, or have become wealthy. You can too. Researchers claim that the world's millionaire population is roughly 35 million, and is expected to reach 53 million by 2019. You only need to be one of them, should you choose to be. So choose to be. These millionaires take a huge variety of forms, niches and skill-sets: rock bands, artists, chefs, chocolatiers, designers, inventors, dog trainers, puppeteers, Lego builders, darts players, horse whisperers, Furby and Slinky sellers; anything and everything and more. Of course 'millionaire' is just one generic measurement. Some may have a little less but have their ideal lifestyle; some may have tens or hundreds of millions, or billions. The commonality in this diverse range of niches is that they've all found a way to monetize their vision and convert their passion and latent form of non-monetary wealth into cash. This might be through scale, reach, leverage, service, marketing, sales, inspiration, being the best, investing, compounding, or just continual mastery of their wealth.

Everyone is a latent millionaire

You are already wealthy. Everyone is wealthy, in his or her own unique form, and you must never forget it and continually embrace and give yourself permission to accept your own uniqueness and genius. This doesn't make you an egomaniac, it is simply who you are. Conversely, you, I and every millionaire have polarized non-wealth in anything that isn't or hasn't been important enough to us. In this area we are all a total and utter non-genius! You should see me dance; I could ruin any good song. I look just like a newborn baby horse trying to walk for the first time. I'm not about to convert my latent dance talent into millions, although interestingly I am mentoring a Strictly Come Dancing dancer (the best one), so hopefully I can help him do that. I may not be able to dance, but I have my own skills and latent wealth to share. A millionaire is no better or worse a person, and nor are you. We're all a genius who can teach and inspire others, in our areas of highest value. For many, money is a non-genius area, or an area they'd like to improve their genius in. Perhaps this is the reason you are reading this book.

Better to die with money than without it

Many people end up working for a third of their entire life, doing something they hate, working for someone they don't like or respect, to barely make ends meet. They don't do what they love, and they don't become wealthy doing it. They sell themselves short and sell themselves out. They convince themselves that wealth is beyond their reach, and accept a lifestyle below their innermost desires and possibilities. They convince themselves that money doesn't make you happy and that the love of money is somehow wrong or bad, and therefore protect themselves from feelings of failure or inadequacy in the pursuit of what they really want. And then they die.

Imagine just for a utopic moment, that you aren't being judged at all, by anyone, around money and wealth. Imagine that you are totally immune, like Teflon-coated Kevlar, to criticism from others, from the upbringing of your parents and the voice of doubt, guilt and fear inside your head. Would you settle for a crap rusty car and a holiday once a year where rats get better food? A school for your kids that doubles up as the local prison? Or would you, just for this idyllic moment, allow yourself to dream? Perhaps a car that can start itself? A holiday where you aren't filling kitbags with the 'all-you-can-eat' breakfast? A school for your kids where swearing isn't grammar? Could you, for the sake of this hypothetical dream, allow yourself to have and enjoy more money, and maybe even to have a love affair with money? Remember, no one is judging you. Go on, say this: 'I LOVE money'. Go on, say it again: 'I. LOVE. Money.'

I dare you to say it out loud. Say it in front of someone. Chant it like a mantra. There you go, you did it. You said it. It's out there. I hope your partner isn't writing the divorce papers or trying to find you a straitjacket on eBay. But doesn't it feel good to really admit that you are worth more money, and that you deserve your fair share, and that it doesn't make you a bad person? Because that is exactly how it is, in reality and not ideology, for the 17 million millionaires on the planet. The question is, will you be one of the 53 million by 2019? No one is born with the sole function of just about making ends meet, selling out their dreams and only paying bills. No one's unique purpose in life is to simply consume oxygen and be a drain on public resources. Everyone is born with a unique purpose to serve humanity and make a difference to the evolution of the species. If they weren't, they wouldn't be needed. It's just that so many people haven't found their unique purpose.

The aim of this book is to help you figure out how to monetize that. To find more people to serve. To take on bigger challenges. To solve bigger problems and develop systems and strategies around them. To scale and sustain, and convert your unique wealth into the physical cash form. To become the true definition of 'wealthy': 'Wealth is well-being and prosperity in the form of money, caring and service of yourself and others'.

13

The purpose and nature of money

The purpose of money is to create an efficient, fair and universal exchange of value to serve the growth of humanity. It is to cope with an uncertain future trusting that you can store value today for a purchase tomorrow, or further into the future.

Money, firstly in the form of a physical commodity such as precious metal coins and later fiat money (money that is deemed legal tender but is essentially valueless as it isn't backed by a physical commodity), replaced bartering as a system for exchange of value. Money has four main universally recognized (economic) purposes:

1 A medium of exchange

Money is more efficient than a barter system. In a barter system, where one good or service is exchanged for another directly, without a universally recognized and accepted exchange mechanism, you need two parties who want to exchange their goods for the goods of the other party in the right, equal and fair quantity at exactly the right (and not delayed) time. This isn't easy if one farmer has a cow, and a cobbler has a pair of shoes. How do you equally and universally measure the value between them? This is known in economics as 'the double coincidence of wants'. You rarely get this double coincidence in a barter system. Liquidity is much lower, and fewer transactions occur because of the need for a double coincidence. You have knock-on barter issues too. If you have a dead animal that you exchanged for three pairs of shoes, and now you need to buy land, the inefficiencies have continued along the transaction chain, passing on the inefficiency. In addition, you have storage and divisibility issues with your dead animal or other commodity.

Money is durable, even more so now that it is made of polymers, and so in addition to suitability for storage, it can be exchanged many times over without decay, unlike the dead animal. Money is divisible which many commodities are not, and highly portable and liquid. Money is also deemed legal tender, and so is relatively resistant to counterfeiting, and therefore more easily protected by regulation.

2 A unit of account

Money gives us a more standardized way to measure and compare value. This helps in the understanding of economic principles like profit and loss, inflation and general accounting. Because you know what £10 is, a £10 loss is more easily and universally understood than the loss of part of a dead animal. £10 is £10, no matter how far along the transaction chain you go.

Prices are in constant change due to currency fluctuations, increases and inflation, stock market performance and confidence, economic cycles, (Br)exits, disruptions and so on. If you have a standard unit of account, like a pound, dollar or euro, you have standardized account measurement. Imagine factoring inflation and currency fluctuations into the value of your dead (now smelly decaying) animal?

3 A store of value

Money acts as an efficient, non-decaying and standard store of value. It can be saved and retrieved at a later time and still hold the same value. It provides a coping mechanism for an uncertain future, known in economics as 'radical uncertainty', by giving trust that today's store of value has the same or similar value tomorrow or in the future. Radical uncertainty is the kind of uncertainty that statistical analysis can't deal with. This characteristic of a store of value isn't exclusive to money. Property, precious metals, watches, jewellery and other goods also store value efficiently. However money is the most liquid, being instantly transferrable, exchangeable and universally measurable. Anything non-liquid will have a higher exchange cost, and most other goods are perishable so their value will decrease through storage and deferring payment or exchange.

4 A standard of deferred payment

With a barter system, you can't defer payments until later because of the risk of decay, devaluation and difficulty to store and exchange. Money solves this problem as it stores and retains value efficiently. Of course you do have inflation, but that is a relatively slow devaluation of money compared to alternatives.

Despite its flaws, a barter system has some advantages. It can replace money as the method of exchange in times of monetary crisis, such as when a currency is either unstable, in hyperinflation or economic crashes, or simply unavailable for conducting commerce. It can also be useful when there is opaque information about the credit-worthiness of trade partners or when there's a lack of trust. *Money needs trust to function. Money is trust.*

Money also creates relative fairness. It is a way of measuring your personal value, contribution and worth, equally and relatively. If you spent hours or days making a shoe, while another person spent years farming, raising and grazing the cow, how would you compare the inherent value between the two? By converting the stored value into money. Money is a standardized measure of worth, and you will measure your own later in this book.

In summary: money is nothing but an efficient, fair and universal trusted store and exchange of value to serve the evolution of humanity. There are myths, fallacies and delusions many people place on money as a 'meaning' which clouds the truth. Societal, familial, media or self-imposed limitations and ceilings are distractions from your real nature. Money is the accepted system by which you can turn your passion into your profession, vocation into vacation, and ideas into reality in fast, efficient and tradable ways. And there are virtually limitless amounts of it. Are you game for making some more?

The nature of money

Money has no inherent nature, other than that imposed and transferred onto it by a government or individual. How your individual beliefs, emotions and habits affect your personal money flow (your personal GDP) will be detailed later. Those who have succeeded in making vast amounts have transcended imposing their, or anyone else's, beliefs onto money. They've gained enough wisdom to see through all the filters, distractions and emotions to see it for its true nature. Once you do this you will start to see with real clarity, predictable patterns of money and people using it.

The nature of money in the current fiat, capitalist system tends to obey the following overriding laws and patterns:

Money devalues over time

Money devalues relatively over time due to inflation. Inflation is an average, general increase in prices and fall in the purchasing value of money. 'Average' because individual products and services can decrease in relative price and purchasing value too. *Money today is worth more than money tomorrow.* This is known as the 'time value of money'. This has shown consistency since precious metals that were used as currency were re-melted.

Other potential causes of inflation could be the introduction of other or new currencies that scale (e-currencies like Bitcoin), interest rate drops encouraging lending, spending and money supply, or a reduction in the quality or quantity of goods (assuming money supply remained constant). Whatever increases prices or supply of money generally leads to inflation, and the opposites are true for slower inflation or deflation.

Inflation of money is ultimately a reflection of life's purpose of progress and evolution. The desire for growth makes human beings want to continually increase prices and quality of services. Growth or greed for more money, more goods and the world's resources increases the supply, and so reduces the relative value. Population growth drives inflation, as money is divided between more people. You can use this knowledge to your advantage by embracing your ever-increasing self-worth, and your ever-increasing prices relative to that, and the ever-increasing number of potential customers. You can constantly improve your service knowing that your money will increase because that is the perpetual nature of money. And if you don't, your value relative to the value of money will decrease.

Money flows from those who understand and value it least to those who understand and value it most

Money operates under predictable laws and principles. It is people, not money, who manage or mismanage those principles. Let's test this concept: if you won the lottery today, what would you do with the money? Those who understand and value it least would list all the things they would spend it on and where and how they would squander it. You wouldn't hear them talking about investing it in their education, investing it for a return, protecting it, insuring against loss and building enterprises with it. If they valued it, they wouldn't spend it on transient liabilities. If they understood it they wouldn't waste it on consumables and depreciables.

If you asked that same question to someone who valued and understood money and wealth, first they'd say that they don't play the lottery because they don't leave their money-making abilities to a '1 in 13,983,816' chance (UK lottery odds of drawing six numbers). Then they'd list how they would invest it to create commerce, gain a long-term sustainable and compounded return, invest in and build assets that pay passive income, protect it, build a team and hire specialist accountants and tax advisors to preserve it. They'd use the income from assets to spend.

Money does not distribute equally; that is not its nature. Money does not move to those less fortunate, more deserving or more spiritual. That is also not its nature. Money simply tends to move from those who value and understand it least, to those who value and understand it most. And it tends to stay with those who manage it well and move away from those who manage it poorly or without respect.

Expenditure and receipt balance

There is an equal economic and monetary balance of receipts and expenditure: all spending and receiving balances exactly and equally to the total money in a given economy. Those who value money least have higher relative expenditure than receipt, and those who value it most have higher relative receipt than expenditure. Money tends to flow in volume to the few who know and understand the most about money, which is why you have the 80/20 principle of the super-rich. The top 3 per cent of Americans hold 54.4 per cent of all US wealth, according to Fed research in 2014. The top 3 per cent hold over double the wealth of the US's poorest 90 per cent of families.[1] Why does this surprise so many people? Why do so many people think this is unfair? This is the nature of money. Where does that 54.4 per cent of the nation's wealth come from? The 'poorest' 97 per cent. It doesn't get stolen from them or confiscated by government (most of the time). They spend it! They literally give it to the wealthy, and then complain how unfair it is.

Money is an energy exchange and therefore continues to flow

The law of 'conservation of energy' states that 'energy cannot be created or destroyed'. The total amount of energy in the universe never changes, it merely exchanges from one form to another. Money flowing is an exchange of energy in the form of ideas, trade and transactions, debt and credit, service and value, and solutions to problems, between a buyer and seller. If energy through money didn't flow, it wouldn't continue to exist as a form or serve its purpose of continued exchange. And even when more money is printed, it isn't a new creation of energy. It is energy changing form into money and then continuing to exchange. An idea and decision drives the printing of more money, just as ideas and decisions drive all other non-monetary wealth. Even if you set fire to physical money, all that happens is that the value and energy of that money is transferred into the remaining money existing in supply, according to the 'quantity theory of money'. Ironic isn't it, that 'burning' money just makes everyone else wealthier. I wonder if The KLF thought about that when they burned £1 million? This is a metaphor but also literal of what the first-world poor do: waste their money transferring its energy from their 'possession' to other people's, quickly and freely.

Money flows towards service and value, not work and time

Money tends to flow from those who don't offer service and value, those who consume rather than produce, to those who offer value, service and solutions to problems. Time and hard work are not proportionately related to money. Value and service are. People want ease and happiness, and use money to buy it. People exchange their stored energy latent in money into products, services and information that make their lives better, not in what took the longest or involved the hardest work. *If money is energy transfer, increase the energy transfer and you increase your money.*

14

Currency, flow and cycles

Currency is 'a system of money in general use (in a particular country), which is widely accepted and circulated', according to the *Oxford English Dictionary*. It is the paper and coins in circulation. *All currency is money but not all money is currency.* The origins of the word gives insights into its true meaning: it is derived from old French *corant* meaning 'running, lively, eager, swift' (the present participle of *courir* 'to run') and from Latin *currere* 'to run, move quickly' (persons, things). It also is defined historically as 'condition of flowing'.

This knowledge of the origins of the word can help us to understand the properties and behaviour of money in circulation. An economy only works if money is in constant movement and exchange. If everyone stored cash under their mattress, there would be less in circulation and the flow and velocity of money would decrease. This is known as the 'paradox of thrift'. On the one hand it is smart to save money, but if everyone saved money the flow of money would dry up. The paradox of thrift was popularized by the renowned economist John Maynard Keynes. It states that individuals try to save more during an economic recession, which essentially leads to a fall in aggregate demand and economic growth. *For an economy to grow, money needs to flow.* This is why central banks often print more money in a recession, to kick-start the flow of money.

The paradox of thrift can happen in times of fear or deflation, though usually only in relatively small percentages. If it were extreme we'd end up back in a non-cash or barter system. In short-term, low percentage volume it would actually increase the value of money, but if it were extreme it would devalue it significantly, because the nature of money is to flow, to transfer energy (that isn't created or destroyed, just exchanged).

Let it be free to flow

When money stands still, it's no longer money. Money needs to move and flow to function. This is why saving, storing and hoarding money will never make you or an economy wealthy. Over time the value will erode with inflation. The energy will be latent. No service or value can be given and exchanged if money stands still. Money is effectively a carrier or transporter of energy, value, exchange and trade. It moves back-and-forth-and-back-and-forth-and-back-and-forth hundreds and thousands of times before it decays or goes out of circulation. It's like a fibre optic that carries information. This should be an epiphany to many, because it means that one single bank note, let's say an English £50, could be worth £50 multiplied by the amount of times it circulates through the British and global economy. This is known as the velocity of money. The lifespan of a £50 has been estimated at 41 years before it becomes unfit for circulation. The polymer notes, with increased durability over the current cotton derivative, could last over a century, the Bank of England estimates.

If you get better at sending money back-and-forth, using it for its function to flow and transfer value, to exchange and trade in the form of energy, you give it life. You let it serve its nature and purpose, and so you are rewarded and remunerated. *Money loves speed and hates friction.* The more friction, the less money flows (or it flows at a slower speed), and the less friction, the faster money flows and in greater volumes. Currency is liquidity, and liquidity is how quickly an asset can be converted to cash at a predictable price. Currency has liquidity as defined and dictated by you.

You *start the flow*

I was taught by one of my mentors to tip big, not at the end of the meal but as soon as I walked in the restaurant. At first I was resistant, I didn't have money to just give away, and I wanted good service first, before I decided if and how much to tip. This showed my limited understanding of the laws and nature of money. When I changed my attitude, I was amazed how kick-starting the initial energy exchange created extra value. It created more energy in the form of better service, referrals and gratitude, and a chain of energy flow that would attract more money to me. It took faith at first, but it is the true nature of money and so the only way to speed up the velocity your way. The friction started inside my head, and this mentor of mine knew that. In removing my friction, money was allowed to flow from me, through me, and to me, again.

Of course, saving money is a part of getting your financial house in order. You don't just give it all away frivolously but, as you will learn later, saving is only one of seven steps to becoming wealthy, and will not make you wealthy in isolation without the other six steps. Savings barely keep up with inflation and you can't leverage energy transfer and velocity in a stored savings account.

Nature abhors (and fills) a vacuum

According to Aristotle 'nature abhors a vacuum'. Aristotle based his conclusion on the observation that 'nature requires every space to be filled with something, even if that something is colourless, odourless air. The idea is that empty spaces are unnatural as they go against the laws of nature and physics. Nature contains no vacuums because the denser surrounding material would immediately fill the void. A void is nothing, and nothing cannot rightly be said to 'exist'. And so it is with money. Money follows the laws of nature, so money abhors a vacuum, in that money will fill the void. There can be no empty space, so money will move from one place to another, in constant flow. I would have argued that my bank account was a 'vacuum, void of colourless, odourless air' back in 2005 (though not as eloquently), but I was clearly filling other people's voids for them quite nicely, and filling my void with debt! Damn it.

This is part of the balance that keeps money constantly in flow, and keeps currency in 'current'. You are able to leverage this natural law because an idea, service, solution, product, sale and promise are all potential voids that will suck in the 'denser surrounding material' – your money and more money. Money is very much like air and water, in that it continues to flow and circulate. You just need to open the floodgates more.

The law of vacuum prosperity

If you want to attract more material wealth into your life, then create a void that nature will fill. If you want new clothes, sell your old ones on eBay or give them to charity. If you have clutter, you have no space to fill. This is known as 'the law of vacuum prosperity'. Anything you want in your life needs space to fill, so clear the space. This could be any material item, but it also should be space in the mind. If you pay a bill begrudgingly, you have not created a vacuum as you are filling space with resentment.

Clear your headspace as well as the physical space by allowing appreciation to predominate your thoughts when paying bills, not just when receiving payments. Let go of the lesser for the greater, in physical and emotional forms. The lesser blocks the greater. A low wage blocks a high wage. Moaning blocks gratitude. You can't put more water in a full bucket so leverage this law and have faith that your voids will fill with wealth and riches.

Money loves speed

You know now that money loves speed. It is my intention to repeat the important concepts throughout the book to programme your mind for spontaneous wealth, so please don't one-star me on Amazon for repeating the fundamentals. Economic concepts like the velocity of money and GDP show that the faster money moves, the more economies grow. The paradox of thrift shows that storing or reducing the flow slows and shrinks the economy. And so it is with you and your money. You are wealthier not just through what you store, but through how much flow you create. The wealthiest people have not only retained the most wealth, they have accelerated the flow of money for them, through them and to others around them. If you look at what people perceive is 'stored', it isn't stored at all; it is constantly moving in and out at higher and higher speeds. One million pounds of savings, for example, is much more likely to have been built up over time: money-in-money-out-money-in-money-out, with ever-increasing amounts of money-in than money-out, than in one absolute static capital sum. You might have had a personal GDP of £100 million to store £1million.

Money doesn't come from you, it comes through you

Money doesn't come from things. People may perceive money comes from a product or item they sell, an electronic transfer, a hole in the wall (ATM) or even an asset that pays income (if their knowledge of money is good). Because money is made by machines that are made by man, and money is a reflection of and service to humanity – *all money actually comes from people, not things*. But even seeing that money comes from people is a one-dimensional, one step removed viewpoint. Bob Proctor (a world-renowned motivational speaker and coach) once stated that 'money does not come from people, it comes through people'. Imagine you are receiving a monthly pay packet, most likely electronically. The perception may be that the money has come from the bank as you see the account details on your statement. In fact it has come from the HR department who make payroll. It came to HR via permission from the MD, CEO or owner, who really controls the money through the company. But that money came from the customers and clients. That money came from their family or their boss or spouse or a loan, and so it continues through people, not from people. This 'through people not from people' concept has only 'six degrees of separation'.

Six degrees of separation – or 3.9

Six degrees of separation states that anyone on earth can be connected to any other person across the furthest points on the planet, through a chain of acquaintances that has no more than five other connections. For example, your friend knows a friend, who knows a friend, who knows a friend, who knows a friend who 'knows Kevin Bacon'. Hence this also is known as the 'six degrees of Kevin Bacon'. Recreating a famous experiment done in the 1960s, 40 parcels were given to people randomly picked around the world, as part of a programme testing this theory. They were challenged to get the parcel to a scientist called Marc Vidal based in Boston, via someone they knew on a first-name basis. Three of the parcels made it to Mr Vidal, and on average took six steps to get there.

In more modern and more socially networked times, Microsoft examined its instant messenger network of 30 billion electronic conversations between 180 million people. Its researchers concluded that any two people are, on average, apart by 6.6 degrees of separation. Research from Facebook showed that 'each person in the world' is separated from every other individual by an average of 3.5 other people through its social network.[1] Because of social networks leveraging the Internet that leverages the speed of light, the world is essentially getting smaller and smaller. Researchers studying connectedness on social networks have now suggested that the average number of acquaintances separating any two people, no matter who or where they are, is not six but 3.9.

Because money comes through people and there are between 3.9 and six people separating you from anyone else on the planet, you are much closer than you think to all the money you could want. You may not get the money on the first degree, but you may on the second or third. Too many people have such a short-term view of money that they repel the first person. This might be by accepting rejection, not asking for a referral, selling too hard, selling too soft, or simply not seeing the full six degrees of the worldwide network. Imagine for a moment if you made such an impact on the first person with awareness of how close we now are to each other, how much your mindset and skillset of money would grow. Imagine if instead of seeing the next step in a sale or request for money, you saw the following opportunities of currency, flow and exchange:

- Your reputation
- The 'mind-space' you own in their head

- How 'viral' you are
- Referrals to you or about you
- They know someone who knows someone
- Your attraction, magnetism and inspiration

Imagine how the following would change, or your view of these would change, if you had even just a second- or third-degree view, rather than a first-degree view:

- Raising finance
- Pitching business ideas
- Finding deals, assets and property
- Marketing your business
- Selling your products, services and ideas
- Getting debt paid off
- Attracting staff and partners
- Finding jobs
- Sharing a grand vision and inspiring others

You could say that this is simply long-term thinking versus short-term thinking. I think it is much deeper than that. It's more strategic and leveraged. It's what creates attraction over repulsion and pull rather than push. Imagine if, like a mind map, you could physically see the connections you were making, and your positive, money-magnetic reputation and brand going viral through the six degrees network. *Just because it's ethereal doesn't mean it's not real.*

The best way to receive is to give

When you give, you create a vacuum that nature and money want to fill, so you receive more through giving. When you give you speed up the velocity of money, so you receive more, faster. When you give, you reverse the paradox of thrift and increase rather than decrease personal and global economic growth. You are literally creating a global bank account the more you speed up the flow and currency of money. To speed up the velocity of your money, increase your personal GDP and make and give a lot more cash, there has to be a deeper belief that it exists in abundance. If you feel there is a limited supply, or that you have a limited ability to attract it, you will hold onto it for dear life. If you feel that your economy is affected by *the* economy, it will be. This fear, scarcity and thrift will close the supply to you, because you get back what you give out. If you give none out, you get none back. The paradox that exists in money is that you need to save well, but not hoard. You need to share well, but not overspend. You need to charge fairly, but not be greedy. You need to be selfish to your own needs, but also concerned for the needs of others. Either extreme will be unsustainable and put out of balance the natural flow and velocity of money. Money starts in your mind, so your mindset towards money determines your mastery of money. This book is dedicated not just to the skillset of money but the mindset of money too.

Boom–bust cycles

Just like seasons, economies have cycles. Micro and macro economies have cycles. Global, national, local and personal economies have cycles. Cycles are a natural part of life and money, striving to maintain balance and order.

When I was younger, I used to wish it would never rain. I also used to wish that Coke came out of the school taps (Coca-Cola, of course). However naïve and innocent that is, many people have this one-sided 'I-wish-I-could-have-all-summer-and-no-winter' mindset towards money, cycles and economies. It seems that many people have this attitude to boom–bust cycles. That they can be one-sided. Or avoided. Or that they will be different this or next time. Or that they'll be the same. Or that they can be controlled. *Cycles follow the nature of money and mankind.* There will never be a constant where a personal or global economy will have consistent, steady, on target growth for the rest of time. Risk and reward are intrinsically linked; they are two parts of the same whole, like fear and greed. When people are bullish and sense opportunities they will tend to move towards one-sidedness of greed (growth). When people are bearish they will tend to move towards the opposite one-sidedness of hoarding and defence. People don't behave consistently. People are not linear or logical. People are predictably emotional. They tend to overcompensate actions and emotions, and balance swings from one extreme to another. Things rarely stay in local or national balance, despite being in universal balance.

Many economists concerned with logic miss the 'ego' in economy. Economists don't separate *the* economy from *your* economy. Economists and policy makers are trying to 'solve' the issues of swings in the economy with hypothetical models (like the grand auction or perfect competition) and systems that assume a predictable future set of patterns and behaviours. They make the assumption that consistent predictable balance could and should be achieved. This is perhaps an illusion because people have emotions that overpower logic, and all emotions are necessary, or they wouldn't exist. Here's the paradox of imperfection: we still need to strive for perfection for growth. We need and desire to strive for an unattainable perfection and an unattainable perfect balance. Perfect competition is unattainable because some people play victim and others cheat or game the system. Radical certainty is unattainable because we don't know what will happen tomorrow.

(Rob) Moore's Law?

I'm optimistic about the impact you can have personally and globally, in your pursuit of wealth and money. I realize that striving for unattainable perfection could sound pessimistic, so let's be clear: I choose to be in a game I have a better chance of winning. A game I can control. A game in which I can make a meaningful difference. I'd love to encourage you to do the same. Instead of blaming, complaining, justifying and defending events out of your control, like presidential elections or rich-greedy-unfairness, focus on you. Then if you strongly believe that you want to change the system, make so much money and create leadership and influence that you really can make a difference. Like them or not, but Arnold Schwarzenegger and Donald Trump did just that. They put their money where their mouth is, became successful themselves and leveraged that money and influence to get in powerful positions.

I believe the best game that you can control is your personal economy, and how you use that to impact your local, national and then global economy. This is the inverse of trying to change the system from the top down, where you have little to no control. It can take 20 or more years to get yourself high enough up the ladder to have a position of authority in the 'system', only to realize there are layers of politics and bureaucracy that undermine the control you thought you'd have to make an impact. I recommend that you choose to change the system by changing yourself. Change the system from the bottom up, not the top down. This is how Bill and Melinda Gates, then joined by Warren Buffett, have chosen to do it. They have shown how to balance selfish and selfless in the pursuit of personal, national and global wealth and contribution. Be the change you want to see. *Start with you, then let wealth flow through you.*

Volatility is good for business

Volatility is good for business, because money moves faster and more freely. There are always challenges in a recession, but you will have more opportunities if you are open to them. As there are likely more overall problems in a recession, there are therefore more overall opportunities to solve them. Money is just moving in a different direction. Higher-level problems get higher-level pay packets. Prepare now for the next recessions and crashes. Be ready to buy low. Be ready to leverage and have cash reserves to go 'shopping'. Not just shopping, but power shopping, like January sales in Harrods!

Factors often overlooked regarding boom-bust cycles

1 **New money and people:** Each 'cycle' is different and experienced by people who didn't experience it first-hand last time. They can't learn from the 'mistakes', and they didn't feel the pain personally, because they weren't at the coalface back then. Each cycle shows unique characteristics. Even if lessons from the last cycle were learned, the current cycle

will be different. It will be driven by different people, industries, wars, asset classes, meteorological conditions, and other unpredictable events and phenomena. The trigger for each crash is different, and cannot be predicted, otherwise it may not happen.

3 **Balance is not balanced:** Balance is a constantly moving entity. Like a pendulum that swings from one extreme to the other, through the entire range of the radius, only ever at a fixed point for a transient moment in time, so a 'cycle' and 'balance' performs. To think that equilibrium can exist for a prolonged period of time is as delusional as thinking a pendulum will remain at the centre more frequently than anywhere else in the radius. Don't expect balance; expect continual movement through the range. Embrace and leverage it.

4 **Sheep:** Everyone else is doing stupid things. The masses follow the masses. The masses can be uneducated and under illusion, so expect the market to move with the masses, not your or any one commentator's ideals. Why would any one banker stand up in the boom and shout, 'This won't last. It has to stop. Everyone, stop making so much money and taking such big bonuses (including me)!' People tend to do what others are doing, and what serves their best interests at the time.

5 **The nature of growth:** Human nature is to grow, just like part of the purpose of life is to grow. You want to get better next year, not worse. Companies, governments and financial institution's main targets and measurements of success are growth. So it's against human and corporate nature to accept, predict or plan for any incoming 'busts', but strive for 'booms' (growth). This perpetuates busts.

6 **Bias:** No matter what happens in a market, *human beings will see the world the way they see it, not the way it is.* They believe what they choose, not what is. They act on self-interest mostly in the short-term that will create balance shifts in the

future, like the swinging of the pendulum past the centre to the extremes. Perhaps this is what Nick Leeson and Bernie Madoff did? We can all convince ourselves of anything.

7 **Greed and fear:** People tend to think things are worse than they are when they are bad and better than they are when they are good. Fear and greed drive the markets to and from the extremes (and not towards the centre) because the markets and money are a function to serve humanity, and emotions are an expression of humanity. This is explained by George Soros as 'reflexivity'. Reflexivity refers to circular relationships between cause and effect. A reflexive relationship is bi-directional, with both the cause and the effect affecting each other in a relationship that can't be distinguished as cause or effect. In economics, reflexivity refers to the self-reinforcing effect of market sentiment and resulting reality, where rising prices attract buyers whose actions drive prices higher still, until the process becomes unsustainable (boom) and then the same process operates in reverse leading to the resulting bust.

8 **Momentum:** When markets are moving with momentum in a particular direction, most people don't have any other options than to go with it. Or the other options are harder. It is harder to change the direction of a force than it is to go with the prevailing velocity. Everyone else is doing it, so 'relativity' changes the 'norm'. For example, when more people get more loans to buy houses the relativity changes by normalizing credit or risk and increasing prices. So what do you do, stay in or downsize to a smaller house while everyone else is leveraging up, or borrow money and gear up like everyone else?

The economy is what it is (not what we think it should be). Rather than trying to change what can't be changed, or blaming the state of the economy for everything that is wrong in the world, leverage it. Leverage the knowledge of flow, currency and cycles to create change, wealth and money from the bottom up, not the top down. Remember *the* economy is not *your* economy. *You can be booming while the economy is busting.* Create change internally and don't rely on external factors outside of your power and control.

The time will *never* be right. The market will never be in a state of perfect equilibrium. *You are the constant in every cycle.* Service, value and solving are the constant in every cycle. Making people's lives faster, easier and better are the constant in every cycle. Focus on these, have awareness of where we are in the cycle (as much as you can know), and set about making more money and making a difference. *Innovate, iterate and adapt. See the downside in the upside and the upside in the downside.* Plan for the worst but shoot for the best. Study trends and solve future challenges before the masses. Specialize. Hybrid-ize. Evolve. Roll up your sleeves when things go wrong and fix them fast. It's all within your power. The best thing about being rich is not the money, it's the things you learn and the person you become along the way.

15

Fair exchange

When I was starting out and attempting to forge a career as an artist, my art was cheap. That wasn't because it was crap (before you say it). And it wasn't because I'm from Peterborough and my Dad is a northerner from Huddersfield either. I'd convinced myself it was because people in Peterborough didn't have any money. I knew the canvas and material costs, and as those costs were low, it felt greedy to charge high London prices.

Recently, I stumbled upon a story that I wish I'd read when I was setting out. Picasso was sitting in a Paris café when an admirer approached and asked if he would do a quick sketch on a paper napkin. Picasso politely agreed, swiftly executed the work, and handed back the napkin, but not before asking for a rather significant amount of money. The admirer was shocked, 'How can you ask for so much? It took you a minute to draw this!'

'No,' Picasso replied, 'It took me 40 years!'

And there it was, right in front of me like a sumo-slap in the face; the clearest explanation as to why I was significantly undercharging for my work. I was only valuing the cost of the materials, and not the time, investment, total cost, opportunity cost, awards and degrees, commitment, pain, passion and dedication to art since I was three years old. That was over 20 years of experience I wasn't valuing or pricing in to my work. The message is strong. Your prices must include your life's work, education, experience, desire to serve, solve and care, and the sacrifices you've made. If they don't then you'll experience the feelings I felt of guilt, embarrassment, bitterness and lack of self-worth. You'll resent your buyers for paying a lower price that, ironically, you set. Of course value is subjective and relative, so the value as perceived by the buyer is also part of the value-determining, fair exchange process. You can't just slap a huge price tag on if the seller doesn't think it is fair either. *It is the balance of fair value and fair price that creates fair exchange.*

An exchange (or transaction) has to take place for you to receive money and wealth. You give a product or service that someone perceives has value to them so they willingly exchange payment in equal value for it. Fair exchange is a minimum, usually two-way, exchange between a buyer and seller. For fair exchange to take place the seller must add value as perceived by the buyer, and the buyer must exchange equal monetary value as perceived by the seller. Only under fair exchange do you have free monetary flow, and therefore wealth. A market or an individual governs the perceptions of fair exchange, sometimes separately, like art, sometimes in unity, like the price of fuel. Prices always tell the truth, because they are the agreement between what the seller will accept and the buyer will pay. I've created a proven, replicable formula for wealth. It involves Value (V), Exchange (E) and Leverage (L). For sustainable fair exchange to take place, giving (value) with fair remuneration and receiving with fair payment need to occur in natural balance. This idea is discussed further in Chapter 26.

Giving without (fair) receiving

Value without (fair) exchange or remuneration isn't actually value at all. Most people don't value what they don't pay for. Have you ever been given a book for free that's got dusty on the shelf? You may have increased your 'shelf-development', but free advice is worth every penny and most people don't value it. If you'd paid £500 for that book, would you read it? Why of course; you'd probably shove your partner over to the far end of the bed and give it pride of place between you. You might read, love and caress it every night and morning. Value is a perception that money quantifies and puts something ethereal into a tangible and specific form.

Many poor people who struggle to make significant wealth don't realize they're actually creating and attracting scarcity by pricing their products and services too low. I now know that's what I did. I thought that there wasn't anyone in Peterborough with any money to buy my art, when in fact the inverse was happening. My low-priced art was attracting low-paying customers. Even worse was that it was repelling higher-paying ones. I had guilt, fear and worry about pricing my work higher. In turn, I devalued my self-worth and worth the world gave to me. I felt unfair exchange was happening to me when in reality I was creating unfair exchange myself.

If you don't price highly enough, no one will volunteer to give you more money than they perceive to be 'fair', just to help you with higher, fairer pricing. No one is going to give you more money just to lift your self-worth. That has to come from you. If you price too low the fair exchange balance will be out, and there will be consequences of unsustainability due to zero or negative profit and resentment from the seller. Zero margin and resentment will perpetuate a lower self-worth and poorer relationships with clients. The buyer, in turn, will perceive a lack of value, despite paying a low price. This attracts more of the same because of the laws and nature of money. Ironically the solution is so very simple. *Put your prices up!* I will detail how to do this in more detail in Chapter 43.

Receiving without (fair) giving

Because money reflects and serves humanity, which is an amazing paradoxical balance, the other extreme of unfair exchange is also unsustainable. Examples of illegal or unfairly gained wealth are often cited as a counter to fair exchange, and more about a need for power. Perhaps it is true for the short-term that you can make money dealing in drugs or running the government of a communist society, but these are extreme and rare examples. If you study history you will find most, if not all, of these instances of excessive greed and power are unsustainable, and the consequences are often in line and scale with the greed. The balanced result could be huge debt, prison or worse. Anyone who exerts excessive power for gains more towards the self than the whole of humanity usually gets unseated, overthrown or, in extreme cases, killed. You don't see many war criminals and drug dealers topping the Rich List year after year. So, if receiving occurs without fair giving, or someone offers a product, service or idea and the remuneration is too high (or value too low), there will be consequences. People will feel disappointed, ripped off or worse: conned. They will spread the message aggressively, which will affect your reputation and reduce future sales. A good message will be shared four times and a bad one 11, according to 'The secrets of word-of-mouth marketing'.[1] Sales may, at first, spike until the lack of value has been proven, and then it will reverse because the price exceeds the market ceiling, or there was a lower perceived value than the level of remuneration.

Give and receive equally and gracefully

It is important to observe both extremes of fair exchange, and strive to strike a balance. Wealth is momentum and velocity of the laws of money in action, and you can only build and sustain it through continued fair exchange. Too much extreme in favour of the self and perceived value to others is reduced. Too much extreme in favour of others, and worth and sustainability of the self are reduced.

PayPal realized that sending money by email was going to be massive, that one company would dominate it, that it was relatively easy to do, and that nobody dominated it *yet*. They quickly tried various things as a route to market. Initially, they provided no added value or incentives for customers to use their services, and that was their biggest challenge. They needed organic, vigorous growth. So they gave customers money. New customers got $10 for signing up, and existing ones got $10 for referrals. Growth went exponential, and PayPal increased the gift to $20 for each new customer. Their flexibility and increased value, first, proved to be a major asset. PayPal was swift enough to change course in time to go public in 2002 and later get bought out by eBay for $1.5 billion. The current value of PayPal is between $49 and $51 billion, all off the back of giving first.

If you operate under fair exchange, you increase your self-worth because you feel adequately remunerated for your time and work. This, in turn, helps you increase your prices and value. You are able to make a profit, which means you can increase the scale of your service and reinvest in quality and value. Furthermore, as you increase your prices and value, you attract a better quality of customer who values what you offer, and is willing to pay more. As they pay more you can give and serve more, creating a virtuous cycle of growth and contribution, increasing the velocity of money and augmenting its nature. This is another reason why increasing your prices is important.

16

Spirituality and materialism

Spirituality and materialism are often seen as unconnected polar extremes. 'Materialists' or capitalists might think that spirituality is hugging trees and holding hands singing 'Kum Ba Yah'. Spiritualists and libertarians may deem materialism or capitalism to be about greed, power, self-interest and bling over caring and sharing with others and the planet. I make these generalizations not because I subscribe to them, but rather to reflect generic social stereotypes. Everyone is a unique individual and we all exhibit all traits. The deeper my research goes, the more evidence I find to support the concept that the material and spiritual are as one – part of the natural balance and order of humanity.

Spirit without matter is expressionless and matter without spirit is motionless. To declare, 'I want to be spiritual and not materialistic' or 'materialistic not spiritual' is to state a paradoxical contradiction. In order to fulfil a material desire you require a spiritual mission. Everything is spiritual and material in one. To quote Dr John Demartini: 'Spirit without matter is expressionless and matter without spirit is motionless.'[1]

Spirit without material substance can't exist in a physical form. It is simply a void. But material without spirit is like being a stone – with no function, direction, purpose or life.

What does this have to do with money? When you are part of the process of creating matter or you are, for the sake of societal stereotypes, 'materialistic', you are bringing spirit to life in the form of matter. Artists who put their soul into a painting or watchmakers who put their passion into a timepiece are able to express their passion through material items that you fund by exchanging money for them.

In order to possess opulent wealth or material items, you have transferred energy and spirit, economy and gratitude to the seller. You have helped the seller fund their enterprise and share their expression of soul and passion with others. You are part-funding their vision that contributes to humanity. You have rewarded the seller for their work and created an environment of fair exchange. You have helped increase their personal economy, pay their overheads, feed their family, educate their children and pass on their knowledge to the next generation. Without the buyer of material items, many services wouldn't exist, and while many people will argue that yachts and supercars are unnecessary extravagant expenses, if they served no function, they wouldn't exist. The material items are a true expression of the beauty of spirit. You have likely looked at a painting or car or piece of furniture and thought it to be beautiful. This is because the designer or creator has expressed their passion and spirit in order to make the item. It is also giving through spirit.

Giving or creating spirit?

It could be argued that the best form of charity is education and enterprise. While it feels good to donate money, many people feel it doesn't all go where it is intended. Some charities spend a significant amount of donated money on corporate events, salaries, accounting and other expenses. This is not to expose charities' practices. The apparent amount of money that goes directly to the cause you donate to varies wildly depending on which sources you consult. But if charity is the standard, generalized form of monetary spirituality, then there's a lot of waste and misinformation. A small percentage of your donation may go directly to the cause, and the true gifts of education, knowledge (spirit), and enterprise (ability to work and earn), aren't given by handing over £10 a month on direct debit to your chosen charity.

Materialism is ultimately charity and spirituality in the form of purchasing. The more expensive an item, the more likely more spiritual work went into it, and the more recipients benefited from it, more taxes were levied on it, which went back into repairing roads, defending your country, upkeeping hospitals, paying carers, keeping water clean, and much more that is easy to take for granted.

Of course, materialism can be greed and grotesque opulence too. *Have* possessions but don't *be* possessed *by* them. That's the natural balance and life paradox reflected in money. The pursuit of money and material items, with the humility to continue to learn and grow, giving value and serving others, is a benchmark of your progress towards your goals. It's also a feedback mechanism for your contribution and progress towards your vision.

It is society, religion, media and other external influences, which can become your inner voice that attempts to convince you of the sins and judgments of materialism. This is not the balanced truth. Many of the people who've contributed most to humanity created and made vast personal fortunes. We will study them later in this book.

The more material items and wealth you possess (while staying humble to and honouring the balance of spending vs investing), the greater the economy you create locally, nationally and globally. You increase GDP by spending more, and the economy around you grows. Materialism and money is charity, earned by the seller. You donate more and help more people, and in turn keep the seller learning and growing by earning money and creating service. Charity without fair exchange and transaction can reduce service and earning for the recipient.

Materialism and money inspire others to create more economy. How many people ever got inspired by a rusty old car that you drove? Materialism in a spiritual, humble manner shows others they can get rewarded for their efforts and service too.

A gift or a curse?

Of course, there are downsides to materialism, but you can't receive without giving. So give more to receive more. A measurement of receiving more, and therefore giving more, is materialism. It is the intention of spirit converted into matter. If you are viewed as generous, you'll receive more in return. You need to spend and increase the flow of money, to attract more money. Many suggest that wealth is best tasted and shared through experiences rather than objects of desire. Experiences can be materialism too; after all, it takes material wealth and money to create and enable amazing experiences and memories for yourself and others. If you prefer experiences to materials, then good for you: go for it. People might not see expensive holidays and dinners as materialism, but how are they any different?

Materialism is seen as selfish by many people who take a more philanthropic or spiritual viewpoint. What they often don't see is the amount of philanthropy and spirituality in materialism. Many people put a huge amount of time, passion and creation into material items. It takes five to six months to build a Rolls-Royce. It takes one man five hours just to polish the radiator. A minute repeater or a tourbillon movement in a Patek Philippe watch takes eight years to craft. Patek Philippe employs 1600 people whose livelihoods depend on 'wealthy materialists' buying watches that cost tens or hundreds of thousands of pounds, as do their families and children growing up. So when you wear that watch, you carry that spirit forward. Any philanthropy or charity that is undertaken or donated by the employees or families of Bentley or Patek Philippe is created and caused by the very people who can afford to buy the watches. And because energy is never created or destroyed, it is a myth that while one person spends £50,000 on a watch, someone in the third-world loses out. It is simply spirit flowing thorough material items that continue to flow spirit through others.

Bang and Olufsen design beautiful audiovisual equipment. It could be called art through sound and vision. The flair, passion and dedication of the designers and technicians come through the material items that they create, and the materialist gets to enjoy. Sure, some people like material items for how it makes them feel or how they will be seen by others, but for many it is also about enjoying the beauty in material form. In that respect it's not that much different to enjoying nature itself, or the great feeling of giving to others.

Many people choose to buy only organic or ethically-sourced food, so that their money goes to good causes. And so it can be buying material items. You can buy the Tesla over the petrol guzzler. You can invest some marketing budget in Google Ads, who gave

$144,606,000 to non-profit organizations and schools nationwide in the US in 2011. Certain credit cards include incentives such as the opportunity to give back or donate to various organizations and good causes, just for using your credit card and being a card member from companies such as American Express and Capital One. This is a great way to give back to society. With these credit cards, you don't have to donate money, you can either donate your time, points, miles, or rewards with a credit card you may already be carrying. *Much spending and materialism can be second-stage philanthropy, where the next flow of money after the initial transaction can have a charitable element.* You can be wise and ethical with your choices, if that's important to you.

The materialist becomes the spiritualist through their spending and first- or second-stage philanthropy, creating jobs, economy and welfare. This happens both directly via taxes on direct purchases (VAT in the UK) and indirectly through contributions via employment (national insurance in UK), corporation tax and other 'duties' and 'stealth' taxes. This spending and increased economy funds all the 'spiritualists' living off that same system who may be creating a deficit through housing and welfare support, or being kept by hardworking partners.

I don't see it as a one-sided argument that people are either fully materialistic or spiritual, greedy or giving. There is materialism and spirituality in everything, in different forms, equally balancing each other. Just remember that the law of attraction without action is just a distraction. Don't just sit and meditate and expect bullion to fall out of the sky. Decide, act and turn all that spirit into cash.

17

Capitalism and leveraging the system

Capitalism is a non-perfect yet relatively efficient system at creating fair competition in a free market, with a motive of profit. It creates a coping mechanism for a radically uncertain future, and quantifies and stabilizes labour and value that can be fairly and quickly exchanged.

Capitalism is based on private ownership of capital and assets, and the production of goods and services for profit, as opposed to production owned centrally or for common and social distribution. Production is for voluntary exchange, in part self-regulated by fair competition, fair exchange and supply and demand, and part regulated by anti-trust laws. Capital is freely accumulated and invested by private, not state, decision. Work is fuelled and financed through wage labour. Taxation redistributes state-needed funds.

Capitalism sometimes gets a bad press during and after crashes, busts and recessions, often from those who don't value or understand money, often from freedom-seeking libertarians, socialists and communists. John Maynard Keynes said of capitalism: 'Capitalism is the astounding belief that the most wickedest of men will do the most wickedest of things for the greatest good of everyone'.[1] Yet what other system balances and aligns so efficiently self and humanitarian interests? Capitalism is an effective (but non-perfect) meritocracy that incentivizes entrepreneurs and innovators to create enterprise, jobs and money, equally serving the self and others, and then supporting infrastructure and services that benefit everyone, through taxation. Perhaps the major flaw in socialism and communism are the disincentives for meritocracy and growth, in that an entrepreneur may feel disempowered to grow and serve because of perceived unfair redistribution and lack of profit incentive. *If markets aren't free then trade doesn't flow and grow.* It could also be seen to encourage entitlement and non-competition, because human beings have selfish, as well as humanitarian, motives. Even in an idyllic non-capitalist system, history has shown that a few people with the power behave almost as dictators and extreme capitalists. Many people overlook effective redistribution mechanisms such as welfare and benefits, which are funded by capitalism, and are also very 'socialist' concepts.

Capitalism funds roads, hospitals, police, healthcare, water, sanitization and benefits to those less fortunate. Entrepreneurs and innovators generate revenue, supported by fair competition controls, regulation and some protection, that they are taxed on (heavily). I'm not going to rant about tax because I buy into and benefit from a capitalist system, enjoying the benefits of redistribution that I don't have to pay for, thanks to the revenue generated through taxation. I feel a sense of value that I contribute to this through VAT, NI, capital and income taxes, rates and more that my companies create and increase the velocity of our local, national and global economy.

There are tax reliefs and incentives to innovate, create jobs, bring buildings back to life and create enterprise. I am free to make a fair profit without a large chunk of it being redistributed, competition keeps me balanced between personal motives and serving humanity, and prices regulate themselves. If my performance or fair exchange slips, my competitors win my business, and I have to up my game. If I get in early, I gain advantage. If I help more people, I gain advantage. The more money I make personally, the more I contribute to the GDP of the economy. There are fair fines and penalties for abusing the system and fair rewards for embracing it. Capitalism is one of the great inventions of man, yet the system is much maligned and misunderstood by many. Seek to gain a balanced view, and not the victimized and brainwashed one-sided story. The former governor of the Bank of England, Mervyn King, says of capitalism: 'Over many years a capitalist economy has proved the most successful route to escape poverty and achieve prosperity'.[2]

Important factors in sustained, effective capitalism

The main important, media-distilled factors to consider for capitalism to sustain and serve are as follows:

1 FREE MARKET

An economic system in which prices are determined by unrestricted competition between privately owned businesses. The prices for goods and services are set freely by consent between producers (vendors) and consumers, in which the laws and forces of supply and demand are free from any intervention by a government, price-setting monopoly, or other authority. A free market is the opposite of a regulated market, in which governments intervene in supply and demand through price-fixing or laws creating barriers to market entry. Prices are allowed to reach their point of natural equilibrium without intervention and a free market typically entails support for entrepreneurship, innovation, highly competitive markets and private ownership of productive enterprises.

Although free markets are commonly associated with capitalism, they have also been advocated by free-market anarchists, market socialists and some supporters of co-operatives and profit sharing. Free markets are non-perfect due to the fine balance and non-balance of greed and growth, regulation and freedom, monopoly and redistribution. The main characteristics of a free market are:

FREEDOM OF CHOICE

Owners, businesses, consumers and workers are free to produce, sell and purchase goods and services. Their only constraint is the price they are willing to buy or sell for, the amount of capital they have and fair regulation such as anti-trust.

SELF-INTEREST

The market is driven by everyone trying to sell their goods or services to the highest bidder, at the highest margin and lowest overheads. Although the motive is selfish, it works to the benefit and balance of the economy over the long run because this 'auction' system fairly prices all goods and services, accurately depicting true supply and demand at any given point in time.

COMPETITION AND PRICE TRUTH

The forces of competitive pressure keep prices moderate and self-regulated. Prices are fair and efficient and always tell the truth of the market. As demand increases for an item, prices rise thanks to the law of demand. As competitors see there is additional profit to be made, they start production, adding to the supply. This lowers prices to a level where only the best competitors remain, serving the producer and consumer equally. How you value yourself and your products also emerges in truth through your pricing. Prices too high or too low will be rejected by the market and supply and demand.

AN EFFICIENT SYSTEM

A market economy is completely dependent on an efficient market in which to sell goods and services. An efficient market balances freedom and regulation with buyers and sellers. It balances individuals and firms who have equal and open access, and the same information upon which to base their decisions. All are at liberty to enter, leave and participate in the market as they so choose.

2 PROFIT MOTIVE

Why would any producer, entrepreneur or business owner build something meaningful if they felt that their hard work would be undermined and their profits redistributed? Without the self-serving motive for profit, production and productivity could dramatically reduce, and ultimately not serve humanity. Self-preservation will almost always override humanitarian interest, due to primal survival instincts. Much like when you are told to put your oxygen mask on first before you help your children in the event of a plane crash, when faced with a decision between saving yourself or helping someone you don't know, most people will choose the self. This is human nature, and so it is human nature with money to seek profit and the ability to control our own overheads, expenses and margins. With theoretical socialist and communist redistribution, this ability to self-preserve and control our lifestyle risks being taken away, and so the future becomes uncertain. Innovation, scaling, employment, exploration and taking risks are all discouraged. Entrepreneur creators don't want to feel that they are funding the entitled, and that their efforts are not fairly rewarded or, worse, being taken away. Co-operative alternatives have not scaled or thrived throughout history. Most publicly owned entities have been carved up and sold off to the private sector to fund or bail out the public sector. Too much regulation, control and taxation means that profit makers either circumvent the rules or relocate to other tax havens. With too much freedom, however, greed will take over and this will not serve the wider society. To this end, the law of supply and demand balances and controls pricing in fair exchange between the producer and consumer, innovator and employee.

3 SUPPLY AND DEMAND

Demand for an item, such as a good or service, refers to the market pressure from people trying to buy it. Buyers have a maximum price they are willing to pay and sellers have a minimum price they are willing to offer. The point at which the supply and demand curves meet is the equilibrium price of the good and quantity demanded. Sellers willing to offer their goods at a lower price than the equilibrium price receive the difference as 'producer surplus'. Buyers willing to pay for goods at a higher price than the equilibrium price receive the difference as 'consumer surplus'.

The model is commonly applied to wages in the market for labour. The typical roles of supplier and consumer are reversed. The suppliers are individuals, who try to sell (supply) their labour for the highest price. The consumers are businesses, which try to buy (demand) the type of labour they need at the lowest price. As more people offer their labour in that market, the equilibrium wage decreases and the equilibrium level of employment increases as the supply curve shifts. The opposite happens if fewer people offer their labour in the market. Prices tend to be higher when either supply is lower or demand is higher, with one usually resulting in the other. Prices tend to be lower when either supply is higher and in surplus, or demand is lower, again with one usually resulting in the other.

4 Fair competition and meritocracy

When people are rewarded on merit, it tends to encourage more of the positive behaviour. When people are rewarded by entitlement, it tends to encourage entitled or victim-like behaviour. The profit motive rewards on merit, and fair regulation ensure that fair profit remains fair, legal and beneficial to wider society, as well as the individual or company. Competition in the right manner and spirit drives innovation and growth way beyond what co-operation could achieve. I'm sure Coca-Cola would have been smaller, lazier and less customer-focused had it not been for Pepsi. Likewise, Steve Jobs was motivated by his competition with Bill Gates and Microsoft. The Russians and the Americans have competed for space innovation and exploration. Competition with each other forces capitalists to reinvest as much of their profits as they can afford to keep their means and methods of production up-to-date and to gain competitive advantage. This, in turn, benefits the consumer through better products and services at ever-reducing prices. As everyone is a consumer, we all enjoy the benefits of competition driving prices down and innovation up. Fair competition has probably driven nearly all mankind's progress and funded all humankind's research and development. Because growth evolves mankind, competitive capitalism has served mankind much better and more globally than other systems to date.

5 Fair exchange, regulation and redistribution

In under-regulated capitalism, the motive for producing goods and services is to sell them for a maximum profit. This can lead to greed, which can result in a 'profit at all costs' mentality. This could manifest in exploiting workers, underpayment, drastic reductions in cost and quality, reduced health and safety, a lack of care for the environment and illegal activities. Necessary 'merit' goods and products may not be produced because the margin isn't high enough, and that may not serve society, like rural hospitals. Yet 'demerit' goods like tobacco and alcohol may be a strong focus due to highly addictive profits. Regulations and taxation, if balanced well, can solve the majority of these problems while still enabling the innovator to make a fair margin. It is a thankless task to be at the helm of regulation, and for the most part we enjoy a safe and fair environment. Demerit goods are heavily taxed which can then fund merit services. Anti-trust, competition and monopoly laws are in place; IP, image rights and patents can be gained; early adopters can gain large margins; and taxation increases the more an innovator produces. Other competitors are allowed into a market place which self-regulates pricing and value. Unethical and illegal activity is minimized.

With over-control or regulation the opposite occurs, where unfairly perceived control or redistribution de-incentivizes innovation, competition, service and profit. Or a dictatorship occurs where the very few controlling the policy, regulation and economy gain vast wealth, greed and power at the expense of the mass population. Many of the alternatives to capitalism have inherent problems.

Fight it or follow it?

Is it better to learn and leverage the existing system or complain and attempt to change it through empty rhetoric? Is it better to resist it or embrace it? All of us in a capital system are capitalists by virtue of being in the system. Learn the intricacies of the system, and you will benefit from it. Seek to control and change only that which you have the power to change. It is far easier to go with the flow than fight against the tide. Honour money and capitalism for what they are, not what you think they should be. The titans of wealth have made this important distinction, as you will learn in the three commonalities of the wealthiest people in history. And if you still want to change the system badly enough, become so rich with money, power and influence that you actually can. It will be a lifelong cause, but the billionaires have this power. If you follow the concepts in this book, you can leverage capitalism for ethical and sustainable wealth and riches.

The future of capitalism?

Bill Gates has called for capitalism to contribute more effectively to the big social and environmental issues of the emerging century. His plan and adaptation of capitalism is 'creative capitalism'. A working definition might be 'capitalism which places the resolution of social needs as a primary goal of economic activity, rather than a secondary consequence'. Gates spent many of his earlier years creating vast wealth, and now he is using his later years to leverage it for the greater good of humanity. That is a worthy model to follow to balance social and capital interests.

Richard Branson has coined a system 'Gaia capitalism'. A working definition might be 'a socially, globally responsible and sustainable capitalism that helps the world heal itself'. He has pledged $3 billion of future profits to fight climate change that wouldn't be possible without the initial leverage of capitalism. Many of the best businesses in all niches are taking a holistic approach and setting an example of responsible capitalism, while still being entrepreneurial, visionary and profitable. Smart companies are also gaining competitive advantage from being among the first, and you can too.

These are sustainable, ethical models for the future that leverage the fundamentals of capitalism which have proven longevity. The very billionaires who leveraged capitalism so effectively have witnessed the social power of capitalism, if used as a force for good. These titans of wealth are using their power and influence to make positive change in the world, balancing making and sharing wealth to sustain our species. I whole-heartedly support them in moving capitalism into the new age of capital-philanthropy, and maybe you do too?

How to leverage the system

You are incentivized to set up a venture with a fair balance of freedom and protection. You can serve and sell immediately with freedom to reach a global audience with ever-decreasing overheads and risk. Prices regulate themselves and you increase them based on a meritocracy and the more value you give. You get tax breaks to maintain a sustainable profit margin and you generate significant revenues for the state. You are free to build assets, income and profit, and encouraged to re-invest to keep your product and service competitive. Money is moving faster than ever and all the information you need is out there to have more of it flow to you. The more money you make under fair exchange the more you benefit and contribute to society, and the more your self-worth increases.

> Capitalism demands the best of every man – his rationality – and rewards him accordingly. It leaves every man free to choose the work he likes, to specialize in it, to trade his product for the products of others, and to go as far on the road of achievement as his ability and ambition will carry him.
>
> *Ayn Rand, Philosopher*

A commitment starting now…

Sections 6 and 7 of this book will help you to gain a deeper understanding of the monetary system, laws, strategies and tactics to know more, make more and give more money. But for now I'd like you to make a commitment to money. Just as you would commit to healthy eating and exercise, commit to a continued, life-long passion and study of all things money. Start with these:

- Embrace the technology and innovation of money and surround yourself with it.
- Study future trends.
- Look to solve meaningful problems.
- Look for super-specialization opportunities and disruptions that leverage the network concept.
- Turn yourself into an extended bank account (later chapters).
- Surround yourself with smart, wealthy people.
- Adapt to change and continually look to improve your value and service.
- Keep nudging your prices up.

- Plan for the worst and then go for the best.
- See upsides to the downsides, and downsides to upsides, before the masses do.
- Get perfect later, get started now.
- Roll up your sleeves when it goes wrong and keep on keeping on.

18

Capital, equity and income

There are three main ways to produce money, excluding debt or leverage. Let's look at each one:

1 CAPITAL

Capital refers to any financial resources or assets owned by a business or individual that are useful in growth, development and generating income. It can mean:

- Funds raised to finance and grow a particular business or project
- Accumulated wealth of a business in its assets minus its liabilities
- Stock or ownership in a company.

While it may seem that the term 'capital' is almost the same as 'money', there is an important difference between the two. Money is used for the purchase and sale of goods or services, and therefore has a more immediate purpose and use. Capital, however, also includes assets such as investments and stocks: assets that are more long-term and could store future value. Capital involves the aspects of a company or individual that help build and improve it, that form its base for generating revenue.

2 EQUITY

A simple umbrella definition of equity is 'assets minus liabilities', or 'total asset value minus all associated debt'. The variations of equity would usually take the following forms:

- An owned stock or other security.
- The amount of the funds contributed by the owners (stockholders) plus the retained earnings (or losses) on a company's balance sheet. In property, it is the difference between the current fair market value of the property and the amount of debt the owner still owes.
- (Equity exists in) stocks, fixed-income (bonds) and cash or cash-equivalent asset classes.
- When a business goes bankrupt and has to liquidate, the amount of money remaining (if any) after the business repays its creditors.

Equity is one's ownership in any asset after all debts associated with that asset are paid off. For example, a car or house with no outstanding debt is considered entirely the owner's equity because he or she can readily sell the item for cash, with no debt standing between the owner and the sale. Stocks are equity because they represent ownership in a company, though ownership of shares in a publicly traded company generally does not come with liabilities.

3 INCOME

Income is money received by an individual or business, especially on a regular basis, from work, investments or capital. Here are the different income streams:

- Exchanging time for money in the form of work. Net cashflow from the sale of assets (can be defined as capital).
- Residual income from assets (income that continues to be generated after the initial set up; also known as passive or recurring).
- Royalties (income from IP such as music, film and patents).

Money, money, money

It is important for sustainable wealth that you have and balance all three types of money. If you have all capital and no income your money is 'lumpy' (irregular), delayed and susceptible to market changes. If you have all income from work (exchanging time for money) you risk a life change, loss of passion or health, or change in regulation making you redundant and drying up your only source of income. While it could be argued that residual income is the best source, if you aren't also focused on preserving and growing capital, then your overall net-worth may be lower. You will also be more exposed to irregular shocks, unexpected costs and disruptions.

How much time and weight you put on each depends on your current skills, values, existing models for making money, age and attitude to risk. In your late teens and 20s you may focus on your ability to earn well on your time, skill-up, save and gain experience. In your 30s you may invest accrued savings into some assets, build your savings for marriage, start a family and buy a bigger family home. In your 40s you may look more into the future and build a larger capital base for your pension and legacy, grow your asset portfolio and look to develop residual income streams. In your 50s and beyond you may want to overtake your earned income with passive income from your assets, and wind work and time-exchange right down. Or you can do it all, now, if you are the serial entrepreneur. The sooner you start to build the three main sources of money, the more you will make, grow and give.

(Il)liquidity

Capital is (more) illiquid and income is (more) liquid. Liquidity is defined as 'a measure of the extent to which a person or organization has cash to meet immediate and short-term obligations, or assets that can be quickly converted to do this'. Or, the speed at which you can get your hands on cash. Whilst this may sound necessary, it is simply a benefit (or upside) that has drawbacks too. Generally the more liquid the asset, the lower the return, and the more illiquid the asset, the higher the return. Of course there's no guarantee of either, but this rule tends to stand. Property is one of the most illiquid assets, taking months to liquidate, but has consistently proved to be one of the best performing asset classes.

So a balance of liquidity to meet short-term obligations and expenses, and illiquidity for higher returns and protection from spending, inflation, fee skimming and even theft, will grow and sustain your wealth. You aren't going to see a couple of men in balaclavas pegging it down the street with your house over their shoulder anytime soon. But cash in your pocket is more exposed to theft, inflation, spending emotions and low returns.

Lumpy and recurring

Another balance to maintain, and have both of, is *lumpy* and *recurring* income. 'Lumps' of capital are great for protection, coverage for irregular and unexpected shocks, coverage of many months' or years' worth of expenses, security, collateral and more, but are very illiquid and delayed. For example, a property refurbishment or conversion project could take one to three years to complete, with no income until the final day. But then when the capital comes in, it comes in big, as long as you have been able to cover the overheads for that timeframe. The recurring or residual income covers the overheads, maintains lifestyle and reduces the need to sell time for money. One without the other leaves you exposed on one side of the balanced equation of sustained wealth and money.

Leveraged and unleveraged

If you have all unleveraged capital, you aren't maximizing its earning potential and power. If you are over-leveraged, you may not have any capital at all and you may be at risk from small market movements or bank recalls. Look to balance your leverage such that you are de-leveraged enough to sustain sudden changes in the market and drops in asset prices, but leveraged enough to use your capital as collateral to get good-debt bank lending so you can scale your asset portfolio. As an example, if loan to values (LTVs) to buy property are 65 per cent to 75 per cent, which means you require a 25 per cent to 35 per cent deposit and the bank will loan the remaining capital, then don't leverage any higher than 75 per cent. Allow your asset base to reduce in loan to value to around 50 per cent with capital repayment, capital growth or both, and then if it drops further look to gear back up to 50 per cent or 55 per cent. This would be a guideline strategy, and yours would depend on age, risk profile, current access to finance, current asset base, interest rates and banks' willingness to lend.

Cycle and counter cycle

Each asset class will have its own cycles of high relative capital value through to low relative value and underpricing. Each asset class is both connected to all others, and independent. There are micro and macro cycles. For example, interest rates, inflation, the state of the economy, politics, regulation and social implications will all affect the cycle of each class locally, nationally and globally. While property prices are high, gold and precious items may be low, and vice versa. Exchange rates between countries will have implications, and in times of high inflation, non-monetary liquid assets may have higher relative values than more illiquid assets.

As you build your wealth, it is good to have a spread of capital, income and equity across different classes to balance, de-risk and arbitrage the cycles and counter cycles.

Risk and reward

Risk and reward are another pair of poles that exist not separately but as one. Higher risk, higher reward, but higher risk! No guts, no glory. Risk is a balance of optimism and skepticism. It is unwise and dangerous for your sustained wealth to stereotype yourself as either one of the extremes. You also want to be aware of your natural tendencies, and work on the other part of you (or get partners and team members who possess your opposing qualities). Other areas of risk to consider and mitigate are political risks and impact, especially prevalent in industries like oil. Regulatory changes, common in the financial services industry. Reputational and legal risks, like Donald

Trump had with Trump University while President Elect, where he had to settle at $25 million. Age-tolerance risks have to be factored in, as do your timeframes for business and investment. Your level of experience and knowledge or performance in a class also impact risk. There's capital risk, income risk and dividend risk. Finally there is blindside risk, which is risk you can't predict or plan for. So you'll want to plan for that, too!

You can't separate risk and reward. Without reward, why would you take on any risk? But you can't expect all the upside with none of the associated risks. Most people are 'risk one-sided'; they either fear taking any, play too safe and as such never experience much upside reward, or they take too many risks without protecting the downside or understanding that the high risk doesn't guarantee high return. *If you don't risk anything, you risk everything.*

If you add risk scenarios to capital, equity and income, you can protect and grow your wealth. You can risk income more than capital, because you have the ability to earn it back relatively quickly or it may come in again the next month, passively. If you risk big capital lumps, you also risk losing big capital lumps and you may have no protection capital left for irregular shocks. Wealth is built best if risk is low at the outset, because the less capital you have to lose, the easier it is to get wiped out. Increase your risk only when you have multiple layers of capital and multiple streams of income.

Multiple streams of income

Multiple streams of income have their obvious, sexy benefits. In addition to the 'more than you can shake a stick at' income that you have from multiple streams, you also have multiple layers of protection and coverage. If you have high time-value earned income in the form of consultancy (high hourly rate), passive income from assets (property and stocks), protection capital in the form of an unencumbered house you live in, some physical assets, bling, books, IP, patents, income from a movie you directed, or if you wrote Slade's Christmas number one *and* designed the Dyson vacuum, then *you* should be writing this book! While you can't do everything, multiple streams of income in the three forms of capital, equity and income are a very real proposition, and a major common factor in the wealthiest people I know, have studied and experienced personally.

I wrote some models on how to create multiple streams of income in one of my previous books *Multiple Streams of Property Income*. While based on property, it covers important concepts for building multiple income streams including how many asset classes or streams to manage at any one time (between one and three), how to scale and systemize them and when to add the next stream to your portfolio (once you've systemized the last one and tested the new one). You'll want some unrelated income streams in case one stream gets disrupted, but also dovetail streams to leverage existing experience, like setting up a lettings agency once you have enough properties in your portfolio.

You can see that *capital, equity* and *income* are all major players in vast and sustainable wealth and money. You can also see that they balance and complement each other, have different functions, benefits and drawbacks, and peaks and troughs within their own cycles. The more you balance and grow each class of money, the more money you will make and build a fortress of protection around you. The more assets you build, the more it serves others too, like a property owner who houses tenants, gives letting agents more income, gives jobs to refurbishment teams, plumbers, gas safety engineers, maintenance people and more.

SECTION 5

Money values, beliefs and emotions

In this section we explore upbringing and how this influences an individual's mindset around money. What beliefs haven't served your personal wealth, or worse, repelled it, and what are the opposite and alternative beliefs? How can you control your emotions around money and begin to reprogramme your beliefs to make more without guilt or fear of being judged? We pick through specific beliefs that are common in people with money issues and offer the counter beliefs that could grow and scale your wealth.

19

Values and vision

Your values are the areas that are most important to you, in all aspects of your life. They are abstract concepts that serve as guiding principles, such as freedom, honesty, equality, family, fun, wisdom, teaching, travel, golf, business, recognition, your career and so on. They filter everything you perceive, think, decide and act upon. *You experience the world through your values.* If you went through a shopping centre you would notice the shops, people, signs and concessions that link to your values. You'd be virtually blind to things not linked to your values.

The problem, at an individual and global level, is that most people don't really know who they are, at least not consciously. They have many conflicts and aren't able to be truly authentic. They don't honour their own values and uniqueness. They mould themselves on, and are subordinate to, others who are more clear about what their values are. The first step in honouring your values is knowing what they are.

It is liberating and inspiring to discover and live according to your values. It is not an overestimation to say that the discovery is life changing. When you see yourself and others you care about around you step up, become truly authentic and who they are meant to be, their world changes in an instant to be a more fulfilled, inspired life. To awaken this genius inside you (that's already there, and doesn't need 'fixing'), first you have to give yourself permission, and secondly you follow a simple process.

So, first of all, do you give yourself permission?

If so, then the second step is something to look forward to (in Chapter 25, coming soon – look for a 'Positive health warning'…).

Vision

Do you have a clear picture and outcome of the purpose you want your life to serve? The legacy you want to leave? How you want to be remembered? The difference you want to make on this planet? These are important life questions that most people don't consider. Give time and attention to these as you read, and know that we all have a purpose, and that includes you. If we didn't, we wouldn't exist. Don't let yourself accept that you can't find it, and don't let others put out the flame of your grand purpose.

Clarity

Clarity of vision is important. If you're not clear on your vision, no one else can be either. If you aren't clear on the difference you make to others, then they won't see how they benefit from it, and so won't be inspired to buy your products or services or serve you towards your mission. Your inner, most tangible thought becomes your outermost reality. See your destiny both clearly in a future vision, but also living it now, day to day.

Your vision is the ultimate manifestation of your values lived with inspiration. Your vision is the roadmap for your life, guiding you in each moment through crossroads, tough choices, setbacks, diversions and transient periods where you lack clarity and experience confusion. We all have moments of distraction, overwhelm and confusion and it is a clear vision that minimizes those roadblocks.

Most people on the planet don't have a true 'vision', which explains why most people on the planet don't feel purpose, inspiration and achievement. If you don't know what you want or what your destination looks like, you're never going to get anywhere. A vision could also be seen as a purpose, and living a life *of purpose* means living life *on purpose*.

Without a vision and purpose, you have no direction, like a sat nav that guides your journey to no destination in particular. If a human being serves no purpose, they become irrelevant to the evolution and survival of the species. This goes some way to explaining why so many people wrestle through their lives looking for the meaning of life. I believe the meaning of life is to find your true unique purpose so that you add value to humanity and therefore evolve the species.

> The purpose of life is a life of purpose.
>
> *Robin Sharma*

This also goes some way to explaining why those with a bigger, clearer vision become successful, evolve the human race, leave legacies that inspire others and create and enjoy vast wealth. Those with no vision, direction or purpose often feel empty, depressed, experience being both broke and poor, and sometimes even resort to suicide.

In Viktor Frankl's moving book, *Man's Search for Meaning* (1959), the Austrian existential psychologist created a theory called logotherapy. Unlike Freud, who said our main motives are sex and aggression, Frankl surmised that our dominant driving force is to find meaning in life. Frankl experienced something that Freud never had. In the 1940s, Frankl was held prisoner in Nazi concentration camps. Frankl lived that reality. He felt the horror of losing everything only to be tortured and terrorized. With all the agony and brutality, what kept Frankl from giving up his relentless fight for his life was purpose. He found meaning in his struggle. That's what gave him the power to push forward through unimaginable pain. After escaping the concentration camps, Frankl published *Man's Search for Meaning*, sharing his experiences and an overview of logotherapy. A quote by Nietzsche nicely sums up his philosophy on how people were able to survive the camps, without losing the will to live: 'He who has a *why* to live for can bear almost any *how*'.

> In some way, suffering ceases to be suffering at the moment it finds a meaning.
>
> *Viktor Frankl*

That is the power of purpose and vision: unimaginable inhumanity and torture defeated by vision and purpose. Purpose is what gives us the strength to carry on, if not through dire conditions, then through difficult changes, transitions, relationships, and activities, all of which will present themselves on our path to vast wealth and money. Purpose-fuelled visions give us clarity, focus, and hope that things will be bigger and better.

An immortal legacy?

An immortal legacy, which what most of the wealthiest people in history have in common, is the natural outcome of a grand vision. Legacy and vision are great partners in driving each other, and you, towards vast and sustainable wealth. The desire to do something meaningful that is bigger than you, and outlives you, forces the vision to be national or global and not just local and personal. Conversely a grand vision drives your actions and the support of others towards your legacy that outlives you. We all desire inside us immortality of our spirit and the difference we made on this planet. After all, who wants to be insignificant and forgotten? An immortal legacy will leave and pass on life at the end of our personal wealth. It is a natural inclination of humankind, as you will know if you are a parent with the desire to leave legacies in the form of wealth and knowledge to your children. What a waste it would be to reach the end of your life and have your wealth and knowledge die with you.

An intergalactic vision?

Some people go further and have an astronomical and intergalactic vision. Leaders like Elon Musk, Peter Diamindis and Richard Branson are taking us to new planets. They see the world as their playground, and the scale of their vision has exceeded a global scale. The greater your vision, the greater your service to yourself and to others. The best way to increase your wealth and money is to increase the size of your vision from personal to familial to local to national to global, and maybe beyond to astronomical. When your financial purpose and dreams are focused on more than your personal, immediate material needs, when they encompass the entire globe and all of humanity, a magical financial magnetism begins to emerge, because people are attracted to you.

Little causes attract little wealth, great causes attract great wealth, and immortal causes attract vast wealth.

20

Your beliefs and where they come from

Your beliefs are what *you* believe to be true. They drive what you stand for and what you stand against. They are your morals that drive your judgements. There are few vehicles that exaggerate your beliefs and bubble them to the surface quite like money. Money is universal and connects and concerns us all. *It's a myth that money changes you; money simply exaggerates your traits.* Money will always and only make you more of what you already are. So your money beliefs will be linked to your other beliefs, but money will amplify them. If you already give to great causes, more money will increase the donations. If you have addictions, money will fund and fuel them too.

Where your beliefs come from

The following areas will, to a greater or lesser degree, dictate your beliefs:

- Family
- Geography
- Economics/politics
- School
- Mentors/teachers
- Religion/faith/spirit
- Friends
- Media.

Your levels of exposure to these will form your beliefs. You may have heard the belief enough or seen compelling evidence of it through a person or media. You may have felt enough pain or pleasure around an event or series of events to form a belief. Your beliefs become your reality as a result of external factors that have shaped what you believe to be true, but the reality is that they are not real. Seeing is not believing, believing is seeing, and you do not see things as they are, you see them as you are. Everyone's beliefs are real to them, but they are not the external reality. They are your own filters and experiences that you have for your unique perceived reality.

And so it is with money. You could have had one parent or father figure who worked hard their whole life and never earned much money, who had a poor relationship with money, was in debt and always struggled for money, and hated the moneymen and the system. You could have formed that same view of money. You can't help it and it isn't your fault, because that is your only proof. Your view and beliefs of money are simply stories you are telling yourself about it, and many of those stories are fiction.

> If you are born poor it's not your mistake, but if you die poor it
> IS your mistake.
>
> *Bill Gates*

Many people blame themselves and experience guilt and shame around their financial situation. Of course, many people blame everyone and everything else too. It is important to state that you don't know what you don't know, and if you've had an upbringing that has given you a poverty mindset, or personal proof of scarcity, envy, guilt, disgust and other emotionally charged beliefs around money, then you can't help but take on those beliefs. That is your only evidence. So you must not blame yourself or beat yourself up for them. You must not blame those who imposed those beliefs on you either, as many people do, because they didn't know any different, or better, either.

While it is interesting and important to go through all the poverty beliefs, it is important not to dwell on the past and to move forward fast. The stories you have told yourself that have kept you safe and comfortable are about to be disrupted, in the next chapter.

21

Wealthy vs poor money beliefs

For every belief there is an equal opposite belief. For everything you hold true, someone else thinks it is a falsehood. For every belief you hold, there is a valid, polar opposite belief, even if you don't agree with it. Most people spend more time worrying about money than dreaming about money, and more time dreaming about money than thinking about money. For some strange reason many people wear their poor beliefs like a badge of honour, like there is some kind of esteem and pride in poverty. In this chapter we will line up each polar opposite belief that the extreme rich and the extreme (first-world) poor have, hold and believe to be true. That way you get to see both sides of the equation, and make an informed decision which belief you want to *choose* to see as truth, and which serves your life.

It is important to distinguish the difference between being broke and being poor. Many wealthy people have been broke. Temporarily not having money doesn't make you poor, unworthy or unable. It's just a phase and learning experience necessary to earn the next level of wealth. If you have a 'poverty' mindset, you are likely to always be poor. If you are broke, you can change your life and money situation around. Many millionaires have been broke, more than once, only to rebuild their vast wealth, often even bigger than before. They didn't *own* being poor. You can take all their money but you can never take what they learned and who they became.

Imagine if, as you grew up, instead of being presented with extreme and polarized beliefs, you got to see both sides simultaneously, and could pick and choose those that served you? Well, we can't change the past, but we can impact the future. Here they are from a decade of research and meeting, face to face, hundreds of thousands of people who held both of these extremes to be their truth. Do you want to be 'not poor' or 'very wealthy'? Choose wisely, my friend.

POOR BELIEF: 'MONEY IS THE ROOT OF ALL EVIL'
WEALTHY BELIEF: 'MONEY IS THE ROOT OF ALL GOOD'

This is one of the most misquoted quotes around money. *Money is not the root of all evil, evil is the root of all evil.* If it were true that money is the root of all evil, or even 'the love of money' as is the original biblical quote, then before there was money, there would have to have been no evil. This, of course, isn't true. You could even say we are less savage and barbaric as a race since money and technological advancements. That is open for debate. Humanity is the root of everything that serves humanity, so humanity is the root of all evil, and money is an amoral vehicle for that evil.

Conversely, money is also the cause of all good, because humanity is also the cause of all good. Money cures disease. Money creates charity. Money buys time to give back and help others. Money solves problems that poverty cannot. Sure, someone could use £20 to fill a magazine with bullets and go and shoot 20 innocent kids at a school. But someone could also use that same £20 to leave an £18 tip for a £2 burger, or feed a third-world family for days or weeks. Money is simply the vehicle to serve the human will. To which side you believe money leans, for good or for evil, will dictate how you use it and what you attract and repel.

I used to subscribe to the belief that money was mostly used for immoral means, and because of that I repelled it all, as I did not want to be identified as immoral. The very thing that could have served and scaled my morality was being repelled by my one-sided judgement of others. The irony is I had no real experience to make this judgement: I didn't know any millionaires and had never even tried or tested using money as a root of all good. It's sad to think I wasted seven or eight years being bitter. My hope is that you don't experience this, your children don't experience this through you, and if you do, that today is the last day you do.

POOR BELIEF: 'YOU NEED MONEY TO MAKE MONEY'
WEALTHY BELIEF: 'YOU NEED IDEAS, ENERGY AND
SERVICE TO MAKE MONEY'

While having money attracts money in the form of interest, compounding and leverage, in the wrong hands money will soon evaporate into consumables and liabilities. So it can't be stated that you need money to make money, but more specifically that money can make you more money if managed well.

According to Entrepreneur.com, 62 per cent of all billionaires are 'self-made'.[1] This means first-generation billionaires with no inheritance or gifts of billions. According to Thomas J. Stanley: 'I have consistently found that 80 per cent to 86 per cent are self-made. That also applies to deca-millionaires'.[2] So if we take these figures to be true, the evidence suggests that it is something other than money and inheritance that makes money. I would suggest all money originates from a thought, that leads to an idea, that leads to a decision, which leads to an action, that leads to a result, that then gets tested, tweaked, improved and scaled. Everything that we can conceive that is in physical form has come from an intangible idea. Thoughts and ideas could be in the form of caring, serving, solving, making life easier, faster, better, easing pain, curing illness, new information, IP, patents, copyright, products, services, subscriptions, franchises, licences, assets, and more. And none of these are incumbent on start-up capital. They require vision and action. You will find the money along the way if the vision is clear and you can inspire others to buy into that vision.

I used to think you needed money to make money – because I didn't have any. Because I didn't have any, I wrote off my ability to make any. Therefore, all these assets to make money that we just covered never came to me because I wasn't open to receiving them. If I'd met the 'now' me in 2005 I'd have thought, 'He must have been given loads of money.' This is a very easy, convenient story which I would have told myself in order to feel OK. I would also have thought, 'What a twat!' It is ironic that I've become everything I once hated!

POOR BELIEF: 'THE MONETARY SYSTEM IS EVIL, UNFAIR AND CORRUPT'
WEALTHY BELIEF: 'THE MONETARY SYSTEM IS AMAZING AT QUANTIFYING VALUE AND ACCELERATING MONEY'

Capitalism is a system that allows any individual to make a fair living, merging self-interest and service in equal balance. Making money creates economy, service, employment, taxes and benefits to others.

Fair and perfect competition flourish and value is exchanged universally. There are regulations and anti-monopoly laws that keep the balance between greed and giving. The limited liability set up for entrepreneurs limits the liability to the company and not you personally, so that you are not stringently penalized for taking extra risks. There are very few things in the way of taking your inspired idea and turning it into service and money, other than yours truly (you, not me!).

POOR BELIEF: 'DEBT IS BAD'
WEALTHY BELIEF: '(GOOD) DEBT IS GOOD'

In my experience people have the following attitudes to debt:

1 They get into debt buying liabilities spending what they don't have.
2 They want no debt at all and only buy or invest in something 'if they can afford it'.
3 They leverage good debt to buy assets that produce income.

These go, in order of smarts, from 1 'silly' to 2 'safe and secure' to 3 'smart and leveraged'. It is true that debt for consumables, depreciables and liabilities is going to make you broke then poor. The first stage of moving from broke to wealthy is knowing you can only spend money you have, can get and can afford, for amenities and necessities. Do not get into debt that compounds buying liabilities that drop in value, because you get hurt in three ways:

1 You have debt that costs money and attracts more debt.
2 The liabilities you buy with debt go down too.
3 You have the opportunity cost of not investing the money elsewhere.

Once you've cleared liability debt, and followed your rule to only raise debt for assets, then you can invest in 'good debt' assets that cover their overheads and produce income. This will be detailed in Section 6.

POOR BELIEF: 'YOU HAVE TO WORK REALLY HARD TO
MAKE MONEY'
WEALTHY BELIEF: 'YOU HAVE TO MAKE MONEY WORK
REALLY HARD FOR YOU'

Sure, you have to work hard enough not to have to work hard. You
have to load up the front end so you can receive all the backend and
you have to set so you can forget. I'm not saying, 'Sit on your arse,
meditate and do nothing and the abundance of universal riches will
rain on you.' Even the most spiritual of beings know that spirit and
matter require faith *and* work. There is an African proverb that says,
'When you pray, move your feet'.

But, there comes a point where you hit a ceiling of hard work.
The harder you work, the less you earn because you hit the ceiling
of your hourly rate, the limited time you personally have in a day.
Your salary stabilizes but you work longer and longer. Even a pay
rise doesn't equate to a balance of all the time you have put in. Many
people who have good salaries have very low hourly rates and value.
Value and earning potential are not directly linked to time and effort,
especially when you are an entrepreneur. When enterprises and earning power are structured correctly, we multiply the value of our time
exponentially. A few hours of very high value 'work' could translate
to millions in lifetime income through assets, systems, software, leverage, information and IP, patents and copyrights, people and processes.
You could say you need to work hard *and* smart. Use your vision
and knowledge, not your hands and your sweat. Invest in assets that
preserve time, not money exchanged for time. Leverage the time of
others and do not spend all of yours.

POOR BELIEF: 'IF I MAKE MONEY IT WILL BE AT THE
EXPENSE OF OTHERS'
WEALTHY BELIEF: 'IF I MAKE MONEY IT WILL BE WITH
AND SERVING OTHERS'

You only make money at the expense of others through theft and
deception. Provided that is not your money-making model, then
people pass money through themselves to you through choice,
because they perceive value. They want what you are offering

more than the money they are exchanging for it, thus you are serving them not screwing them. If you want to increase the money you receive, then increase your service and value and you will get more money from more people willingly and with gratitude. If people resent giving you money, you can take this as feedback that they have been forced or leveraged, and that will build ill will and resentment that will cost you in the future. Care about people enough to serve them, then charge in accordance with fair exchange and increase your fees as you increase your value. Other people in the world may screw people to get money. This may have formed your belief, but this is unsustainable and, like booms and busts, there will be a correction and redistribution of the wealth and money. If you watch for long enough you will see it. Enron, Madoff, Leeson (whatever and whoever) looked like they were doing well from the outside, but it never lasts. What serves, sustains and scales is fair exchange.

Another version of this belief is that 'it's better to give than it is to receive'. This is really poor maths. For every giver or act of giving, there has to be a recipient or an act of receiving. One simply cannot happen without the other. So how can it be that giving is better than receiving? No, it cannot be. It is not better, it is equal. It is a 50/50 simple maths equation: the same number of people have to receive as to give. In reality, society, parents and media have conditioned us to believe this myth that it is better to give than to receive. Let's bust this myth. It is both good to give and good to receive. It is necessary for fair exchange. Most poor people need to learn how to be better receivers. What is wrong with receiving gratefully what someone wants to give? How would you feel if you'd taken time, energy and love to purchase or give an act of kind service to someone you care about, only for them to give it back to you and refuse it? You'd tell them to sod off, or at least you may think it. Many people are giving that strong message out to the world that they are not worthy receivers. What happens to people who give out energy that they are not worthy receivers? They receive nothing.

POOR BELIEF: 'I DON'T HAVE THE TIME TO MAKE MONEY'
WEALTHY BELIEF: 'I DON'T HAVE THE TIME TO DO LOW
VALUE TASKS'

Bill Gates and John Doe have the same amount of hours in a day. It
is a total delusion for people to say, 'I don't have time' because we
all have the same amount of time in a day. What they really mean is
'It isn't important enough to me now'. If people think they don't
have time to create wealth and make money, then it simply isn't
important enough to them. They may wrestle with this, because
superficially almost all of us want to make more money, but subconsciously most people want comfort or some other value more
than they want money. Everyone performs tasks in line with their
values. A mother may want to make more money but will focus her
time and energy on raising her children. Gamers may want to make
more money but will spend much of their time on the console.
Once we stop declaring that we don't have time, and start organizing our time and priorities in areas that either make more money
or are linked to our highest values in order to monetize them, then
we free up time and allow more money in. You'll either fill your
time with high income-generating tasks (IGTs) and priorities, or
other people will fill your time with theirs. Have you ever felt
that you got to the end of the day, got none of your own important work done, but spent lots of time dealing with other people's
emergencies? This is because you didn't have important priorities
planned, but they did for you! *You either have a plan or you're a part
of someone else's.*

The rich and wealthy are very strict and strategic with their
time. They know their time value, hourly rate and areas of high
priority that 'move the needle', and will focus on performing *only*
those functions. They will leverage, outsource, delegate, decline
or delete all other tasks. They are not necessarily smarter or more
gifted, just more aware of the value of time and priority. There's
more than enough time in your day, week, month, year and life to
create vast wealth. So much like money, do you see time as being
abundant or scarce?

POOR BELIEF: 'I CAN'T DO IT; I'M NOT GOOD ENOUGH'
WEALTHY BELIEF: 'I HAVE GREAT VALUE THAT THE
WORLD NEEDS AND I AM THE BEST AT SOMETHING
I CAN MONETIZE GREATLY'

You can. You are good enough. If anyone can, you can. You are a unique genius. If you have any doubt in yourself that this book hasn't already answered, then go and read or listen to the autobiographies of all the people you admire and would like to be more like. I love listening to anything about other people's successes, because the evidence that recurs over and over, after listening to hundreds is that they *all* had challenges. They *all* started at some stage and with much less than they have now. They *all* built from the ground up. They are *all* a disaster in some other areas of life that you are a master at. They have *all* made many mistakes. They *all* still experience challenges, despite being at the top. Therefore, they are *all* normal people, and they are *all* just like you and me.

It's not what happens to you it's what happens within you. Be inspired by your idols, but don't hold them on a pedestal. Stand on the shoulders of giants, not at their feet. Learn from your mentors, own the traits of the greats but acknowledge your own unique abilities. Follow the systems and lessons those before you have experienced to accelerate your wealth and money. Follow the trail already blazed and seek help from those who've been there before. What is hard for you now was hard for them, once, back at the start, but is easy for them, now. And so it will be for you, soon enough, my friend.

POOR BELIEF: 'I DON'T DESERVE TO BE RICH'
WEALTHY BELIEF: 'IT IS MY CALLING AND DESTINY TO
MAKE AND SHARE RICHES'

You are worthy of wealth and riches. Being worthy means to have and give worth simultaneously. Your self-worth increases with your permission to yourself to be and feel worthy. Give yourself permission to accept wealth and give wealth. Believe that it is your calling and destiny, just like the titans of wealth do, to accept vast wealth and riches. This belief may be linked to beliefs about your parents, or that you don't have the ability, or represent painful experiences that shattered your self-worth. But this cannot overshadow or deny your true calling and destiny. Accept and be grateful for it and allow it to come through you.

I have done plenty of stupid things in my life, especially with money. I have made many bad financial decisions. I have been too giving and too greedy. I have self-loathed for many years, beating myself to a pulp about all the mistakes I made. It's taken a serious amount of personal development and endless happy-clappy courses and chants, but if a grumpy bastard like me, back then, can change, then so can you.

POOR BELIEF: 'I HAVE TO PAY ALL MY BILLS AND EXPENSES FIRST AND THERE'S NOTHING LEFT'
WEALTHY BELIEF: 'I PAY MYSELF FIRST, THEN I PAY BILLS AND EXPENSES WITH WHAT'S LEFT'

First-world poor people pay themselves last, after all the bills and expenses. There is never anything left, or as Jim Rohn said 'there's too much month at the end of the money'. Because there will always be expenses, there will never be anything left, so you need to reverse the process and Pay Yourself First (PYF). If you PYF then you force yourself to get by with what you have left, and your expenses are reduced accordingly. If you Pay Yourself Last (PYL), it is *your* money that gets cut accordingly. This is much simpler than people think. They think they can't afford to PYF, but the reality is they can always afford to pay themselves something. They can start the process and change the direction of the money flow from out to in, no matter how small the change is. Even if you just paid yourself £50 to Save And Never Touch (SANT) that would soon accumulate. As you earn more, you SANT a higher percentage. You are changing a belief and behaviour as well as an action and outcome.

Your business isn't a real business if it doesn't or can't afford to pay you. The overhead isn't real. It should be higher. If you left, no one would come in and do the work you did for free, so why should you? So many business owners don't pay themselves for years to keep the costs down. They wear not paying themselves like a badge of honour. No one would buy a business, or they would lower the price, if the valuation didn't include fair salaries and dividends or drawings for the owner(s). If you were replaced, which you would likely be at some point after the sale, high-level executive people on big salaries with big recruitment fees would have to be brought in. They'd have to be trained at an expense. So if you want a real business, and you want real money, start paying yourself first, fast and now. You *are* worthy. It *is* fair. This belief can have links to other beliefs, such as you don't deserve wealth and money, or that money is made only at the expense of others.

POOR BELIEF: 'PEOPLE WILL JUDGE ME AND THINK I'VE CHANGED WITH MONEY'
WEALTHY BELIEF: 'PEOPLE WILL JUDGE ME ANYWAY...'

People will judge you no matter what you do. People will judge your rusty car just like they will judge your shiny red car. People will be inspired by your wealth or feel comfortable with your poverty. People will hate about you the very thing that is great about you. At any one point someone will love you and someone will loathe you, simultaneously, no matter what you do. Someone will hate your face. Plenty of people hate my ginger beard, except my Mum. The important fact here is that people are *not* judging you; they're judging you based on their experiences, beliefs, attitudes and values. They are judging themselves through you.

I used to think that as I got better people would be less bitter. Ha. What an idiot I was to think that. The bigger you get, the more you will be judged. The better you get, the more you will be scrutinized. Once you stop looking for the one-sided fantasy of everyone liking you (or disliking you), you can gain back all that wasted time and energy spent being who everyone else wants you to be, and be who you really are. I think you want to be wealthy, that is my suspicion. Am I right?

If you are a career-focused mum, non-career-focused mums may judge you for making money a higher priority than your kids. If you are an artist who creates a craze in music, film or art, and you cash in, others who haven't made money from their art may call you a 'sell-out'. If you are a business owner who makes hard decisions, has to fire people and negotiate big contracts, people may call you cold or greedy. People will call you what they see, not what you are. You know who you are. You know what you've been through. You know the sacrifices you've made. Embrace the critics just like you embrace the fans. You can't have one without the other. Let them judge you how they will and do not allow either the criticism or the praise to go to your head. Just be you and do what you do.

Other forms of this belief are that 'my friends will think I have changed'. I'd be more worried about myself if I *didn't* change. We grow, or we die, there is no standing still. Change is healthy, natural and necessary for sustained success. You can and will change to become a better person with more wealth. If your friends really are friends, they will grow with you, or accept who you are becoming. If they don't, it's OK to gently let them go. No hard feelings, just let them drift in their direction while you power into yours.

Money changes chemicals in the brain

More compelling evidence that money does indeed make you happy, is discovered by studying money and the brain, in particular the neuro-transmitter 'dopamine'. Dopamine is known to be the body's natural reward system. It is responsible for many of your good feelings, especially the naughty ones like lust, power and addiction. The scientist David J. Lieberman, author of *The Science of Happiness*, describes happiness as 'the continual progression toward meaningful objectives'.[3] The four primary chemicals of happiness are dopamine, oxytocin, serotonin and endorphins. They are released in the brain when you make forward progress towards meaningful objectives. Money is progress. Continued making of money is progress. Money attains goals or is a goal to attain. Money buys the very things that make you happy, that trigger the chemical releases in the brain. Money is meaningful, because it affords meaningful things. Because the chemicals in the brain are addictive, so is money. You often hear very wealthy people talk about money and the business of making it as a sport or addiction. Addictions can be good and bad, which is why many people think money is bad. But money is just money, and a tool for happiness, as defined by Lieberman.

Imagine if you stayed broke and poor

Imagine for a moment if you lived the rest of your life in poverty. Imagine being a drain on everyone around you and a victim to all circumstances. Imagine having to ask or beg for handouts from people just to pay your bills. Imagine working really hard but never earning enough to do the things you love with those you love. Imagine becoming a slave to a boss you don't like working for in a company you don't like. Imagine becoming a person you don't like. Imagine having no security for your future, fees for your kids' education, no pension, no savings and no hope. This is not your destiny. But if you continue to subscribe to imposed and one-sided beliefs that first-world poor people have, then you risk some, or all, of these becoming a reality. A lack of money leads to much of our pain in the world, or at least it exaggerates it. It affects our relationships and is the biggest cause of divorce. It deprives people of doing the *very* thing they love, because the things you love take cash to fund them or to fund the time and freedom to do them. It creates a vicious cycle of working to live but never truly living. It compounds its nature and the debt and unhappiness get worse. It creates fear, envy and resentment. It can even create serious, real-life health issues. It will not get better on its own. Do not bury your head in the sand. Take a stand and address each one of these beliefs that you have previously held, one by one, until you have programmed the new belief over them. Read back through them if you have to. Suspend your disbelief if you have to, because you have to. You owe it to yourself and the rest of the planet to know more, make more and give more.

22

Mastering your money emotions

Do you rule the money, or does the money rule you?

As Warren Buffet, one of the richest people in the world, said, 'until you can manage your emotions, don't expect to have wealth'. You cannot manage more money until you learn to manage what you already have. One of the great barriers to wealth and money is a lack of awareness, understanding and then control of your emotions.

> Excessive pains and pleasures are to be regarded as the greatest disease to which the soul is liable. For a man who is in great joy or in great pain, in his unseasonable eagerness to attain the one and avoid the other, is not able to see or hear anything right; he is mad, and is at time utterly incapable of any participation in reason.
>
> *Plato*

Extreme emotion destroys wealth. Anything that you are infatuated with, or resent, rules you. If you get elated or depressed, the emotions rule you. It's smart to have strategies that override extreme emotions. Money is made, grown and given from strategies, not emotions. Many people will tell you that the purpose of life is happiness, but in the extreme, happiness is an emotion and will cost you money. Polarized emotions, at either extreme, cost you money.

You feel down, you want to buy or eat something to feel better. You feel great, you want to buy something or drink something to celebrate. You buy 'things' to create, cover up or repair feelings, only to feel empty once that emotion has subsided. You want to make more money, fast, so you rush to buy a property, for example. You don't want to wait, so you pay more money, now. The estate agent and vendor can sense it and they cash in. You don't want to miss out, so you pay more money. You want to beat others to buy the property, so you pay more money. Then you convince yourself through confirmation bias that you have made the right decision, or that it is OK because it's an asset, because you don't want to feel bad or look silly. You get excited so you chase too hard, pay too much, go too fast. Then you get disillusioned that results didn't happen and blame, complain and justify. Maybe even give up. Then you start the process over again.

At the other extreme you don't want to make a mistake, so you never do or buy anything. You don't want to look silly in front of others so you never do, try or buy. You beat yourself up that you can't do it, find evidence that you are not good enough, and never get started. You're afraid of failing. You do nothing. You stand still.

You do what you feel you want to do, not what is best for you. You want to win rather than make the right decision. You want to look good rather than do the right thing. You want revenge rather than results. Whatever the emotion, it causes a reaction that isn't you. It is your emotion. Then remorse kicks in: regret, shame, guilt or denial. There are two basic rules of money, investing and general business, in relation to emotions:

- **Rule 1:** You can't make a good buying decision when you're excited.
- **Rule 2:** You can't make a good selling decision when you're afraid.

Many people break both of these rules regularly, and that is why most of them are not in the 0.242 per cent millionaires group. On a simple level, observe the masses, and do the opposite. We all have great intentions until we experience strong emotions. You can work on and develop your ability to manage your emotions. Take yourself and temptation out of the equation. If you're dieting, empty the fridge. If you get emotional about money, don't go to the shops. Don't take any cash or cards to purchase an asset until you have done your research. When you make a money decision 'under the influence' of an emotion, you will likely regret it or have a comedown.

I'm possibly one of the biggest 'addicts' or 'junkies' of emotion you may meet. Obsessive and OCD, I love feeling good and love the feeling that money and all its glory brings. I always have, and that kept me skint. I used to spend all my money on clothes to feel better about myself; the only difference now is that I can afford them. The feeling is still there. There are clearly some unresolved issues from when I was a child that don't need revealing in public. I seem to like nice things, and I haven't fully worked out why yet. For sure I love to be around art and beauty in design and furniture and anything material that expresses passion and creativity. It inspires me. I feel I can almost take the inspiration and love put into a Patek Philippe or Audemars Piguet watch, or Bang and Olufsen, Kartell or Tom Dixon design, and transmute it into what I do. When I used to write poetry (see, I was a *real* hippy), I was most inspired by great music and film and it would come through and improve my own work. It's a balance of appreciating beauty and opulence, without getting addicted to, or managing well, emotions that erode wealth.

At the apex of these strong emotions, I had five TVs in my house (with two bedrooms) and a very expensive hi-fi that was probably too big for the house. I had nice designer furniture that I'd spilt luminous Chinese food on, and nearly £50,000 of consumer debt at 18 per cent to 30 per cent interest. It was like the debt was making me feel so low that I had to go and spend to temporarily feel better, only to compound the debt and the emotions. I know it sounds ridiculous, like someone who's trying to lose weight and eats ice cream to feel better. I've since discovered over a decade later that many other people experience this like I did. Fast-forward to now and I still get the addictive 'good' emotions, I've just learned some rules and strategies from people smarter with money than I was, to control or manage the emotions. Here are some emotions you have likely experienced around money.

Money worrying

People often say that those who think about money a lot are somehow bad, but I thought about money way more when I had none. I constantly worried about it, the lack of it, and all the things I couldn't do because I had none of it. What you appreciate, appreciates, and what you think about you bring about, so my worry of debt attracted more debt. The more I thought about it, the worse it got, which is self-defeating and self-punishing. It affected my relationships, self-worth and freedom. When I was worrying for prolonged periods, it had more drastic effects on my health and well-being (wealth). Research from the Associated Press and AOL found that the risks of several significant health problems increase when people worry about their financial situation, including worries affecting their financial wellbeing. In a comparison of people who had a high level of stress over debt and those who did not, it was found that people with high stress levels were twice as likely to have a heart attack compared with those who did not worry about their financial situation. Other ailments included ulcers or digestive tract problems – 27 per cent of people with high stress over finances reported digestive problems versus 8 per cent of people who had no financial worries. Forty-four percent of people financially stressed reported having migraines versus 4 per cent percent of people with low financial stress. Twenty-three percent of people with financial stress were depressed, compared with 4 per cent of people who were not stressed.[1]

There is an easy way to avoid health and mental problems associated with worry relating to finances. Additional research has shown that people who take an active role in planning and learning about their finances were less stressed and more confident in their financial situations and suffered fewer mental health disorders. According to a TIAA-CREF Institute study, people who are educated about their finances are more likely to save for retirement.[2] Attending a financial-training programme increased people's feeling that they were in control of their finances by 25 per cent, according to a recent Metlife survey.[3] Quite literally, learning about and planning your money and finances reduces your worry and stress, increases your overall happiness and well-being and, of course, gives you better financial results. Common sense? Yes, but it isn't always that 'common'.

Instant gratification

We are all susceptible to this desire at first, because we don't have the long-term experience to make the wiser choice. Usually, if something seems too good to be true, it is too good to be true.

In any area that is not important to us, we are going to give in to instant gratification. You may have tried some short-term motivation techniques to overcome desire: slapping yourself in the face, locking the fridge, getting a coach, sticking Post-it notes everywhere and so on. Motivation is temporary, only inspiration is permanent.

Economists often believe that money is fungible, in that the individual units are capable of mutual substitution. That they are 'capable of being substituted in place of one another'. For example, since one ounce of pure gold is equivalent to any other ounce of pure gold, gold is fungible, and so is any unit of money. I have personal experience of this not being the case, and have observed it like many other people. *Economics is a logical discipline but people are emotional.*

When I was 17 I had a serious motorbike accident. I broke my arms and legs, had severe concussion and was hospitalized for days. My rehabilitation took many months, and I nearly lost the movement of my left arm; I missed much of the second year of sixth form college. The insurance claim was protracted, and after nearly eight months I was awarded £10,500 in damages. I was advised to take the money by the solicitors, as this was a lot of money to me. I proceeded to spend the money within a year. I bought a digital video camera for £1,500 as a present to myself, and a couple of suits – which of course are the first things you need at university! I likely put the small amount left into a savings account, but it soon disappeared.

At this time in my life I was very poor and uneducated in managing money. Looking back, the reason I squandered it so quickly is because I had not earned it. It was almost like a gift, because it was so long after the accident. It felt like bonus money, and somehow not fungible compared to earned money. During this time at university I would travel home very early every Saturday morning, with a two-hour drive, to work three shifts back-to-back at my Mum and Dad's pub. While this probably earned me only £75, I managed that money much more carefully, or at least as carefully as I could when I didn't know how to manage money, because I'd worked hard for it and made sacrifices to earn it.

I have seen this same emotional non-fungibility (I have no idea if that is even a word!) observing others in property, business and self-education. Between the early and mid-2000s, people were remortgaging their houses every two years, and drawing out what felt like many to be free cash. There had been no work, sweat or incremental earning over time for the equity in houses. People were far less discerning with remortgaged money over savings. They'd need little convincing to drop large lumps of cash into overseas or off-plan properties, or a suite of fluffy personal development courses, with little research. Even more interesting is that this money is debt. Money that is easier to come by, like gifts and remortgages, flows quicker and with less diligence than hard-earned tax-paid cash. Some people spend inheritances very quickly for the same reasons. According to Business Insider, you spend 12–18 per cent more swiping your card than when using cash.[4] Not all money has the same value, so be aware and careful of your emotions around money that was easier to come by. Easy come, easier go.

Impatience

The desire to rush (into) something often shows a lack of clarity of vision and values. Impatience could be driven by fear, worry or greed, or be an attempt to relieve pain, a desire to look good in front of others, or a fear of missing out and so on. Most people overestimate what they can achieve in a short time and underestimate what they can achieve in a lifetime. You have more time than you think. Impatience will lead to over-paying for assets and consumables, and you risk others taking advantage of you. There are great deals out there all the time. If you miss this one there will be others that come along. They may even be better.

Retail therapy

Using shopping for material items to make yourself feel better is the classic money-related emotion that can turn into an addiction cycle very quickly. Notice and be aware of your feelings. Follow some simple rules when you want to go and melt your credit card to feel better about yourself:

1 Give yourself a maximum budget.
2 Only take cash or a card with that limit on it.
3 Create a 'vicarious shopping experience' – go with someone who will spend loads (like me), and window shop.
4 Have a rule to never buy there and then, but to come back at the end once you've viewed everything.
5 Don't have coffee or get 'high' before shopping (note to self)!
6 Note down the prices and compare online later.

Reward through purchasing

Spending to reward yourself for something done well is a great technique if used sparingly and deservingly. But many people reward themselves with a £150 night out just because it's Friday. Balance reward for good actions (not outcomes) with saving it up for something worth celebrating.

Vanity spending

This is where you spend to make yourself feel better, get more attention, feel more important or seek love. People will spend more than they earn to get more love, attention, or attraction and to relieve pain. The cosmetics industry is huge. L'Oréal's revenues were almost $3 billion in 2014, and the top 20 cosmetics companies were around $156 billion. You are not alone. If you want to save yourself money, learn to love yourself for who you are and accept the beauty that you already have. You are not broken. You don't need fixing. (Note to self again!)

Guilt

Spending because you feel guilty, in the hope that the guilt will go away with the spending is surprisingly common. It literally over-powers you and forces you to spend money to relieve the strong emotion. Maybe you hurt someone and wanted to repay them? The reality was that you wanted to relieve yourself of the guilt. Maybe you saw a charity ad and it stoked a previous event or emotion in you, and you felt compelled to donate? It's just £10 a month, after all. Maybe you didn't spend enough time with loved ones and used spending or gifts as a way to make up for it? Or to say sorry? Many people are doing this on a daily basis with things they did 20 years ago. This will keep you broke and poor. Forgive yourself and others for the mistakes you made, search for and find the hidden benefits and meaning in them, and your guilt spending repulsion of all money and judgement should be gone.

I have a friend who has lived through cycles of making and repel-ling money for many years. He's a smart guy, and when he's newly into something and inspired by it, he has real charisma. It's new, fresh, the reality hasn't quite kicked in, he's moved away from the last thing, the challenges haven't occurred yet, and it's exciting. The vision and dream of money and results and none of the problems (that the last thing created) is palpable. He could sell ice to the Eskimos at this stage. Sales and business grow, and then it gets boring and more dif-ficult. Money is cashed in, but the reality of delivery and logistics isn't interesting. As soon as the point beyond poverty gets reached, self-sabotage mode comes on auto-pilot. The guilt, shame, fear of being judged and other emotions take over. In full self-destruct mode, he moves away from the customers and partners, leaves the business in the hands of others, relocates to a different city, and searches for the next model, idea or strategy to get those new feelings again. The money is spent alleviating the pain that having the money brings. But then desperation kicks in as the money runs out, and other emotions of scarcity, fear, lack and desperation emerge. This causes more flip-pant decisions about new ventures. Each time this cycle continues it gets shorter and shorter, and the attrition and sabotage grow. It is a sad irony and vicious cycle. This has happened a dozen times or more in the last decade, and it becomes an addiction that perhaps he knows he wants to kick but just can't.

Charity (guilt)

As above, but this time with the added detail that while charity has great benefits, you can live in constant poverty giving everything you have away to relieve an unresolved guilt, shame or fear. The past affects the future. In the end this can turn into bitterness and resentment. Again, look at what you need to forgive and let go of. Why not set up a foundation, make significantly more wealth and use your earning power to not just give money away but build infrastructure and education that really changes people's lives.

Bitterness and envy?

The more emotion you hold against others in relation to money, the more you will hold it towards yourself. If you perceive others negatively, you will resist being in any way like them, because you wouldn't want to be perceived that way. Even worse is all the time wasted and destructive energy, hours or days thinking and feeling bitter towards others as a distraction from your own life. In fact, many people play this as a pattern, being bitter and envious, unconsciously yet intentionally, as a distraction from their own shortcomings. The sad reality is that they most often get their facts wrong. This has fuelled much of my desire to write this book: to get alternative views out there about money and all its benefits. Simply stop 'doing' bitterness and envy. It's not a 'being', it's an activity; an action that you can stop now. Research from J.R. Thorpe of Bustle.com should help:[5]

'Envy is actually intertwined with a very particular form of negative bias: viewing people as seriously good at what they do, but fundamentally untrustworthy or insincere.' Prejudice against the very wealthy (Jewish people and Asians were all put in this category) was rooted in envy of their apparent excellence and how little they seemed to 'deserve'.

The basis for envy is 'wanting what another person has'. It's a part of our development of what can be described as 'self-evaluation', in which we compare ourselves to others and compete with them. Theories of envy in human psychology state 'self-evaluation' developed as part of our evolution, provides the basis for our competitive edge. Envy can produce a 'Why not me?' set of emotions and motivates us to seek a more 'fair' arrangement, so that one person doesn't have more than us and make us feel bad. Envy motivates a desire to take what another person possesses and achieve it for ourselves. Or better it.

Envy can make us physically ill or pained. The brain actually registers physical pain when we're in situations of envy, in a similar way as when we're heartbroken or experiencing social rejection. So ...

Loss aversion

In the same vein as pain, loss aversion is a strong emotion that can fool you into false economy or bad financial decisions. It is at the other extreme to the addictive emotions, but those who are a little more tight-fisted might relate to this more.

In economics and decision theory, loss aversion refers to people's tendency to prefer avoiding losses than acquiring equivalent gains. It's better not to lose £10 than to find £10. Studies by Amos Tversky and Daniel Kahneman have suggested that losses are twice as powerful, psychologically, as gains.[6] This can lead to an extreme or exaggerated risk aversion when people evaluate an outcome comprising similar gains and losses. Would you rather get a £10 discount, or avoid a £10 surcharge? Though traditional economists consider this 'endowment effect' and all other effects of loss aversion to be completely irrational, behavioural finance does not, and nor should you.

The effect of loss aversion was demonstrated in a study of consumer reaction to price changes to insurance policies. The study found price increases had twice the effect on customer switching, compared to price decreases.[7] Humans, it seems, are hardwired to be loss averse due to 'asymmetric evolutionary pressure on gains and losses'. For an organism operating close to the edge, the loss of a day's food could amount to death, while the gain of an extra day's food could lead to increased comfort, but would not lead to a corresponding increase in life expectancy. Notice when you have extreme loss aversion with your judgement and logic; be prepared to make financial decisions numerically and not emotionally. The fear of loss is strong and false economies are compounded. Over years you could be missing out on millions by being a tight-arse.

Strategies to control and manage emotions

People with wealth and money have either been raised to be less emotional around money, or have learned how to control their emotions, desires and addictions; at least to the point where they make more than they spend. They likely have money or money-related enterprises high on their values, or they have linked how making money and creating wealth will serve and meet their highest values. This is more who you are than transient emotions, and so will win in the long run.

To master your emotions is not to deny them or not feel them, but to observe and then understand them. What purpose do they serve? Here are the strategies you can test in your own life to understand, manage and master your emotions:

1 Observe the emotion. Take yourself out of the emotion, and like another voice or person inside you, watch without judgement. 'Oh, that is an interesting reaction, Rob. Look what you did there!'
2 What is beneath the emotion or reaction? Where is it coming from? What in you is making you react like this?
3 Why is it persisting? What are you not learning for it to subside?
4 What is the feedback that you need to own to grow through it? What do you need to improve to master it?
5 How does this emotion benefit you?

6   Isolate yourself. Go to a space alone where your emotion can't disrupt your life or others at that moment, until it subsides.

7   Have a friend 'punch-bag', a go-to person you trust who is discreet and will not judge you. Ask them, 'Can I have a rant please?' Then let rip. Once it's out you may feel a lot better. The storing and suppressing of strong emotions can lead to passive-aggressive behaviours, a full melt down or, worse, illness.

8   Have trusted counsel, advisors and mentors who you can talk with and who are qualified to give smart advice.

9   Wait before you make a rash or emotional decision.

10 Read, listen to and attend courses from the top experts in the field related to the persistent challenge you have.

11 Link the spending or investing to your values. If it serves them, do it, if it doesn't, don't.

Instead of reacting to emotions be proactive with patience, clarity and the ability to see all sides. Listen, learn, receive feedback gracefully, use considered judgement and look for what is best for the outcome and not best for your transient emotional state. Remember that wealth means well-being, so manage your emotions and you'll manage your money. You will make, grow and give (a lot) more money.

23

Self-worth and net-worth

The economic climate is not as important as your emotional climate. *The* economy is not as important as *your* economy. The original meaning of the word *economy* is 'skilled in managing a household or a state'. This could relate to managing yourself. If you have a low self-worth, you will forever have a low net-worth. Are you deliberate or desperate? Are you temporarily skint, or do you have an eternal poverty mindset? If you don't believe in yourself, why should anyone else?

You are worthy

Net-worth is net-worthiness. Self-worth is an inner feeling of being enough. Most feelings of worth are linked to your 'story' that you tell yourself, and how well and much you love yourself. You are worthy of love, from others and yourself. You are worthy of wealth and riches, as much as anyone else. Why shouldn't you be? After all, who decides who's worthy and who isn't? There is no omnipotent higher order that gives out worthiness badges, with you missing out.

It doesn't matter what anyone tells you about your worth and value, because they are judging you on their own values and not yours. It doesn't matter about your past mistakes because we all make them. The past does not have to dictate the future. It doesn't matter who's screwed you over in the past, you can move forward fast. If you want to increase your net-worth, increase your self-worth. This would have benefited me greatly as an artist, and I was ignorant to the link between self-worth and net-worth. Here are some strategies to increase your self-worth in relation to your net-worth:

Forgiveness

Forgive others for wrongs you perceive they've done to you. Forgive yourself for the mistakes you perceive you've made. Let them go. Go back to the previous chapter if you have not already performed this exercise. At first you may resist, but once you find a couple of benefits to the process of forgiveness you will get going and it will start flowing. Every event you experience has simultaneous benefits and drawbacks, supports and challenges.

Gratitude

Be grateful for everything you have and count your blessings. What you appreciate, appreciates, so list in your mind all the things you are grateful for, in whatever form you choose. Writing it down, prayer, visualization, incantations, it is up to you. For the last 11 years, every night, since I read Napoleon Hill's *Think and Grow Rich* (1937), I have been practising gratitude before I sleep, listing all the things I'm grateful for, both big and small. In addition to the mantras and incantations, this has become such a part of my life that I sometimes even forget that I do it. You cannot simultaneously be grateful and feel unworthy. The more things you list in your mind, the more powerful the exercise becomes because it diminishes doubt, fear and low self-worth. What you think about, you bring about, and as an added bonus you will get to sleep much quicker and in a great state. (You could do the same routine in the morning, but at 5:30 am my auto-pilot is locked onto coffee and conscious thought doesn't kick in until 6:10!)

Expect wealth, for it is your right

Expectation theory states that you get what you expect, not what is apparently 'fair' or what you 'deserve'. You are worthy of wealth and money. It is your right, as it is for all. Expect to be wealthy both in the form of giving and creating, and allowing it to come through you. You must allow yourself to feel deserving of riches, much like the story of Picasso's sketch on a napkin. Are you valuing all of your life's effort and work in your fees, charges and salary requests? Everything you have done in your life should be reflected in your worthiness, and it will lead to a vast net-worth. Recount all the things you've done and experienced in your life, go back as far as you can, and list as many things as you can that would add value to your worth, both in your personal feeling of worthiness and as value to contribute to others. Focus on what you have and not what you lack. Focus on what you can and not what you can't.

When you take the things you judge about yourself and appreciate them so much so that it doesn't matter if people judge you, you'll attain great self-worth. The world is a mirror that presents how you feel about yourself. With high self-worth there's no fear of the reflection.

'The Law of Lesser Pissers'

There is a law about how you value yourself and how it relates to others. It is called 'The Law of Lesser Pissers'. A view of this from one of my mentors, Dr John, is: 'If you're given the choice between pissing someone else off or pissing yourself off, choose them every time. People come and go, but you're with you for the whole trip'.

No one can piss us off without our permission; so never let someone else determine your self-worth. They don't know you, don't know what you've been through to get to where you are and who you are today. Being passive-aggressive and bottling emotions inside does a lot of unnecessary damage.

Knowledge and experience

Many people feel their confidence will improve *once* they have knowledge and experience. This is true, but be mindful not to wait until you have everything you need before *you* increase your self-worth. You will never have everything, or all your ducks in a row. Get perfect later. Of course your self-worth and confidence will naturally increase as you learn, work on yourself and gain more experience, but this is a slow process and you mustn't accept that this is the only way to higher net-worth.

You can increase the speed of gaining knowledge and experience, while simultaneously believing in your own value *right now*. Commit to working on yourself more than anything else. If you want business mastery, develop self-mastery. If you want abundant wealth, develop psychological wealth. Declare that you are a life-long student in the areas in which you desire growth. Find the top experts and read all their books, subscribe to their podcasts, listen to their audios, attend their seminars and events, watch their YouTube videos, get mentoring with them and look at how you can connect and help them in return. The more you learn, the more you earn.

Set the goal, then let it go

Are you deliberate or desperate? Sure, you want to achieve wealth and success, but desperation will repel it, as people aren't interested in making you wealthy for your own motives. Set an inspired goal, put it out there to be attracted into your life in whatever form of incantation or visualization you choose, then detach from the outcome and accept the journey. It is a balanced dichotomy for entrepreneurs: you are hungry, motivated and relentless, but those traits while admirable in getting started aren't attractive to others and will block the flow of wealth to you. Too much pressure on yourself or an over-control for a specific outcome can lead to unrealistic expectations that lead to resistance.

Increase your monetary ceiling

We all have a ceiling of money that we earn, and are therefore worth, regardless of our net-worth. This could be your consultancy fee, hourly rate, salary, yearly drawings, fees for your art (product or service), or all your passive income combined. The ceiling is the highest point of your earning power, both in the form of actual pounds and pence, dollars and cents, and also the limit to what you believe you are worth. It is the cap that restricts you from charging more, and is directly linked to your self-worth. Whatever internal dialogue would stop you from dramatically increasing your fees and ceiling is what keeps it at that level. Combine the techniques and information so far in this book, with Chapter 43 on pricing and value, to raise your monetary ceiling and open the floodgates to wealth and money.

Your worth is your wealth

The more you value yourself, the more the world values you. The more you invest in yourself, the more the world invests in you. If you feel worthy, you are wealthy. Your wealth might be in your relationships, compassion, hobbies or sports, area of specialized knowledge, your children, or wherever you hold highest value and have therefore continually focused on. If you are not yet financially wealthy, you simply haven't learned or connected how to convert that wealth into cash yet, and the next section will give you the strategies and tactics to do just that. There are millions of people across the planet who have done this: rock bands, artists, chefs, chocolatiers, designers, inventors, dog trainers, puppeteers, lego builders, darts players, horse whisperers; anything and everything and more. If they can all do it, you can do it. But first, some money repellents to get rid of...

24
BCDJ

B, C, D and J are four of the biggest wealth and money drains. They are absolutely repellent to all cashflow, and people. They put you at effect, not cause; victim, not victor. *You can have money or you can have excuses, but you can't have both.* Absolutely commit now to getting rid of the following four wealth repellents:

Blame
Complain
Defend
Justify

They have their own chapter, as I wanted to ring-fence them and not poison the rest of the book. When you have a virus, you have to contain it quickly to prevent a mass outbreak.

Blame

You can blame the government, the system, the banks, the politicians and policy makers, your parents, your IFA, the media, your customers and clients, buyers and sellers, and the rich evil bastards, but it won't change a thing. None of them care anyway. Actually, let me correct myself, it will change two things: other people's view of you, and your view of yourself. You will become bitter, not better. You will become repugnant and to be avoided at all costs as perceived by others.

We have all been self-inflicted victims of blame. The purpose is not to beat yourself up even further, but to commit now to stop blaming everyone and everything and take full and final responsibility for everything that happens in your life that you can personally control. And the things that you can't control – *let them go*. What a waste of time and energy to whine about the things you have no ability to control, at the expense of all the things you can control.

Complain

As a result of blame, the outlet of frustration, anger, unfairness, guilt and other emotions is to complain. Bitch and moan about this, bitch and moan about that. Does anyone on the receiving end of all the complaining ever think, 'I am really enjoying listening to this. Thank you for the gifts of value you are bringing to my life. Please keep complaining'?

I was listening to Tim Ferriss' podcast, where he received a suggestion from one of his interviewees to do a '30-day no complaining' challenge.[1] What a great idea. Some people will wear a wristband and ping it to feel a sharp pain if they catch themselves complaining. Others will start the 30 days again from the beginning. I encourage you to take this challenge. Thirty days is long enough to form a new habit, and when you get to the end you may have unlearned the bad habit of complaining. It will not only make a huge difference to your outer world and the people and wealth you attract into your life, but it will also have a positive impact on your inner happiness and wellness.

Defend

When you are required to defend your position and decisions it is a total energy drain. Most likely, the people you are defending yourself from do not want change anyway. Many people like picking fights for the sake of picking fights, so how do you convince someone who just wants to fight? The answer is, you don't. Not only is this a waste of time, but it also drains your energy and enthusiasm. You get distracted from your vision. Balance selfishness and selflessness, create, make decisions that are fair and good for you and others, then let people say and do as they please. Practise listening, smiling, thanking people for their criticism; say nothing more and move on. Catch yourself wanting to defend your position, and keep quiet. You will save hours that you can instead put into making money and making a difference.

Justify

To justify decisions and actions may be to doubt them, or yourself. Like defending, it is wasted air and energy. Why do you need people's approval? Unless, of course, they are the people you respect and care about the most. You know the single right action for you and others. You know instinctively if you are being authentic, and that's all you need to know. Often it is best not to tell people the things you are planning and doing so that you don't create as much resistance. Move on. Nothing to see here.

How-not-to-be-rich tips

Here is a short list of 'how-not-to-be-rich' tips based on BCDJ. Do not:

1 Listen to poor people.
2 Read the tabloid newspapers.
3 Take other people's views or comments personally.
4 Follow the masses.
5 Make excuses.
6 Be scared to be yourself.
7 Fight battles that aren't very important to you.

Are you letting your fears, doubts or other people dictate your thoughts, behaviours and actions? Many people indulge in BCDJ not because they are inherently mean, but because they have guilt, shame and fears just like everyone else. Maybe they fear the unknown, ridicule, failure, success, criticism, change, loss, pressure, or standing out. The only way they know how to handle these fears that we all feel, is to lash out at others. Do you relate to any of these fears, and are you working on yourself to overcome them and ensure you don't dump them on the people you care about? You're doing the best, with what you know, so keep going and keep growing. Take full and personal responsibility for everything you can control and let go and accept the rest without blaming, complaining, justifying or defending.

SECTION 6

Money mastery

In this section we reveal the scalable, sustainable and ecological secrets that the masters and titans of wealth have had in common. There are laws that create significant wealth personally and globally, as modelled by the super-rich, not the super-skint, that will be revealed to you.

We give you techniques in how to make and manage (more) money, and then grow it and keep it. We show you ways to use it as a force for contribution.

25

VVKIK

Ordering and prioritizing, from the big picture down to the small details, in order to know more, make more and give more money, is known as VVKIK:

Vision
Values
KRAs (Key Result Areas)
IGTs (Income Generating Tasks)
KPIs (Key Performance Indicators)

Some people have their head in the clouds, others have their face in the dirt. Some people are clear on their vision but aren't managing the details, while others are doing the doing but with no idea where they are going. The VVKIK system will help you have clarity of vision, focus on the highest priorities that will make the biggest difference and give you measurement data to get the feedback to check you are on course.

This chapter is a summary of the 24-page section in my book *Life Leverage*.[1] It is focused particularly on how VVKIK relates to money. If you want the full version, in order to bring VVKIK into other areas of your life, then give yourself the gift of that book once you've finished this one.

Vision

Your vision is the clear picture of the purpose of your life. It is expressed both at the end of your life in the form of your immortal legacy, and lived now, every day. Your vision is the ultimate manifestation of your values lived with inspiration. Your vision is the roadmap for your life guiding you through crossroads, tough choices, setbacks, diversions and transient periods when you experience confusion. Your vision is your purpose lived on purpose.

Your vast wealth will be driven from and as a result of your vision. An immortal legacy, which is a commonality of the wealthiest people in history, is the natural outcome of a grand or global vision. Legacy and vision are great partners in driving each other, and you, towards vast and sustainable wealth. The desire to do something meaningful that is bigger than you forces the vision to be national or global and not just local and personal. A grand vision drives your actions, with the support of others, towards a legacy that outlives you.

Values

Values are the life concepts and guiding principles that are most important to you in all areas of your life. They filter everything you perceive, think, decide and act upon. You experience the world through your values. The most important areas to you in your life are efficient at organizing themselves in order and priority. Your values are unique to you; no one has the same values as you. You are unique. When you are authentic you are the best you, and a better you than anyone else could ever be. It is liberating and inspiring to discover and live according to your values. To awaken this genius inside you, that's already there, and doesn't need 'fixing', first you have to give yourself permission, and secondly you follow a simple process. So first of all, do you give yourself permission? If so, then the second step is the following exercise:

Create a blueprint for your ideal life

⋆Positive health warning: this exercise will change your life⋆
This exercise will give you epiphanies, clarity and focus. It will help you value yourself more and stop self-defeating emotions and delusions that erode your wealth. It will order your life and your actions for intuitive and spontaneous clarity and money. Be prepared now for your life to change and your money to grow. Take the time to do this exercise properly and completely. Isolate yourself from distractions and do the following:

1 Note down what you feel is most important to you in your life. Consider higher levels of abstraction and concepts such as health, family, wealth, freedom, happiness, learning, success, growth, travel, teaching, etc. Keep going until you run out of words or you look at the concepts and don't feel inspired by them.

2 Evaluate the list carefully, then reorder according to what you want to change for your life (like moving money or family up the list).
   To help you do this, consider the following:
   • What do you spend most of your time doing?
   • What would you love to do all day long without external pressure?
   • What do you fill your space with (home, office, car, etc.)?
   • What do you think about consistently?
   • What are you most known for?
   • Where do results already show and not show in your life (whether you like them, or not)?

Try not to second-guess yourself in this exercise by what you think you should think, or what you say to others, or what you want for the future you. Let it be what it is. Honour the process and do it without judgement; let it flow and enjoy it. It is important that you do this now, even if you are listening to this book on audio. Pause me and take some time to do this exercise.

Assuming you have done this, now you have a list to look at that represents you. A mirror of you, your life's guide and what governs every action you take. Imagine if you'd done this at school? Imagine if you knew the blueprint that governed and masterminded your own life. Imagine if you redid this every year or six months of your life to check and adjust and re-co-ordinate.

It is vital to living your ideal life and having abundant wealth that you have your list of life's values with you at all times in your chosen easy-to-access format. You are going through the process of making the unconscious conscious, the invisible visible, and you will need constant reminders while it is new.

One of the very best ways to make your values go from unconscious to conscious is to read your list of values just before you go to bed, and as soon as you wake. It will take two minutes to read the list three times and consider it. Within just a few weeks you will know your values unconsciously and intuitively, and your actions will start to mirror them, in what you do and also what you delegate. Your unconscious mind does not sleep like your conscious mind does. You know that often you dream about things that happened in the day, or strong emotions you felt in reaction to a situation just before you go to bed. So clearly what you think about comes about in your unconscious mind. Now, you have the opportunity to control that, and the ability to self-programme.

As you look at your list of values, you are able to see your passions and pains, vacations and vocations, what you are inspired by and what you need to be motivated for, right in front of your very eyes. Until this moment, you have been unconsciously drawn to and focused on those highest on the list, and away from those lowest or not on the list, and most likely in the order and hierarchy in which they appear. If you don't like what you see, and you want your life to change, then make a conscious decision to reorder your values. A pretty quick thing you can do to attract more wealth and money in your life is to move money and money-related values up the list. Your values can and will change through your life, either organically over time (for example health usually moves up as you get older), from a significant emotional event that was strong enough to force change (like being very poor and it ruining your relationships) or through a conscious decision to change. If you want to make more money in your life, the deepest root of change and the most likely to create fast and lasting riches is a values change, because values drive everything you do in your life.

Values often come from voids, because we place high importance on the things in life that we haven't yet achieved or received. Someone who feels they have an abundance of money will no longer see it as important to them. They have filled the void, and so something will naturally usurp its rank in their values hierarchy, like health, freedom or contribution. This is why yo-yo dieters yo-yo, because their diet is most important to them at its worst point, when the pain is at its height. As soon as the diet is good or the weight has gone, the pain goes and the ice cream comes back into play.

Enjoy doing this exercise. I am very excited for you, as your natural right and innate ability to make and give more money will happen quicker than you might imagine once you focus on your values. Do the exercise every 6 to 12 months. I like to do it in early August and early December, when the UK quietens down a bit and I can get space to think clearly. I redo my vision, values, KPIs, KRAs, legacy, mission, cause and individual goals, which results in me feeling inspired to live life in flow for the next few months ahead.

Ask yourself these questions, and note down some thoughts about your vision and purpose. Start now. Get perfect later. It will evolve so don't procrastinate because you don't think you are worthy of a big vision, or you don't know, or you think it's hard; just get some thoughts out of your head *now*:

- What purpose does your life serve?
- What is the vision of your life that will serve others and outlive you?
- Why is this so important to you?
- What do you want your life to look like in 3, 5, 10, 25, 50 years?
- How do you want to be remembered?

Once you have considered your vision, you can link it with your values. How do your values serve your vision and help you get ever closer to it? Make sure the two are aligned. There's no point saying you want to be on the rich list when wealth isn't even in your top ten values. So take time now to align your vision with your values, tweaking and reordering where appropriate.

If you want some help, or you want to share the process with like-minded individuals, or you want to be held accountable to your thoughts, you can like the following page and share your ideas on my wall. Let me know what you think of the book so far, and share your vision and values. If you tag me in I can help you or give you feedback: www.facebook.com/robmooreprogressive

VVKIK gives you the guaranteed ways (in this order) of gaining clarity, wealth and money in your life, intuitively and spontaneously knowing the right thing to do in the right moment, and therefore the right thing to do in every moment.

How do you know if what you're doing is the right thing, towards the right thing? Do you ever feel overwhelmed or frustrated, or experience procrastination, fear of mistakes or doubt in the right action? Most people start at the wrong place: at the bottom (K). They do more, work harder and stay busy on unimportant tasks to trick themselves into feeling productive and that they are making more money, when in fact they are earning *less* per hour. Their boss, the 'guru' and their conscience tell them to work hard, hard, hard and harder. They dig faster and deeper in the wrong direction, diluting their earning power and self-worth even further.

To check in on your progress and productivity, start at the top of the VVKIK system. The higher up the VVKIK you work, the more the later steps will fall into place and require the least effort.

KRAs

These are the 'key result areas' and are the highest value areas that you focus on to achieve your vision. KRAs are the three to seven areas in which to invest most of your time to make the maximum difference to your wealth, income, company and legacy.

KRAs are often strategic, leveraged tasks and functions such as developing and maintaining relationships, building an amazing network, training leaders, developing systems, raising finance, business planning and strategy, board meetings, constant self-education, and so on.

If you get stuck or dragged into micro day-to-day tasks with low cash value, you have likely lost focus on your KRAs. Detailed, operational and practical tasks are mostly not KRAs – they are 'tasks'. If you feel overwhelmed, confused or frustrated, you have probably been dragged into someone else's KRAs, and they are happily earning on you. You know that feeling when you've 'worked' all day but got nothing done? Harder graft, less craft, and not much money.

On a daily, weekly, monthly, six monthly and yearly basis, check in/against your KRAs that you are performing functions of the highest importance, revenue and that make the biggest difference to achieving your vision and living according to your highest values.

Check to-do lists, tasks and requests by others against your own KRAs. If a task serves your KRAs, do it, if it doesn't, delegate or drop it. Be ruthless. KRAs give clarity. KRAs give you the shortest possible route to the highest possible income. KRAs instantly remove overwhelm, frustration and low-value tasking and get your endorphins flowing, because you intuitively know you are taking the single right action. Progress and momentum make you feel good, and build your sense of self-worth and ability to earn and create more.

If you have staff or hire people, you must create KRAs for their roles. Here are some of the main complaints of employees that cause them to hate or leave their job:

- I don't feel appreciated.
- I have no clear purpose (personally and for the company).
- I don't feel I make a difference.
- My boss doesn't care about me.
- Job expectations are unrealistic.
- Too many projects at one time.

At least four of them (althought it could be argued all of them) are related to KRAs. Your staff/team need clarity. They need to have a clear purpose in their role that is linked to a clear purpose in your enterprise. They need to know what they are supposed to do with realistic expectations to deliver, knowing that the task has high value and makes a difference, and they need to know what to prioritize. If they are performing the highest value functions they can for their career and your enterprise, they will feel like they make a difference and will therefore feel valued and inspired. And they will earn both themselves and you the maximum they can on their time.

The KRAs for your team members, and for you, should be on the job description, at the top. Forget reams of tasks and operations. Write out the role in one clear paragraph, and then immediately underneath list the three to seven KRAs to perform that role. These are the mandatory requirements to fulfil the role, and also a clear guideline of how to deliver maximum benefit and satisfaction to the individual and the enterprise.

In your goals/vision document, with you at all times, you should have your KRAs near the top, under your vision and legacy. At the end of the book I will share with you a gift that has this all in one place.

IGTs

'Income generating tasks' are the highest value to you (or your company) – tasks that align with and serve your KRAs. IGTs leverage your highest possible financial value, and maximize revenue per hour. IGTs are the tasks that achieve the highest, leveraged results directly related to income, in the optimum amount of time, bringing maximum benefit and minimum wastage. IGTs get more done and more earned in less time.

Overwhelm, confusion and frustration in your ever-growing to-do list comes from lack of focus on IGTs and mistakenly giving equal importance to all tasks, or lacking order of IGT priority. All tasks are *not* equal. In golf, 40 per cent of the shots most professionals take are with 7.14 per cent of the available clubs (the putter).

Spending more time and priority on putting practice will increase a golfer's scores the most, in the shortest, most leveraged, use of time. And so it is with focusing on IGTs in highest order and priority to bring in maximum revenue in the shortest timeframe, freeing up the majority of time to either do more IGTs, or more of what you love that isn't 'work'.

You will work out what your current IGT is worth to the nearest pound or dollar, and you will learn a simple algorithm that will help you multiply it by a factor of sixteen almost immediately. Any time that's not filled with high priorities will automatically become filled with low priorities and other people's priorities, who will make money leveraging you.

KPIs

'Key performance indicators' are the important, non-vanity metrics of your business, enterprise and personal goals. They keep you moving forward, reduce mistakes and optimize efficiency. You can't master what you don't measure. KPIs are the vital data sets that tell you in as real time as possible exactly what is happening, or failing, in your business. KPIs become increasingly vital as you grow, hand over control and become more removed or more strategic.

A common mistake is setting up your KPIs too late, or not at all, because they take time, and take time away from urgent, more functional tasks. But that's like not eating because you are too busy working, not learning because you are too busy doing, or not taking the cheque to cash in at the bank because you are too busy working.

KPIs serve your KRAs, because they give real time feedback that operating your KRAs and IGTs are either giving you the right outcome and income, or not. You can test, tweak or change your KRAs and IGTs when you get feedback through KPIs. Because you don't know what you don't know, if you don't have KPIs, you could just as likely and easily be doing the wrong thing, losing money, and working really hard to get nowhere.

Imagine if you had no sales metrics/KPIs in a sales organization. You could be selling lots of something that makes a net loss, not knowing any different. It would be utterly self-defeating, even a touch insane, to do more and more of what is not working. Yet many small businesses don't have enough KPI data. Is it therefore any surprise that up to nine out of ten new businesses fail in the first year, and then eight in ten of those fail in the next three years?

Start compiling your KPIs now, especially income related ones, personally and for your business. Start with the ones that come to mind, such as goals you set that you check in against, metrics for your sales, marketing and financial reporting. From there, build your systems, become less operational and earn more in less time.

Develop your KPIs

To develop your KPIs further, here are some exercises for you:

1 Read books on data/business growth.
2 Ask bigger business owners what they measure.
3 Troubleshoot your business; look to solve problems.
4 Analyse your existing KPIs.
5 Survey your team and your customers.

Asking business owners who've been there before, and have solved the problems you are having or not measuring, will kick out more useful KPIs for you. Ask them what they measure. If you ask the right questions of your team and customers, you get the right answers. What are the bottlenecks? What information do they not have access to? What should you start, stop and keep? Look to solve the problems in your life and business, and you will unearth what you need to measure so that it doesn't happen again. Reading and thinking about your current metrics will spark off ideas about new ones. Failing KPIs create new niche KPIs that are needed to give you overall valuable data. Low staff morale, sickness and absenteeism may be linked to failing KPIs, or retention rates as a percentage of overall staff, or retention rates broken down into left vs fired vs retired. All answers to all problems are hidden in plain sight.

Conclusion of VVKIK

You now have a cyclical feedback loop to constantly stay on track, to be more 'in flow' and less 'on the go' from your highest unique values through to the micro-metrics. You have the system to earn more while doing less. You have a system and hierarchy that gives clarity and direction enabling you to do the things that matter the most to you, serve the most people and manifest your unique legacy and wealth. You deserve to spend time on yourself, so get some quiet time away from the humdrum. Isolate yourself from white noise and work from the top down to know more, make more and give more money.

26

The formula for wealth

There are laws that govern money. The wealthy understand and leverage these laws and the poor are victim to them. Because money moves from those who value it least to those who value it most, wealth will always move to those who know the laws. The formula for wealth is a formula I developed that has stood the test of time and been consistent through every part of the cycle, and can be seen through every titan of wealth over the last 6700 years. It has been modelled on the obsessive and enthusiastic study of the wealthiest people on the planet through history that is a great passion of mine. It is actually quite simple, and it is shared below. You can leverage this formula for wealth just as much as anyone else:

$$W = (V + FE) \times L$$
Wealth = (Value + Fair Exchange) × Leverage

Let's look at each one to help our understanding.

Value (V)

Value is the service you give to other people, as perceived by them. If you serve and solve, and show care and concern, then people will receive value and benefit that they will desire more of, pay for, and refer you to others. People are looking for their problems to be solved, pains to be alleviated, and for things to be made faster, easier and better for them. Time is a scarce resource and most valuable commodity, so anything that leverages or preserves it will hold value that is convertible into cash. If you're ever struggling financially or emotionally yourself, look more at how you can serve others and solve their problems, and you will have part of the formula for wealth solved and more money will flow to you.

Fair Exchange (FE)

An exchange or transaction has to take place for you to receive money and wealth. You have to offer a product, service or idea that someone else perceives valuable enough to pay for, and you have to be open and have high enough self-worth to receive fair payment. When you gratefully receive financial (or other) fair compensation, you have a fair transaction, and repeat business and referrals. Your gratitude will convert to value, and that will be perceived by the buyer. Value without (fair) exchange or transaction will create a financial void in your life, because you will be giving but not allowing receipt. There will be unfair exchange, you will have high overhead to revenue ratios, and your business and income will be unsustainable. You will also build resentment and bitterness. Guilt, lack of confidence, imposed religious or social beliefs, perceived market ceilings and extreme emotions make a transaction too one-sided and unsustainable, on the side of low pricing. This will result in a reduction of value creation, and again will be self-fulfilling.

At the other extreme, if you charge high prices in comparison to the value you give, you will be perceived as unfair, greedy or worse, ripping people off. You may be able to temporarily boost sales because of the big claim, but this will reverse once the reality of the lack of value is perceived. In the end your overheads will rise as you have to compensate in the forms of extra customer service, refunds, PR and damage limitation. This is also unsustainable in the long term, and could lead to insolvency. It is easy to look at others and think they are 'getting away with it', but as with Enron, Madoff and Leeson, in the end the balance will be redressed.

To balance this fair exchange, test your prices and get feedback. *Price elasticity* is a measure of the effect of a price change or a change in the quantity supplied on the demand for a product or service. There are sweet spots that merge and balance the maximum amount a buyer is prepared to pay, and the maximum value creation from the vendor that scales. Interestingly, sometimes that sweet spot is higher than you are charging, or than you might believe. You also want to test the amount of value you create. An increase in value creation will drive prices up. There are ways to increase the perceived value to the buyer with a low actual cost to deliver, such as online-hosted information. Continually seek feedback from your ideal client demographic to keep the value and price exchange in perfect harmony. When you get fair exchange right, the buyer feels they get more value than they pay for without becoming greedy or demanding, they will refer others to you which lowers your marketing cost, and you have gratitude and a service focus which in turn attracts more buyers to you. You value your service, so take care to keep it valuable and improve it.

Leverage (L)

Leverage is the scale and speed of service and remuneration, and the impact it has. The more people you can serve and solve for, the more money you make. The bigger the problem, the higher the transactional amount (as fairness is dictated by the scale and size of the problem). The more valuable the product, service or offer, the quicker it will spread.

You will only leverage and scale wealth for the long term if you have value *and* fair exchange. You could get transient spikes and viral sharing of a big claim or promise, but anything that doesn't serve and solve won't continue to scale because once unfair exchange is discovered, you will be humbled and brought back into balance. In fact it can be very dangerous to scale too fast, because what is broken will exaggerate, or things may start to break if you are not prepared for scale. Also, if you are promising undeliverable value, that will exacerbate with scale and your overheads will increase and margins may even go negative. This is why you hear smart business advisors suggesting not to scale too early or quickly.

Referrals are a sign of Value + Fair Exchange × Leverage (V + FE) × L working effectively, as are leveraged media such as video, TV and other far-reaching media shared by others on your behalf, or going viral. In the world of fibre optics, social media and newer tech disruptions, your Value + Fair Exchange (V + FE) can leverage very quickly. Your business and service can grow faster than ever before. This is why I believe now is the best time in history to create vast and lasting wealth. You can get 10 million views on YouTube, go viral across multiple social media platforms, get millions of likes and shares and get national or global TV coverage. This 'one to many' is leverage in great effect. In the future AI, VR and QE may increase the velocity of scale even further.

V + FE but no L

If you have great Value + Fair Exchange (V + FE) but no scale (L), then you don't create vast wealth. The size of your customer base and the reach of your impact will be relative to the scale of your wealth. You may have a great little business, or have no business at all. If you desire more wealth then you must embrace scale.

V × L but no FE

Conversely, you could have great Value (V) and Leverage (L) but no Fair Exchange (FE). If so you will exaggerate negative margins and unsustainability. You will work harder and longer with more bitterness and resentment, bending to the will of your clients. Your passion and profession will turn into desperation and disillusion. Something will break – either you or your bank.

FE × L but no V

You can have Fair Exchange (FE) and Leverage (L) but no Value (V), and you won't sustain wealth for the long term. This can be one of the most dangerous variations of the formula because you can scale fast on an overpromised claim. In the end, your reputation for not giving value under fair exchange will leverage (scale), and wealth will be rebalanced as stated through reputational costs, defensive costs, refunds and extra service that puts margins in the negative.

An example of the formula in action could be the Post-it Note. Value is created by solving a problem many of us have. In this case it was the need to write something down quickly without having to carry a book around, then the need to put note somewhere it wouldn't be lost, but also where it wouldn't damage anything. A fair exchange is created because the price of the Post-it Note is equal to and worthy of the value. Leverage is achieved with 6,050,000,000 sold each year.

You now have a proven, scalable yet little known formula to build, sustain and scale vast wealth and riches. Focus on the three parts to the formula equally, but in the right order (Value, then Fair Exchange, then Leverage) and hire or partner with the best people in the two areas you are not as strong in. You can then take on the part you enjoy the most. Once you fix or build whichever part of the formula is broken or not created, the floodgates for wealth and riches will open up. You need to keep testing, taking feedback and tweaking as you scale. What worked will change, markets will evolve and new challenges will present themselves perennially. If you embrace this rather than becoming a victim to it, it gives you the best competitive advantage you could wish for.

27

Time–money relationship

They say that time is money. I would also say that money is time. Money and time preserve and serve each other. Most people spend all their time to make a little bit of money to just about cover their bills to delay having free time to the end of their life, only to get to the end of their and have no money or time left. It is a sad irony, but there is a solution: to understand the relationship between time and money.

Inverse relationship of work and money (the myth of hard work)

One of the biggest myths is that to be successful you have to work hard hard hard. Work harder and longer than anyone else, and you will be the best. Make sacrifices and go the distance. Never give up. Keep going when it hurts. Don't be weak. Man up. Smash it. Hustle. Grind. While this may be the case in conditioning for strength or sports at the very highest level, there are many more factors to consider when choosing your vocation and investing your time. The hard workers say 'practice makes perfect', but the smart workers say 'perfect practice makes perfect'.

First, choose the right path to invest time in. It's pretty insane to work harder and longer and make huge sacrifices in a vocation that is unlikely to yield results and wealth. If you put in 60 hours a week in the hope that you will get a promotion every three to five years and an incremental pay rise that doesn't even match inflation, and you delay the gratification of doing the things you love, and it is clear that it takes 30 years to get your salary from £30k to £60k, then working harder and longer is a time drain. It could even be that the next pay grade up is actually a lower per hour rate when you factor in all the extra time.

If you give half your waking life to a technical skill that could become redundant with technological or cyclical changes, and you rely on the state to look after you later in life, then working harder and longer is counterintuitive. If you spend your time working to make someone else rich, without the ability to control the financial upside, then working longer and harder is counterproductive.

Most people think (and teach) that the harder and longer you work, the richer and more successful you get. This is a fallacy. There are stages in building wealth, and while working harder and longer at the start-up stage will push you forward, once you get into strategy, vision, leadership and solving bigger problems, it is almost the inverse: the more you push the worse the results can be. You also get to the point at which hard graft yields diminishing returns.

The 'hard work' model for writing this book

Let's use writing this book as an example. Here is the 'hard work model' for writing this, or any book:

1 Build the knowledge. Read as many books, go to as many events and seminars, and get as many mentors on the subject of money as you can.
2 Gain experience. Spend ten years building wealth and making money.
3 Research. Watch every video, take detailed notes on every book, course and audio on wealth and money. Research all history, data, facts, stories and biographies.
4 Write the entire book. This will take most people years. Most people have a book inside them, yet it stays inside them. Life will get in the way and it will cause you guilt and frustration when you don't commit time to it.
5 Edit the entire book. About as tiresome a process as you could wish to take yourself through, and no matter how many times you read it, you will miss mistakes.
6 Self-publish the book. You have to manage a book printing company. We once had 5000 books printed that all the pages fell out of.

7 Promote and market the book. A book with no marketing is hundreds of hours of wasted time. There were 750,000 books self-published in the US in 2015, and the average number of sales for a non-fiction book was 250 a year, according to the Bowker report, 2016.[1] With 20 per cent of the books selling 80 per cent of the numbers, the remaining 80 per cent of books sell around 50 copies a year. If you bought a stock of 100 on print, you'd have lost money plus hundreds of hours.

8 Update the book. Most books are out of date as soon as you print them. Unless you update them every one to three years, they will stop selling fast.

We will cover the time leveraged, smart-not-hard work model for writing a book at the end of this chapter. This list is the stone-cold reality of most of the honest, hardworking book writers out there. This is my ninth book, so I have personal experience and empathy, and have certainly made most of the 'hard work' mistakes above.

The overtime myth

Overtime is another misleading concept. You think you are making more money, when in reality you are exchanging more of your time with diminishing returns and benefits. Overtime is time you can't ever get back, for slightly more money that you might use to buy more material items, increasing your personal spending, and leaving you in no better a personal financial position. This manifests more pressure as more money has to be earned just to stay in the same financial position, but it now takes more (over) time to achieve, while inflation creeps up behind you.

The conventional employee with the conventional mindset of work-hard-and-take-overtime does create personal wealth and enterprise: for the owner of the business or the state in taxes. Employees can get trapped by mortgages, overheads and illusions of security and 'safe' retirement, but the sad fact is that, at any time, without warning, the state could spend your pension, one single regulation change could make your job redundant, or one decision from your boss could put you out of work.

Being an employee is not necessarily a bad thing, and might be right for you. You could be an intrapreneur in an entrepreneurial enterprise. Valuing, understanding and leveraging time and the time–money relationship is vital to maximizing your earning power. We will return to entrepreneurs, intrapreneurs and employees in Chapter 40.

Not every £ or $ has the same value

Equal units of currency don't necessarily have the same value. Choose how you earn your unit of currency exchanged from your unit of time, very wisely. Here are some options and examples:

1 JOB PRICE

You could have a job price that takes more hours than your hourly rate calculation, so you earn less per hour. If you leverage time better, then you could earn more per hour with a job price.

2 HOURLY RATE

Working more hours to earn more money erodes time. The whole purpose of working is to be able to afford to do the things you love, and that requires time as well as money. Once you are at personal capacity, you can't earn more money, unless you increase your hourly rate, which scares most people and is usually incremental not exponential.

3 MONTHLY OR YEARLY WAGE

You could be earning a salary that has a very low hourly rate, if you are working long hours and taking work home with you. You work harder and longer in your current position, reducing your current salary in terms of hourly rate, in the hope that you will get a 3–5 per cent pay rise. Like the hamster in the wheel, you can get stuck in this cycle working harder and longer for less per hour, eroding the time you have left to do what you love.

In all of the examples above, you're exchanging, or burning, time for money. You can never get that time back so in effect you're reducing your lifespan for a small amount of remuneration. There are ways to maximize your job, hourly or monthly rate so you can still enjoy the benefits of being employed or a contractor, because being an entrepreneur or businessperson is not for everyone.

4 EARNING ON OTHER PEOPLE

If your hourly rate or value is £100, but you employ or contract people who earn £30 an hour, and you get £10 of that, then ten people who work or contract for you replace your hourly rate. This is time and money leverage. You can either reduce the number of hours you work, or earn £100 on your hour *and* £100 on ten other people's hours, doubling your income with virtually the same amount of your personal time. This has limitless scale, unlike the first three methods of earning related to time. If you had 1000 people that would be £10,000 per hour, and 10,000 would be £100,000 per hour. As you hire and contract more people, they will naturally take the tasks that are beneath your hourly value, so an exponential result will be that the more people earn for you, the higher your hourly value grows. Ten thousand people bringing net £10 per hour to you will be £400,000 per week on a 40-hour working week. Your value will be thousands of pounds per hour by this time. You now have the choice to be selective with the type of work you do, or you can work less, or not at all, or you can work and your team can work and you can make more and more money. You are also creating vast wealth through increased service and creation of jobs, and the taxes generated on all the revenues.

5 EARNING ON ASSETS

People need managing, which is a possible time-consuming variable to add to 'earning on other people'. As you scale you introduce levels of management so that managers manage managers who manage managers who manage doers, and therefore your personal management time reduces. You can invest your time into assets, systems, software, stocks and property, which can pay passive income and can take less management than people. Or you can hire people to manage the assets for you. Once time is invested to set up, you can scale up and step out.

Often an asset brings in no income in the set-up phase, which is why people continue to work for an hourly rate or wage as they can't afford or don't have the vision to delay the income. Once an asset is set up, systemized and managed, it will start and continue to pay residual income. As you build up a vast portfolio of assets your income to time ratio gets exponentially high because there is no limit to the amount of assets and passive income you can have.

6 EARNING ON JOBS, HOURLY RATES, SALARIES, OTHER PEOPLE AND ASSETS

As you scale businesses and gain experience making money, you can get income in all five ways. You can still earn per hour. You are happy to exchange your time for tens or hundreds of thousands of pounds. Why not? But you can be selective. You could also invest your time in a 'job rate' developing a large commercial building or setting up a team, Steve Jobs style, to build a new enterprise. You can still take huge salaries, dividends and drawings from all the businesses you have started and then stepped back from. You can earn on the hundreds or thousands of staff in your enterprises and all the assets you have built. You will have multiple streams of income, multiple ways, with multiple leverage and minimum time input, once each stage is set up.

Earning vs enjoying time

Wealth isn't just about money, of course. Wealth is about well-being, which balances free time with abundant cashflow. The choice is yours if you choose to earn on your own time, once you earn leveraging the time of others. You can compound the money and maximize your earning potential, or simply take some time to do more of the things you love. It is not for me to tell you what that should be, but surely it's better to have the choice. It may also depend on your stage of life. They say you have three stages relating to money: the learning years, earning years and yearning years. Perhaps we should change it to learning years, earning years and leveraging years.

Time management models

Here are three essential time management models that will preserve and liberate your time and accelerate your wealth:

The four values of time model

The four values of time are: wasted; spent; invested; leveraged.

WASTED TIME

You can only afford to waste time if you have recurring income coming in. Otherwise you're eroding your time and life, and not earning any money. Ever said to yourself, 'I'll never get that time back?' Enough said. Next.

SPENT TIME

Time spent is time that can have both low and high value in financial or emotional terms, but has no residual, ongoing benefit. Working for an hourly rate, performing an unleveraged task or exchanging your time for money, and being earned on by others, is time spent.

INVESTED TIME

This is time that continues to earn or give leverage long after the initial task was completed. It has residual and recurring benefit that could last a long time or a lifetime.

LEVERAGED TIME

Leveraged time builds on invested time, yet you leverage out the initial task or set up. You completely outsource the building of the business or asset, yet get a share of the ongoing income stream(s).

Passive income comes from time invested and leveraged, as do dividends, drawings and royalties. Salaries come from time spent. There's nothing wrong with exchanging time for money, as long as there is a vision to invest it. *You can work hard for your money or you can make your money work hard for you.* Measure and monitor your time in order to master it. Be strict, ruthless and disciplined in how you invest it. Lead, manage and leverage. It's not about how much you do, but how much the world is doing for you. Ask yourself, 'Will this give me the best return on time invested?' This question will force you to earn the maximum amount of money on the minimum amount of your personal time, creating recurring income to have and do more of the *things you love* that make you significantly more money without burning out or selling out.

IGV calculation model

The only way to know for sure if you are leveraging correctly, that the tasks you are doing are of the highest financial value to you, *and* that the tasks you're outsourcing are beneath your financial value, is to know what you're worth, per hour of your time.

The first stage is to calculate your Income Generating Value (IGV). Your IGV is what you are worth, per hour of work. When you know exactly what an hour of your time is worth, you can calculate accurately what tasks you should do yourself, and what tasks you should leverage out, pay for or inspire others to do for you.

To calculate your IGV, add up the total number of hours you work every week. That includes your job/career, any part-time work, and any time you're putting into asset building; the entire amount of time devoted to earning money. You might work 55 hours.

Now calculate, or roughly guess, how much money you earn in that timeframe. Include all sources of gross income: salary, dividends, interest, property income, etc. if you have it. Include all income not including gifts or loans, and add up the gross amount (not net of taxes, etc.). You may have £1000 in a week. If you know what you earn per month, not per week, divide your monthly figure by 4.3 to get your weekly figure. Now divide the amount of gross income by the total number of work hours, and you have your IGV: your time value per hour. Every hour you work brings in, on average, £x.

In this example: IGV = £1000 / 55 hours = £18.18 per hour

Or, IGV = total income (week) / hours worked (week)

So what does this tell you? Every task that will (or could) bring in more than £18.18, it's OK to do yourself, without diminishing your IGV. But every task that brings in (or could bring in) less than £18.18 per hour, or you could pay £18.17 or less to outsource, *must* be outsourced. If you don't, your IGV will go down. This compounds, because when you free up time from lower value tasks for higher value tasks, you bring in more money which increases your IGV.

This is why people don't get rich working longer employed hours or doing overtime. This is why the rich get richer, because they leverage, outsource and pay for the lower value tasks. In order for this to work for you, you need to be disciplined and have faith in this 'model'. Any task that comes your way that you feel will, or could earn you more than your IGV, do it yourself, because it will pay you to do it. If you keep doing that, your IGV will go up and up and up.

But even more importantly, every task that comes your way that will or *could* bring in less than your IGV, you *must* leverage or outsource it. If you don't, you'll get poorer and you'll actually repel more money than you pull in. Stick to this system and it will change your life and finances forever.

LMD model

This is a system for maximizing your time in relation to money, to manage your tasks so that you get the most done and make the most money in the least amount of time. L1, M2, DL:

Leverage first, Manage second, Do LAST!

When you're busy, perhaps the first thing you think is, 'What do I need to do?' or 'I've got so much to do, where do I even start?' or 'When can I get this done?' or 'How can I do this?'

Now try this: next time you start your task or to-do list, instead of starting with a task, start with what you can leverage or outsource. Who can you get to do the first task you were going to do? And the second? And third? Out of seven or so tasks for the day, if you leverage four of them, and do three of them, you'll achieve more than double the results in less than half of your personal time.

Once you've leveraged out tasks you would ordinarily have done yourself, they don't just magically arrive on your desk the next day in shiny wrapping paper and a ribbon. Any task 'leveraged' needs managing through to completion. Check through your leveraged tasks and manage (guide) them through to completion. Only once you have gone through these two steps should you even consider 'doing' a task yourself. A few small hours moved from 'doing' to 'leveraging' has huge compounded benefits. You might end up leveraging three tasks, having two 'under management' and only two that you actually have to do yourself.

And if you're too busy to invest time, that's probably the very reason you need to do it. If no one can do that task or job as well as you, that's probably the very reason you need to do it too.

28

The commonalities of titans

This is the chapter I've looked forward to writing the most. There is no better way I know of building and scaling vast riches than by learning from the titans of wealth. Some people say the best way to learn is from your mistakes; I say that the best way to learn is vicariously through the mistakes of others. Let them be the crash test dummies and you step in when you know it works. The real, non-get-rich-quick-get-rich-quickest strategy is to model and own the traits of the greats.

The Book of Wealth

Hubert Howe Bancroft, an American historian who wrote 27 publications between 1874 and 1917, published *The Book of Wealth* in 1896. It is a 6700-year history of the wealthiest people in history that took six years to complete. Only 4000 copies were released, in ten volumes, at $2500 each in 1898. Bancroft distributed the book to the wealthiest people in the western world such as the Morgans, the Rothschilds, the Rockefellers, the Vanderbilts, the Kennedys, the Carnegies, the Fricks and the Fords. I would like to pay homage to this book, and everyone I have learned from. If I could summarize for you the common threads in *The Book of Wealth* and the commonalities of the titans of wealth through all of history up to almost 1900, many of whom amassed vast wealth that, once adjusted for inflation dwarfs some of today's billionaires, then they would be: service at scale, material opulence and wisdom of wealth and money. Here are the three commonalities of the wealthiest people in the last 6700 years. The wealthiest people in the last 120 years after

The Book of Wealth was written appear to have these traits in common too. As my personal wealth has increased, I have seen a change towards these commonalities, in part through education, but it seems also in part through desire and destiny from within. The wealthiest people in history share the following beliefs:

1 THEY ARE DESTINED TO SERVE VAST NUMBERS OF PEOPLE

The wealthiest people have all experienced a deep realization that they want to serve vast numbers of people, and to continue to grow, reach and serve more and more. There is no destination or end to this scale, and therefore no cap or ceiling on the amount of wealth that can be amassed. This desire for scale of service dovetails with a yearning to make a massive contribution and leave a lasting legacy. While vast riches are the result, it seems always to be about more than just the money. It is about the memory and the creation of lasting history.

The vastly wealthy will endure the challenges that come with global riches. *The vision is bigger than the resistance from others.* They will solve the world's biggest problems. Their mission seems impossible *not* to fulfill; it seems to be their destiny, and they make the link between service, scale and solving problems.

Two of the wealthiest people in history (adjusted for inflation) were John Rockefeller and Andrew Carnegie. Rockefeller had the equivalent of up to $341 billion ($1.5 billion in 1918), and Carnegie $372 billion. Rockefeller controlled 90 per cent of American oil production, a significant scale and service to his nation, interconnected across the globe. Carnegie is perhaps the richest American of all time? He sold US Steel to J.P Morgan for $480 million in 1901, which equated to more than 2.1 per cent of the entire US GDP. Carnegie disrupted steel production, built a massive steel works larger than 80 American football fields, and by 1900, 11 million tonnes were being produced by Carnegie every year, employing 200,000 men.

You can increase your wealth by making your vision bigger than any fears of scale you may have. These titans have blazed the trail, had thousands of staff, served millions of people, had global-sized difficulties to overcome, and they kept going and growing. In their own ways they showed a great care and concern for humanity, balanced with self-interest.

> 'I believe the power to make money is a gift to be developed and used to the best of our ability for the good of mankind. Having been endowed with the gift I possess, I believe it is my duty to make money and still more money and to use the money I make for the good of my fellow man according to the dictates of my conscience.'

> J.D. Rockefeller

2 THEY ARE DESTINED TO LIVE AT A HIGH, REGAL AND OPULENT STANDARD

In almost all cases of the super-rich, they enjoy opulence. The opulence is most sustainable when balanced between narcissism and altruism, serving the self and others. The high, regal standard of living is about enjoying the finer things in life, but it is also a means to boost the economy. If you have assistants, servants, bodyguards or an entourage, the speed of money increases wherever you go, and you add value and money to every place you visit or reside. You increase the standards through your opulence, and increasing the standards serves more people.

3 THEY HAVE AN AWARENESS OF WHAT MONEY IS AND IS NOT

You cannot scale vast wealth if you don't know what money is, much like you can't repair the engine of a car if you don't know how it works. This is of course common sense, but it was a revelation to me. I used to think economics, business and history was dry and boring. Funny how that has reversed, and now I love it. Money, as you now know, is not good, or bad. It is simply a universal mechanism of exchange of value, a way of storing future value and worth, coping with an uncertain future and enabling fair exchange. Money is credit, which is trust, and debt. Money is spirit converted into matter. The wealthiest people in history have transcended the emotive meanings and beliefs of money, and gained wisdom into how it really works. Knowing this allows you to give yourself permission to have opulence without guilt or fear of being judged. This is very liberating.

Other commonalities of millionaires and billionaires

In studying millionaires, billionaires, business leaders, innovators and visionaries, and being fortunate to have many as friends, I've learned that you can't stereotype one type in the way people think you can. They come in all shapes and sizes, with varying values, in different niches, in multiple countries, sexes and ages. There is no typical demographic billionaire, but there are consistent and persistent qualities to model to convert your latent wealth into millions.

Wealthy people continue to strive to build vast service-based enterprises through a merited monopoly, where you have large market share created fairly through merit, service, fair exchange and increased economy and investment. Occasionally the biggest come up against anti-competition laws, a few maybe through illicit means. Cream rises to the top, customers vote with their feet and they purchase goods and services that they value the most, on merit. While wealthy people will cite some good fortune along the journey, they all endure some harder times and struggle, which likely balance out over time. Society has a way of self-regulating if any enterprise or entrepreneur abuses their power, in the form of customers leaving *en masse*, laws and regulation, smear campaigns, forcing philanthropy as seemed to happen to Bill Gates, and in extreme cases imprisonment and assassination. Do not let this stop you from scaling, just do it balancing self-interest with humanitarian interest.

Visionaries

Everything around you that you call life was made up by people that were no smarter than you and you can change it, you can influence it, you can build your own things that other people can use.

Steve Jobs

Apple now earns $300,000 per minute.

A visionary often views the world as their playground. Billion-aires are the few who realize that the world is pliable, as opposed to static or predetermined. They can see things other people can't see. They are inspired by a new idea, often more so by the bigger, more unrealistic ones as perceived by others. Elon Musk wants to colonize Mars. They see possibilities that offer value and they can visualize scale. They inspire, mobilize people and resources and bring ideas to life, turning ideas into income. You too have the power to manifest your thoughts into a clear vision and mate-rial reality. The visionaries share their inspired message with other people and enrol the masses. Once construction of the plan, peo-ple and materials start, investors come in and finance the vision, and more people are inspired to join and deliver your vision through a mission. Holding and directing the vision gives one power and authority.

Some legacies, infrastructures and buildings took years or decades to build. The visionaries have the capacity to see clearly that far into the future, in terms of unlimited possibilities, and what seems impos-sible to 'mere mortals'. Visionaries raise the standards around them. Virtually all the world's most wealthy believed that they had this visionary power and deserved all the good things they desired. Many of these wealthy people believed they had an immortality factor and their lives and legacies changed the world.

Certainty and clarity

Stay certain and clear, trust yourself and your vision; tweak it every 6 to 12 months and gain ever more clarity. The world's best wealth creators have shown seemingly unbreakable purpose and staying power. If you don't believe in yourself, why should anyone else? No one is inspired by a confused vision. Your certainty gives confidence to others, and a desire to assist and support you to manifest your cause.

Own the traits of the greats and model the masters

It is said that success leaves clues. There are common traits of the greats that you can model and master. You are what you admire, and you already have within you every trait that they have, so awaken them by studying and learning from the greats. Choose the people you most want to be like who've made their mark on this world, identify their traits and embrace them.

There has not been one titan of wealth that I've ever met or studied who didn't spend much of their time with other successful people at or even beyond their level. Your network is your net-worth. Make it a lifelong commitment to seek out, serve and spend time with other titans. You're only successful as those you frequently associate with, so build your network like you would your empire. Seek peers, specialists and mentors. Learn from the mistakes of others. Get connected with the best, from the best. Successful people know successful people, and those with money attract others with money. This will be detailed in Chapter 44.

The optimist and the skeptic

You might hear generic advice that 'millionaires are positive', and that you need to be a 'glass half full' type of person to succeed. I believe this advice to be too simplistic, and generally comes from people who write articles but don't have direct experience. Neither extreme leads to vast wealth and money. Too 'positive' and you become naïve, too skeptical and you never take calculated and considered actions. Richard Branson, arguably one of the most 'positive' billionaires, gives this advice: 'trust your instincts, but protect the downside'.[1] This is a blend of go-getting and risk-protecting. You are not a pessimist but not delusional or blind to what could go wrong either. The titans seem to have an overall positive outlook, one of the ability to empower change and make a difference, but with the ability to put a skeptical hat on when required. Depend on people, but don't let them bully you. Negotiate fairly but firmly. Trust, but verify.

Your ability to turn on and turn off these extremes quickly will augment your earning power. Perhaps you could call yourself a 'realistic optimist'.

Life-long learning

Steve Siebold, who has studied over 1200 millionaires, states: 'Walk into a wealthy person's home and one of the first things you'll see is an extensive library of books they've used to educate themselves on how to become more successful'. He continues: 'The middle class reads novels, tabloids, and entertainment magazines.'[2]

According to *Business Insider*, Warren Buffett estimates that 80 per cent of his working day is dedicated to reading.[3] Tom Corley of Richhabits.net states that: '85 per cent of millionaires read two or more books every month'. Most of these books are on the subjects of career, how-to books, history, biographies of successful people, self-help, health, current events, memory improvement and learning, psychology, leadership, science, new age, inspiration and positive mental outlook.[4]

It is categorically clear from the research I and others who study wealth have conducted, that the wealthy self-study through reading books and articles. They learn from other titans and attend events and courses on business, wealth, money and the subjects listed above. While this research isn't a revelation ('read and get rich'), it really should be. It is not hard to read two good books a month, and according to Tom Corley, if you did read just two relevant books a month then on average you would become a millionaire in 32 years.[5] You are what you think about, and thoughts become things, so in reading and self-studying wealth, you turn what you put into your brain into physical wealth.

Multiple streams of income

According to Tom Corley, 65 per cent of millionaires studied had at least three streams of income that they created prior to making their first million dollars.[6] I've yet to meet anyone with sustained wealth who didn't have multiple streams of income. Many made their initial fortune through one model, but later diversified by investing it into property, stocks, other businesses, technology, IP and other asset classes. No matter how deep and vast, income from one stream is exposed to the risk of disruption and market changes. It is wise to balance capital and income, cyclical and counter-cyclical streams, higher risk–higher return and more consistent, safe income streams.

Vitality

When asked what had made him so successful and amass such a fortune, Warren Buffett answered, 'Three things: living in America for the great opportunities, having good genes so I lived a long time, and compound interest.'[7]

This is far more insightful than it seems at first glance. Warren Buffett is pushing 90 years old now, and has made 99 per cent of his wealth since his fiftieth birthday. The length of his life has helped him amass and compound great wealth. It is not just about being old, and doing it the longest, but also being vital, healthy and maintaining good energy. Illness or fatigue will slow your wealth creation as much as a bad investment decision. Sixty-six per cent of millionaires studied by Tom Corley exercise for 30 minutes or more every day.[8] Many are famed, as was Steve Jobs, for going on long walks. Exercise has been proven to increase energy, brainpower and life span. Fifty per cent of self-made millionaires wake up at least three hours before their workday begins, so you could combine getting up early and exercising, while listening to podcasts and audiobooks, for triple leverage of time.

Test your optimum day

There has been much conflicting advice around how early you should wake and how much sleep you should have. There is a common thread amongst the very wealthy of waking early, so it should be a serious consideration for you. However I also feel, from performing many tests on myself and interviewing some experts on my podcast, that we all have different energy peaks and troughs in the day, and we all perform at peak based on individual variables. Many business people love getting up early, while many creative people love working late. Some people only need five hours' sleep a night; those who exercise hard often need eight. So rather than blindly getting up early and working long hours, test the time you rise, and the amount of sleep that works best for you.

First generation, self-created

Most millionaires are first generation. Contrary to popular and envious convention, they created wealth themselves without inheritance, handouts or lottery wins. They started at the same point as everyone else. Between 80 per cent and 86 per cent of millionaires are self-created. (I do not subscribe to the view that anyone's wealth is 'self-made', hence my choice to call it 'self-created'.) According to Forbes there has been a significant swing from inherited billionaires to self-created billionaires since 1984. According to a January 2016 article at Entrepreneur.com, 62 per cent of American billionaires were self-created.[9]

Teamwork makes the dream work

If you want wealth and money at scale, you'll need a lot of smart people around you. When you start, it's just you, your laptop and your dream. You can outsource and leverage, and you may get to 300k on your own with a couple of virtual staff. You will hit a threshold where the volume of work that comes back to you is too much, and you need mentors, advisors and staff. You start with admin help, PA, office or operations manager, a salesperson, and scale from there. As you grow you will need managers, an MD, a marketing and design department, finance, tax and legal advisors, PR, and maybe an FD and HR manager once you hit around 50 staff. The more you drive your top line revenue up, the more people you are likely to need. A lot of people have concerns or bad experiences about hiring up.

This means that they have let the challenges of scale overpower their vision, and not that it can't be done.

Sam Walton was one of the world's richest men, both in his time and in today's money, once adjusted for inflation. He willed more than $100 billion to his heirs. Walmart had 2.2 million staff in 2015. Facebook are a little leaner with 12,691 employees in the same year, but still sizeable, and Mark Zuckerberg is valued at $54.8 billion. One of the driving metrics of any business is revenue per employee (RPE). I have keenly researched this and have found a range of (on average) $51,000 per employee for a conventional business, up to a high of $1,865,306 (Apple). LinkedIn are at $320k RPE, Yahoo at $375k RPE and Amazon $580k RPE. The tech- and innovation-driven companies have high RPEs, many of which have grown significantly in the last decade.[10]

Behaviours, actions and habits of the rich vs the poor

The following summarizes some of the direct polarized differences between the titans of wealth and the rest: the rich vs the (first-world) poor:

Rich	Poor
Take full responsibility	Blame and make excuses
People commit to wealth	People want and dream of wealth
Think big	Think small
Create	Consume and depend
See opportunities	See problems
Study money	Think being driven by money is bad
Admire the rich	Resent the rich
Have rich networks	Have poor networks
Sell, market and self-promote	Can't sell, market or self-promote – or won't

Good at receiving	Bad at receiving
Leverage	Get leveraged
Keep going	Keep starting again
Give	Drain
Manage money	Mismanage money
Have money work for them	Work hard for money
Learn and grow	Think they already know
Manage fear	Are managed by fear
See the future	Dwell in the past
Listen to mentors	Listen to friends
Balance emotions	Suffer extreme emotions

It is both your right, and your choice, to be rich.

29

Trust economics

All economies are built on one thing above all else: trust. *Money relies on trust.* Micro, macro, local and global economies rely completely on trust to function. If trust fails, the system fails, and fast. A run on a bank is a lack of trust that the money will be safe or payable. Riots and anarchy result in a lack of trust in governments, authorities, banks and police. Capitalism is a system to cope with an uncertain future. The more uncertain the future, the lower the trust.

Trust is measured in monetary policy and society. The more a lender, individual or bank trusts you to repay them, the more likely you are to get a loan. The measurement is even more specifically quantified. The more the lender trusts you, the higher loan to deposit ratio they will give you, or loan to value. The more the lender trusts you, the lower the interest rate will be. The more the lender trusts you, the less security or collateral will be required. *More trust = less cost. More trust = less friction.* Credit is a bet on an uncertain future, and to negate that risk and the devaluation of future money (inflation), 'interest' is charged. The words 'interest' and 'credit' have a history of meaning that reveals part of the function of trust in money. 'Interest' in a literal sense means to be 'interested'.

Charging interest to hedge against future uncertainty and inflation keeps the borrower 'interested' in repaying the loan. The higher the interest, the more 'interested' they are in repaying. The medieval Latin origin of the word *interesse* is 'compensation for a debtor's defaulting'. The origin of the word 'credit' is the Latin *credere* which means to 'trust, or believe, or have credibility'.

Character is collateral

Your character acts as collateral. The better your reputation, responsibility and history, the less friction, and therefore less collateral and interest will be required to lend to, or invest in, you. This is a highly misunderstood concept among the poor, and highly guarded and regarded by the rich and wealthy. Your creditworthiness is your CV for money and your lend-worthiness is trust in your character manifested in increased certainty. This is reflected in credit scores online, which are a scoring system to reflect trust and creditworthiness. The lower the score, the higher the deposit and interest, and collateral is usually required. When these lending laws of trust are broken, as when lenders lend frivolously, with higher loan to values, it is because they trust that things will still be certain tomorrow. Sometimes this trust is over confidence, bullishness or hubris, but it exists all the same.

Cycles of trust

Money flows quickly from distrust to trust. Trust flows in cycles like the seasons. Trust goes from bullish to bearish, certainty to fear, and back again. Every story of boom and bust, growth and decay, highs and lows and ebbs and flows, money schemes to money scams, is based on the level of trust in the individual or institution. Trust that today's store of value has the same value tomorrow. Trust that tomorrow's money will be paid back. Trust in the entire system. Trust in people. Trust in yourself.

You are money

While only a short chapter, this could be one of the most important in the whole of this book. *You* are money, because trust in you attracts money. Money loves speed, and trust increases speed by reducing friction. Commit to doing and continually working on your reputation, brand, mindspace and creditworthiness to manage, maintain and master your personal 'Trust economy'. Subscribe to Experian and check your credit score. Look at what you can do today to improve it. Set up direct debit payments to all your credit cards, and never miss a payment, ever. Do not leave this to chance. If you ever borrow money, do your best to pay it back, no matter how hard times get. If you have to negotiate a longer term or reduced rate, do what you need to do, because defaulting is way more expensive than one unhappy and unpaid lender. It sends a message to the rest of the world that you are not worthy of credit, and not to be trusted. That is the biggest debt you can have, and it can last decades. But you can turn it around starting today. Make every decision to increase your Trust economy, and for your long-term interests. This goes for lending as well as borrowing. Always go for fair exchange; if you become greedy you too will reduce your Trust economy and people won't borrow from you.

Your reputation is proof + trust × leverage. It is everywhere, always.

A higher trust economy reduces friction, which reduces costs and increases profits. You will get referrals and recommendations that will reduce your marketing costs. Your single best asset is trust. Do what you say you will do. Always pay your debts. Do the right thing that you intuitively know is the right thing. Have a longer-term view than anyone else. Help people where you can. Do the right thing even when no one is looking. *Trust is money, and money is trust.*

30
Your personal GDP

Gross Domestic Product (GDP) is the total monetary value of all the finished goods and services produced within a country, in a specific time period, usually one year. GDP is one of the primary indicators used to gauge the health of a country's economy. It represents the total pound, dollar or currency value of all goods and services produced. You can think of it as the size of the economy.

GDP is usually calculated in one of two ways: adding up what everyone earned in a year (income approach), or adding up what everyone spent in a year (expenditure method). Logically, both measures should arrive at the same total. The income approach, GDP(I), is calculated by adding up total compensation to employees, gross profits for incorporated and non-incorporated firms, and taxes less any subsidies. The expenditure method, GDP(E), is the more common approach, and is calculated by adding total consumption, investment, government spending and net exports. You often see GDP as a year-on-year comparison reflected by a percentage increase or decrease.

You are part of this national or global equation and, as such, I believe you should be aware of, measure, target and create your own personal GDP: Your personal GDP (YGDP).

Growth of GDP is both a main aim and metric of economies and countries, and so it could or should be with you. If YGDP is growing, so are you. YGDP drives increased wealth for you and the economy around you. Increasing YGDP requires spending and investing, not just saving and hoarding. It is a measure of the total throughput of money you attract, create and generate. You make more money by creating more currency flow, enterprise, converting spirit into matter, ideas into solutions and increasing the velocity of money. Be the person who increases the speed and flow of money wherever you go. It is a myth that the measure of wealth is in stored value. Yes, net-worth is an important personal metric of progress, and I will be recommending you measure it, but the paradox of thrift concept indicates that storing and hoarding wealth constricts economies, both personal and national. So the real measure of wealth, that balances giving with receiving and caring of the self and of others simultaneously, is the speed of money, the amount of transactions, or volume of money and the total of the spends and the receipts. Because money is dynamic, always in flow and not a one-off transaction, the value of it perpetually increases. It has a single unit of value if stored, but hundreds or thousands of units of value if shared.

For a business to grow, profits need to be reinvested. To get new customers, marketing dollars need to be spent. For staff to grow with you, investment in training and development is essential. The growth of stock is accelerated by reinvesting dividends. And so it is with GDP and YGDP.

Commit every six months, as you review your vision, goals, networth and other KPIs, to monitoring your spending, investing and incoming cashflows. Target growth for all three metrics. Aim to give more to charity, reinvest more of your profits, grow your assets, reinvest the income from them, do more random acts of kindness and giving, take better quality holidays, travel, and have higher grade material items that are important to you. Target a higher velocity of money around you and through you, and your personal wealth will grow, as will the local, national and global wealth. Later in the book we will give you strategies and tactics to increase YGDP.

31

You alchemist, you asset

The definition of the word 'alchemy' is 'concerned with the transmutation of matter, in particular with attempts to convert base metals into gold or find a universal elixir'. It is interesting that inherent within the dictionary definition, and in primary medieval usage for chemists, alchemy was mostly associated with trying to turn metal into gold. We're all looking for mythological alchemy, a way to turn water into wine and lead into gold – the shortcut to success. People are looking through the limited viewpoint of turning matter into a newer form of matter directly, which is much harder than turning spirit into matter, or ideas into gold. Every millionaire, billionaire or whatever-you-want-to-be-aire is an alchemist, in the truest, most relevant form. Thoughts turn into physical gold. Ideas turn into physical gold. Decisions and actions turn into physical gold.

Embrace the gift that you have inside you as an alchemist of your values. You are not broken. You do not lack anything. It is all there. You can convert your latent wealth into cash form through 'You alchemy': survey, serve, solve then scale. Every material solution was at first an ethereal problem. All printed money was once spirit. What a gift we all have inside us. The problem is that for most people it is still inside them. Be an alchemist not a pessimist.

You asset

To bring to life the alchemist inside you, you need to work on, develop and improve yourself. You are your best asset; invest in yourself wisely, and pay yourself the best interest. The more you learn, the more you earn. Your money can only grow at the speed you grow. Commit to investing in yourself. You are worth it. If you don't value yourself, why would anyone else? Some leveraged areas of self-investment are:

Knowledge (education)

There are three parts or stages to building your knowledge: what you learn, what you learn about who you are, and who you become. Character is collateral. Trust is capital. To work on yourself is to work on your business and your money. You may have read all of the books in the Peterborough library (about six), but if you let your emotions, beliefs, past and future get a hold over you, then knowledge means nothing. These are the three stages of self-awareness to self-mastery in business and money, as well as in your personal development:

A: SELF-AWARENESS

How aware are you of your strengths and weaknesses? Do you over or under play them? How aware are you of how others perceive you? How others see your strengths and weaknesses? Are you aware of your energy highs and lows? Your emotional triggers and reactions? Do you know your values and what you accept and will not stand for? What you love to do and what you want to leverage out? The mistakes you make over and over? This is a continual journey, but the more you know yourself the more you can grow your wealth. Re-evaluate your performance with a 1 to 10 score every six months.

B: SELF-EDUCATION

How much are you investing in yourself? Are you outsourcing your weaknesses? Are you surrounding yourself with the right team to balance your personality traits? Are you getting out of their way? Are you challenging yourself or is your ego surrounding you with those who will only say 'yes'? Do you have mentors who are at a higher level than you? Do you read and listen to audio daily? Do you do relevant training courses to fill your brain with the food it needs to grow your business? As above, review these questions and score yourself out of 10 for each. If I could sum up the two main differences between the debt-ridden grumpy bastard me and the new, not always as grumpy, me who is rich enough to be hated by the old me, it would be these two things that my mentor told me would change: *the books I've read and the people I've met.* Expand these two areas and you expand your wealth. Here are the main areas you can work on that give you the highest return on self-education:

- Books and audio programmes
- Courses, workshops, seminars
- Coaches and mentors
- Networking and masterminding with smart people
- Watching biographies, documentaries and YouTube videos; listening to podcasts
- Reading intelligent and factual publications
- Subscribing to experts' blogs/websites/social media
- Questioning convention and listening intently.

If you make money, you can just as easily lose it, but once you have learned something of value, you can't unlearn it. You can always leverage it, like a physical asset you own forever.

C: SELF-MASTERY

Do you plan your day around your energy levels? Are you self-aware to second-guess yourself and your bad habits? Do you challenge yourself regularly to grow? Do you constantly work on yourself? Do you take feedback graciously and learn from everyone? Do you leverage and delegate to your team, inspire them with a vision and support them in growing too, serving them as much as yourself?

Experience (applied education)

It should go without saying, but all the books in the library won't do anything for you if you don't get off your arse and do something about it and with it. Education and experience are different, because experience is applied hours of learning, then effective hours of applied learning, then perfecting the applied learning. And it's never ending. Get perfect later. Start now. Do not be like most people who are sitting on their hands waiting until they have enough experience to then be confident. That is a paradox. If you never do anything because you're waiting to be perfect, you never do anything. As perfection is unattainable, go for good enough first, fast, and now. Pursue excellence over perfection. Experience will come, and it will get easier and more leveraged over time.

Myths of self-made

No one can succeed alone. I used to think you make your own success with your drive, hard work and making your own luck; that you can be 'self-made'. This thought process came after an epiphany from seven years of feeling like a victim and that I had no control over my own destiny. So it was progress, but it was attritional. It got me started, but it also limited my progress. You can't do everything. You can't be everywhere. You need great people, great friends, a great <u>team</u>, an extended business network, smart advisors and partners, support, accountability and community. A B team beats an A player every time. A team of A players can carry you to great heights and you can achieve mastery and money with a great team that you lead and inspire. Or, if you are more of a supporter personality or intrapreneur, you can support leaders and find your own part to play and value to add within the team.

We are interdependent as a species balancing self-interest with humanitarian interest. When you help others it feels good and does something for you in return. We seem to be designed to work in communities. Look at how the golfers completely change in the Ryder Cup: camaraderie and spirit that you never see for the two years between competitions. Cristiano Ronaldo gives much of his credit to his agent and long-time family friend, Jorge Mendes. Andy Murray cites Ivan Lendl as the main reason for turning his career around. The self-made ones are in fact the ones who have many great others 'making' them.

'Self-made' is a media and cultural myth and story for success. It is a soundbite to the reality. It could even be deemed to be selfish – what about all the others who helped you to where you are? There is no 'I' in team. Visionaries and leaders not only are not self-made, they make others. Leaders create other leaders. This is how virtually all the business and world leaders and high-achievers operate. Don't do it on your own, because you can't and won't do it on your own. Get out of your own way. Be a self-created billionaire by taking responsibility, creating visions, solving problems, and make it part of your mission to attract all the best people so you can build a team that goes to great heights together.

Network (social and business)

Most people are working too hard to be rich. Most people think that working harder on more operational tasks is going to lead to an early retirement of doing nothing. If you study the people perceived by society as being the most successful, the ones that movies are made about and statues are built of, most of them were visionaries and strategists. And every single one of them, without exception, had one thing in common: they had great people around them. The people could have been in the form of a great wife to a powerful man, great employees for a business owner, PAs, VAs, Operations Managers and MDs, great team members for a sportsman, great mentors, coaches and advisors, great agents, accountants, tax advisors, great sages and muses, and spiritual healers.

Your network is your net-worth. And your relationship with that network defines the amount of money you leverage from it. One of the biggest factors in your success will come down to your long-term relationships and the trust and goodwill you build, creating leverage from your contact base who will work hard serving you and your vision. The more business you generate for your network and the more money you help them make by giving them employment or contracts, the more money you will make.

One of my companies and investment vehicles is property. To buy and manage property you need to leverage brokers, conveyancers, commercial solicitors, banks, private lenders, JV partners, commercial lenders, agents, builders, letting agents, estate agents, refurb teams, business advisors, millionaires, billionaires, tax specialists, accountants, business partners and employees, specialist consultants (marketing, PR, sales, design, tech, etc.) and more.

You don't have all the answers and all the knowledge on your own. Build the best possible network you can, because it is your path of least resistance and least effort to maximum results. Build your network like you would your favourite collection. You could spend up to one-third of your working week building and managing your network and that would not be wasted time. The best people have had all of the problems and pain, and have solved them and grown to a higher level. If you're smart, you get to leverage all of that and stand on the shoulders of giants. It is totally attritional and very slow to keep going through that process yourself in the name of 'learning on the job' or 'not spending money on courses and mentors'. Building and investing in your mastermind of peers, coaches, mentors and specialists should be one of your highest KRAs.

Mentors

There are mentors you pay, and mentors you beg/bribe/stalk with nice free lunches. There are mentors you know locally and nationally, and mentors you don't, but you follow all their work. I used to think you either have mentors or you don't. I was wrong. We all have mentors, it's just that some of us are surrounded by people unqualified to give free advice that's worth every penny, with no experience behind their opinions. Will you have good ones or bad ones?

You will still have to forge your own path, but you will follow the trail already blazed and save 80 per cent or more of the time, mistakes and challenges learning from someone who's been there and done it. I see three main areas in mentoring:

A: ROLE-MODELLING

Strategically seek out people who've got the lifestyle you want. Wine, dine, interview, grill and stalk them, persistently but politely. Analyse their rituals, habits and behaviours. Tap into their already leveraged network for double leverage. The people who were once your idols will become your peers, friends and business partners in time, and your bank balance will start to look like theirs. There's no need to feel guilt that you're only getting to know them for their money, because we are all getting to know people for our own motives. Look to offer value to great people where you can, and they will equally gravitate towards you.

In *Think and Grow Rich*, (1937) Napoleon Hill discusses creating the mastermind in your mind. He would close his eyes and imagine in detail being around a boardroom table with all the titans he admired, like Andrew Carnegie. He would visualize a process of bringing his challenges to them and asking them what they would do. At first the old me thought this was a little woo-woo, but one credit I must give myself is that I will often suspend my own disbelief and give things a try. So I started this process in 2005, and have been doing it ever since. Many of the people I visualized have since come into my life and network, and to date we have moved through our biggest challenges. While I know there is more to come, I know even when I'm alone, I'm not alone. I don't recommend you share this strategy with the poor as they will likely think you have lost the plot. Do it for yourself, it's none of anyone else's business.

B: MENTORING

I don't know of a successful sports or business person that hasn't had (multiple) coaches and mentors. You can learn from your own niche or industry, and different fields. You can have personal paid coaches, successful business mentors, 'free' peer groups, paid masterminds, and you can study and read up on successful people and enterprises.

One of the most valuable hobbies/studies I've added to my life over the last decade is reading biographies and autobiographies. You get great insights into leaders in their fields: their ethos, traits, life condensed tips, insights and strategies.

Having mentors has made a huge difference in my life. It has many benefits. It has saved me from my mistakes, protected me from bad advice and relieved the pressure of having to know and decide everything.

C: Masterminding

A mastermind is a collective of 'master minds', smart people who get together to help each other combining unique and complementary skills that are more powerful as a whole than the sum of its parts. I am a member of many mastermind groups as a mentor and as a peer and wouldn't be without them. You get some of the biggest insights, benefits and strategic direction from putting great minds together and letting them create solutions and solve problems. Someone 'around the table' or in the group has the answer, a different way of looking at the challenge, or knows someone who can help. You don't know to ask the questions you didn't know to ask. You get as much benefit being a 'voyeur' on other people's business discussions, whether in the same industry or a different one. You can often borrow innovations for your own niche. You learn being the mentor as well as being the mentee.

Plan, see, do, review, repeat

As the alchemist of your own material life, start with a clear plan of what you want to create. It has been said 'be careful what you wish for, you just might get it'. Create a clear and definite plan for all the strategic, spiritual and material goals and desires you require. I've found that you can get better at leveraging what many call the 'Law of Attraction' with practice and iteration of your planning and goal setting. When I started I would have had a few generic financial targets, but over the last decade I have been planning the following year each year (including my lifetime goals). My plans have become more specific, focused and holistic across all life areas. I share the link to my personal goals and vision document below, to save you the decade of testing.

In your planning, vision and goal setting, target all main areas of your life, how you want to be perceived by others, how you want to be remembered, the legacy you want to leave, all areas of material wealth you want to manifest, your philanthropic causes, parental and familial goals, business and personal financial targets, all broken down. The more specific you are, down to the type and model of car you want, or location of your vacation, the more other people, your subconscious mind and the unknown powers of the universe can help you.

The goals and vision document

Leverage the goals and vision document I'm about to share with you, or use it to create your own version. Use your favourite format backed up on the cloud. Read it every morning as you rise and every evening as you go to bed, when your subconscious mind is the most open and impressionable to commands. Review the entire plan every six months. Check in regularly as you feel progress is slow, and tweak if necessary to be more clear. As you achieve small milestones tick them off or write the progress in brackets alongside the goal. Set the near short-term goals to be closer to realistic, and the longer-term goals to be more optimistic. Always do your yearly goals against your lifetime ones, so that they work synchronously. Practise picturing the goals vividly and you will improve your manifestation power. And, of course, take consistent action and both your conscious effort and unconscious system will go to work bringing about what you are thinking about. Here is the link to the goals and vision document to leverage your time and money: http://tiny.cc/RMGoals

Health and well-being (wealth)

Live long. Enjoy life. Take good care of yourself, the best asset you have. Exercise. Eat well. Regularly check your health and make lifestyle adjustments accordingly. It is very true to say that 'health is wealth'. Let me remind you of what three main components Warren Buffet credits to his vast wealth: 'Living in America for the great opportunities, having good genes so I lived a long time, and compound interest'.

You may not be able to control your genes, but you can make a huge difference to your health if you take responsibility. Don't be one of those rich people who neglect their health in the pursuit of money, and regret it later.

Passion and profession, vocation and vacation (merge)

Do what you love and love what you do. Don't spend all your life working for money only to have no time to enjoy the rewards. I believe the secret to sustained wealth, well-being and happiness is not to have hobbies you love and a job you hate, but to merge your passion and profession, vocation and vacation. Imagine if there were no risks to starting again. Imagine if you were guaranteed all the help you needed along the way to do what you love and love what you do.

Create your ideal work–life balance

Imagine if you could create your ideal work–life balance. Well you can, now. Here's how:

1 Choose a vocation with a path of least resistance and limitless *upside* that *you* control.
2 Choose a vocation that's a vacation and a profession that's a passion.
3 Study what the most successful people whom you admire or idolize do, and copy (most of) it.
4 Know what to keep going at, and what to give up on.

These will be detailed in Chapter 44.

You really can have work and life as one passion without worrying about work at home, and home at work. You will make far more sustained wealth monetizing a passion rather than accepting a profession. You are an alchemist of wealth and riches, self-created from your thoughts and spirit into matter and money. This is part of the *Money* philosophy, and your guide towards a full and rich life with more cash than you could shake a stick at.

32

Your extended bank account...

... isn't the cash in your bank or savings. Most people measure their ability to spend, save, invest or borrow as 'cash collateral' in their accounts. But everyone runs out of money, even the rich. Most people don't even have even a month's worth of living expenses in savings. Even if you had savings that you could live off for the rest of your life in the bank today, in around 14 years, at average inflation, you'd need double that.

Your bank account is the globe. Money from anyone, anywhere is available for you to withdraw. You are an alchemist of money from any and every source, through any and every person. Your real bank account isn't cash savings, or digits in an account, but networked access to people and systems that connect people, that you can draw down on. It is the sum total of finance through your leveraged network. The more people you know, the more money can flow. The better the relationships and trust you have with people, the less the friction of Your (personal) GDP (YGDP). The more money people have in your network, and their network, the more freely and fast money flows through them and to you.

When you need cash you have 'limits' in your bank account of credit or overdraft. The further beyond the limit you go, the higher the fees and interest. Your extended network removes these limits and makes access to cash limitless. Liquidity is leveraged.

Invest in your network like you would a physical asset. Find the right people, connect and care, build the relationship, create exchange of value and continue to nurture the relationship for as long as you are both alive. Be so great that they refer their trusted network to you. If you did this with just ten great people, you'd have unlimited funds to make and give more money. It is said that you are the sum of the five people you spend the most time with: you become the sixth. Be strategic about who you spend your time with and look to be the least experienced or least wealthy person in your network/circles. You will get dragged up to their level much faster than with people at or below your level who are likely to hold you back.

The rich build networks, the poor work

Bill Gates was very fond of forming partnerships with people who were the top dog and he was happy to be the 'sidekick', because it unlocked new opportunities for him and the potential to learn from other successful entrepreneurs who could teach him a thing or two. Bill Gates, often at the top of the rich list, credits part of his success to his mentor Warren Buffet. During an interview with CBC, Gates credited Buffet for teaching him how to deal with tough situations and how to think long term. Gates also greatly admires Buffet's 'desire to teach things that are complex and put them in a simple form, so that people can understand and get the benefit of all his experience.' It seems that learning from and leveraging his network has paid off for Bill because at a spending rate of $1 million a day, it would take him 218 years to spend all his money!

The 'chain of mentors' doesn't stop at the top, it's why and how they get to the top. After reading Benjamin Graham's book *The Intelligent Investor* in 1949, the author became Buffett's idol. The book changed not only his investment philosophy but also the course of his life. Buffett applied to Columbia Business School where Graham was a professor. Buffett got to know his idol personally. Later Graham hired Buffett to work at his company, and the two cemented a strong friendship that led to and had a big impact on Buffett's transformation into the billionaire investor he is today.

Similarly, in an interview with talk show host Charlie Rose, Mark Zuckerberg talked about his inspiring mentor Steve Jobs. 'He was amazing,' said Zuckerberg, 'I had a lot of questions for him.' He described how Jobs gave him advice about how he could build a team that was as focused as Zuckerberg on building 'high quality and good things'. 'If you ask any successful businessperson, they will always (say they) have had a great mentor at some point along the road' says Richard Branson. Branson wrote in a British newspaper: 'It's always good to have a helping hand at the start. I wouldn't have got anywhere in the airline industry without the mentorship of Sir Freddie Laker.' Branson believes the first step to finding a great mentor is admitting you can benefit from a mentor: 'Understandably there's a lot of ego, nervous energy and parental pride involved, especially with one or two person start-ups. Going it alone is an admirable, but foolhardy and highly-flawed approach to taking on the world'.

Some are calling the age we are in the 'recommendation age' as time seems so scarce. We are looking to turn to people we trust and get good recommendations from them for our key business and financial decisions. We simply don't have the time anymore to do everything. Others are calling our current economy the 'connection economy' for the same reasons. Connecting people has real, tangible value, right now. It adds value to others who are time scarce, and that value reflects on you. Despite being intangible, it might be your most valuable resource. But then all money is intangible in spirit until you convert it into cash. Go where the money flows and some of it will flow your way. Infiltrate events and networks of high net-worth and liquidity to increase your own.

How to create and leverage your network

We can all improve upon and grow our network. Could you get yourself out more and meet more smart people? Sure you could. Could you be strategic and cherry-pick events where wealthy and successful people hang out? Of course you could. Get to as many places as you can that have good people attending, then select over a few months which ones to focus on and keep going back to. You could test charity balls, business angel events, flying clubs, high-end gyms, sailing clubs, golf clubs, rotary clubs, boat shows, business and property expos, city property or business networking events; there are many places where you can rub shoulders with wealthy and successful people. If you know someone who knows someone wealthy, at the right time ask for a connection. Look at how you can offer them value, spend up to one third of your working time building your network, and have it as one of your main KRAs.

The secret smart people know is the smart people they know.

Rob Moore

33
Gratitude and appreciation

Appreciation has growth power. Appreciation raises your consciousness, and ingratitude lowers it. Whenever you fail to appreciate what you give and receive, you literally block the channels through which wealth can flow to you. That blockage is a sense from others that you are not trustworthy, you don't care, you aren't grateful or you don't value yourself. It makes you less attractive.

'Appreciation' derives from the Latin *appretiare* meaning 'to set a price on' (see also 'appraise', meaning 'to rise in value'). What you appreciate rises in value, and by appreciating you, you rise in value. Gratitude is a deliberate emotion that results from appreciation. You only experience growth when in gratitude, even if the event seems at first to be a challenge or problem. You could have the attitude that you 'learn or you earn'. You will feel grateful whether you make money or experience challenges to improve. You will either appreciate financially or personally. You simply can't lose or feel negative in the state of gratitude and appreciation.

For this to give you ultimate earning power and leverage, you'll need to grow into appreciating all events and outcomes, not just the ones you desire. It is easy to appreciate a bank transfer coming in, but what about bills, outgoings and expenses? Every time you pay a bill or expense in the state of resentment or ingratitude, that's the message you send out, and so what you will get back. Leverage the law of vacuum prosperity. Forgive yourself and others for what you are unappreciative of, for this resentment or anger will fill any void fast. From now on decide to send out a new message. Whenever you receive a bill or an invoice, be grateful that somebody appreciated you so much that they advanced you money, a product or a service. Be grateful that you are opening a void to be filled with money. They had the confidence and trust to invest in you, and you're now making a payment of appreciation back to them. You are fuelling their economy and increasing Your personal GDP. You are storing future goodwill to be cashed in later. Instead of begrudging the expense, remember how what you're paying for has served you, and pay that bill in a state of appreciation and gratitude. Give gratitude for what you've already received and for being able to pay for it, and watch how it appreciates your relationship with wealth. When you feel different about sending wealth into the world, the world will feel different about sending wealth back to you. Transactions are no longer about gain and loss, as most of the first-world poor view monetary transactions, but about increased flow.

If you don't value and appreciate yourself, why should anyone else? If you are not grateful for what you have and who you are, then others won't have gratitude to work with you and send wealth your way. You are worthy of wealth and riches, and gratitude will appreciate that sense of worthiness. A great way to appreciate your value is to practise gratitude on a daily basis. You can do this by catching yourself throughout the day and just allowing yourself be grateful in any moments that naturally arise. When your child lovingly clings to your leg, when the coffee kicks in, when you get a smile from a stranger, when someone lets you in a queue. Thank the small things as well as the big things. Gratitude is a practice that becomes a habit that grows your wealth. Each night as you close your eyes, list in your mind in visual detail all the things you are grateful for. This has a triple leverage benefit because it will programme your subconscious mind, get you through sleep problems and probably send you to sleep quicker anyway!

Say 'Thank you' as much as you can throughout the day. You will attract what you thank others for. Put the energy of gratitude out and let it flow back in ever appreciating monetary value to you.

34
Philanthropy, cause and contribution

The greatest of evils and the worst of crimes is poverty.

George Bernard Shaw

Sarojini Naidu, a poet and close friend of Mahatma Gandhi, berated Gandhi for his attempts to live in poverty. 'Do you know how much it costs every day to keep you in poverty'? she is reputed to have asked him. Gandhi's response is unknown, but it is clear he was not offended, and understood that he knew the accusation to be true. He knew how much every train journey and bespoke arrangements cost the state because of the adoring millions who flocked to see him. They had to schedule special trains and reserve a whole compartment for him because of the crowds.

Charles Keating, the American banker known for the infamous 'saving and loan scandal', donated up to $1.25 million to Mother Teresa and was one of her main backers/donors. Robert Maxwell contributed significantly to her work. She didn't hesitate to accept money from crooks because she said: 'I can make it good'.

The point here is that all philanthropy, charity and contribution are a result of a capitalist system and those who master it. All of the world's greatest philanthropists have either been vastly wealthy themselves, or their chosen poverty-stricken lifestyle, like Gandhi and Mother Teresa, has been fuelled and financed by the vastly wealthy. Wealth that has been contributed by the state is fuelled and financed by the private sector, which is financed by the vastly wealthy. More examples include:

- Genghis Khan owned vast tracts of land in the Mongolian Empire, reputed to be one of the largest empires in history. Despite his great power, history suggests Genghis never hoarded his wealth and shared it with soldiers and commanders.

- John D. Rockefeller donated more than half a billion dollars to various educational, religious and scientific causes. Among his activities, he funded the establishment of the University of Chicago and the Rockefeller Institute for Medical Research (now Rockefeller University). He also helped J.P. Morgan mastermind one of the biggest banking bailouts in history, in 1907, raising £25 million in 12 minutes, performing an act as a financial saviour that now only central banks acting as lenders of last resort would undertake.

- Andrew Carnegie built a leadership role as a philanthropist for the United States and the British Empire. During the last 18 years of his life, he gave away to charities, foundations and universities about $350 million, with special emphasis on local libraries, world peace, education and scientific research. With the fortune he made from business, he built Carnegie Hall and founded the Carnegie Corporation of New York, Carnegie Endowment for International Peace, Carnegie Institution for Science, Carnegie Trust for the Universities of Scotland, and the Carnegie Hero Fund.

- Christopher Cooper-Hohn co-founded the Children's Investment Fund Foundation in 2002. He has donated upwards of $2.5 billion of his own money into the fund and that much again to other charities.

- Li Ka-Shing, who made money from property, hotels, airports, construction, phones, steel production, electric power and shipping, gave $1.5 billion of his own money to his personal foundation and has promised to give at least a third of his total net-worth (estimated in 2011 to be north of $26 billion) to charity.

- Azim Premji donated more than $2 billion to his personal charitable foundation. This entity is dedicated to improving India's state schools through teacher training and upgrading school curriculums. His efforts have positively impacted more than 2.5 million students at over 25,000 schools nationwide.

- Sheikh Mohammed bin Rashid Al Maktoum, ruler of Dubai, pledged to donate $10 billion to his personal charitable foundation dedicated to closing the 'knowledge gap between the Arab region and the developed world'. The foundation supports start-up entities and other entrepreneurial endeavours and has also aided humanitarian causes such as efforts for disaster relief in the Horn of Africa.
- Carlos Slim Helú, CEO of several phone and communications companies, has donated more than $10 billion to charity, but has also said that the economic security provided by the jobs he has created is just as important.
- Mark Zuckerberg has a net-worth of $56.3 billion, and has emerged as a major philanthropist. He started selling Facebook shares worth nearly $95 million before taxes quickly after pledging to give 99 per cent of them to public-interest causes. In 2015, Zuckerberg and his wife Priscilla Chan launched the 'Chan Zuckerberg Initiative' whose initial focus area is 'personalized learning, curing disease, connecting people and building strong communities'. He has donated $100 million into education and $105 million into healthcare.

When I was skint I couldn't even bring myself to commit to a £10 a month direct debit for Oxfam. When I had no money, I was a drain on society. I was a consumer, living off loans and credit supplied indirectly by vast producers like the billionaires just mentioned. They were making and giving billions while I was off down to KFC licking people's fingers for food. It's only since I've been open to wealth and money that I've been able to contribute to the causes that matter.

Capitalism is philanthropy

All charitable money or services are financed by capitalism, and therefore all philanthropy is capitalism. If you want to donate or give time to charitable enterprises, you either need a lot of money to donate, or you need to be backed by a successful capitalist, or you need capital that creates income to free your time to contribute.

> You don't make a living by what you get. You make a living by what you give.
>
> *Winston Churchill*

It is both a great power and a great privilege to merge your desire for wealth with a great cause to fight for. The cause that is greater than us grows us and attracts others to us; it literally makes us attractive. It is more powerful for you to get in touch with that cause now, while you are building your vast fortune, not *once* you've built it. You will have stronger wealth power when people sense that the money that flows through you also goes somewhere worthy. Use your capital and position of fortune as a force for good. Wealth in combination with powerful causes, in wise hands, can be used to build cultures and masterpieces in any form. All of the magnificence we get to experience and enjoy now, is fuelled by the balance of capitalism and philanthropy.

Many causes and charities have a value to someone driven by a void. Oprah Winfrey was abused as a child, George Soros experienced Nazi Germany occupation and survived the siege of Budapest, and those voids and pains are being filled by their balanced capitalist and philanthropic ventures. What void do you have that could fuel an important cause that could make a difference to the world? Take time to consider what you feel passionate about fighting for. What's your cause? It's wise to have a cause that has close meaning to you. List as many reasons as you can why wealth coming to you will benefit you and the world you serve. Set goals that leave a legacy far beyond your lifetime.

> If you don't have something challenging and fulfilling to awaken for in the morning, you won't rise and shine.
>
> *Dr John Demartini*

Money flees from those who have no purpose for it, and flows to those who do. The universe will 'meet you halfway' and support your philanthropic ventures by sending people and solutions your way in line with the scale, value and magnetism of the cause. In turn, you will be able to partner commercially with these people and monetize the solutions for 'enlightened self-interest'. A great purpose gives you the courage and resourcefulness to transcend your own limitations and achieve great riches.

Enlightened self-interest

Enlightened self-interest is a philosophy in ethics, which states that a person acting to further the interests of others (or the interests of the group or groups to which they belong), ultimately serves their own self-interests. Use this philosophy to create equally balanced self and humanitarian interest, and receiving and giving in ever-increasing amounts. Your philanthropy does not just have to be monetary. It could be more valuable for your legacy to be in the form of education and support more than tithing. Giving someone money who doesn't know how to manage it yet does not serve them as much as awareness, awakening and knowledge. This is why many of the greatest philanthropists invest in education as much as donation, and set up foundations. Your greatest legacy over and above the millions or billions you leave behind could be the generations you educate and inspire. You can start this now, even if you don't yet have vast wealth, because your most precious commodity is time, and you can invest time now in the care and education of others.

RAOG

A great way to kick-start philanthropy and the flow of wealth to and through you is to perform RAOG (Random Acts of Giving). Thank people often with well thought-out and personal thank-you notes. Acknowledge important life events such as a birth or wedding or birthday. Give random gifts to people you know and people you don't. Do kind acts for people you know and people you don't. Small things lead to big things. Make someone's day every day.

It is both your right and your responsibility to be a giver and receiver of wealth. With all the information and opportunity at your fingertips in the developed world, poverty could be perceived as selfish and not caring for humanity. If you care for humanity then you produce more than you consume and you give as well as receive. Great people make great fortunes and give great fortunes. Raise standards around you and raise wealth within you.

SECTION 7

Strategies and systems

In this section, we reveal the vehicles and mechanisms to know more, make more and give more money. We move from belief, mindset and concept to the finer specifics and details of making more wealth. If you were initially attracted to this book because you wanted to be introduced to techniques to make money, this is the section that could be most relevant to you.

35
Leverage

Leverage is achieving more, with less: more money with less (or other people's) money, more time with less time (or less of your personal time) and more results with less effort (or less of your personal effort).

> Give me a lever long enough and I could move the world.
>
> *Archimedes*

Most people are unleveraged, conditioned to believe that 'working harder' means you'll earn more money. You have to 'graft' and 'sacrifice' in order to 'earn a living'. Living is your right, you don't have to 'earn' it, you should be living it. Everyone experiences leverage: servant or master, employer or employee, leader or follower, lender or borrower, consumer or producer. Each serves the other, but one leverages and the other is leveraged. You're either utilizing leverage, moving towards your inspired vision, earning on other people's time, money, resources, network, systems, experience, skills, or you are being leveraged to serve someone else's grand vision.

If you work for someone else and you're not happy, or you work for money and that money stops when the work stops, then you are being controlled by the leverage of others. They are earning from you, you're lower down the value chain, earning less yet you're working hard. You probably have the least control and freedom, and you're possibly unhappy. Most people are made to believe that time, work and money are directly related. Millionaires, billionaires and visionaries know they are inverse. You're taught to work hard for money, but you need make your money work hard for you. You're taught that longer hours and overtime earn more money, but in reality vision, leverage, leadership and building your network and team to fulfil these actually creates vast and lasting wealth.

However, of the 25 richest people in the UK, *none* of them are employees. *All* of them are founders or recipients of businesses. They are all employers, business owners and investors. All the visionaries across the globe are wealth creators, change makers and risk takers. Millionaires and billionaires earn money and preserve time on other people's time, resources, knowledge and contacts. Just take a look at the billionaire lifestyle. Are they really working 'harder' than the miners, servants and cleaners? No. Leverage is learnable and you can learn the same strategies and tactics they know, have learned, and are using to make money, preserve time and make a difference.

Leverage is easier than ever, due to the Internet, fibre optics and all the apps and systems that leverage them. You can outsource many operational tasks. You can employ a virtual PA who you can pay by unit of time, to free your time to focus more on Income Generating Tasks (IGTs). Five hours of outsourced non-IGT work might cost you £40, and those freed five hours can be invested back into building your business or buying a property that might bring in £30,000, and thousands of pounds per year residual income for a lifetime.

A leveraged asset

Let's use the example of investing in property, seeing as it is one of my passions and business ventures, and a common model of the super-rich. You have the 'entrepreneur/investor' type, and the 'landlord' type. While investors have landlord duties such as regulation, management and maintenance, many landlords are hands-on and unleveraged. They are often self-employed people, or performing landlord tasks as a time-consuming second job. They often get involved in refurbs, painting and decorating, collecting rent and other operational tasks. Of course these tasks are important, necessary and, were they not done, the properties would not flow cash or be of a good standard for the tenant. However, an entrepreneur/investor will have a grander vision, keep to the strategy, employ and outsource all these regulations, management tasks and maintenance to others, freeing their time for higher-level IGTs. Then they can scale. This example and thought process is the same in most other niches or industries.

It can be a hard shift for many ingrained with values passed on from hardworking parents from a different era/age of 'get a job, work hard, get your head down, make sacrifices and don't take risks'. Most self-employed people feel the need to control all areas of their small business. They gain significance from being the boss and getting stuck in. They can get protective about handing tasks over to others because no one can do their job as well as they can. They think they can't afford to pay people, or that they can 'save money' by DIY. They start doing everything to minimize costs, but that ends up lasting their whole business life. While it does stop some wastage of costs, it creates huge wastage and de-leverage of time. It involves doing a lot of things you don't enjoy, and that you aren't good at, for not much money. DIY: destroy it yourself.

When I first got into property, I thought viewing properties, going through the purchasing process, dealing with mortgage brokers, refurbishing, renting out and managing tenants was going to be my daily vocation. I was energized, enthused and motivated at the start, as most of us are when things are new. But it ended up being a grind (for me). After a dozen purchases and on my way to financial security in my first year, I had a major epiphany where I asked myself 'Is this really what I want to do with my life?' The reality was I wanted the baby, but not the labour pains. I wanted the property and cashflow, but I didn't enjoy the nuts and bolts of management and maintenance. But I was knee deep in it now. I was making money, and that was becoming a trap I feared I might not get out of.

Without a vision and leverage, property − one of the best asset classes in the world − can be a hard job like any other, with messy stuff to deal with and people who don't always value you. But it also puts people regularly on the Rich List when they master leverage of time, money, resources, ideas and people. Most other businesses are the same: rewarding when leveraged and defeating when too tactical.

Around a year in, I decided that I didn't want to have my property *business* like many of the part-time overworked landlords I knew. I looked at ways I could get other people to view, offer, buy, rent, refurbish, manage and maintain my properties, while still making my fair share of the income. For me it was a binary choice: leverage up or get out, and thankfully I was in too deep to get out easily. This wasn't about trying to pass the buck or shirk responsibility; it was a moment of clarity of what I really wanted for my life.

I discovered partnering with Mark Homer that there are people who value the tasks you find hard (or hate). Some even love them and earn their own living doing them well. Talk about a revelation to me. Not just someone who could do what I could not, but someone who actually *loved* all the stuff I was a disaster at. I didn't know people out there even existed. If I could leverage this all out, I could grow, earn more, do more of what I loved, *and* create commerce, jobs and economy. This had not occurred or been taught to me anywhere in the previous 26 years.

The non-get-rich-quick get-rich-quick strategy

Leverage is the non-get-rich-quick, get-rich-quick, quicker, quickest strategy for business, money and life. It is the real shortcut to success, freedom and time preservation. Earning a little on a lot of people is far more vast and scalable than earning a lot on just you. It is far better to earn £10 per hour on 10,000 people than £1,000 per hour on just you.

When I first started my first real business (I don't count being an artist because I didn't have a clue about *real* business then) in property, my business partner and I did everything ourselves. We 'hustled'. We probably didn't do too badly, kept costs tight, protected the downside and reduced risks. We'd only just set up shop and the biggest recession and property crash in history happened. But looking back, we could have achieved more, faster and smarter, without increasing our risk too much, if we'd got out of our own way. We should have leveraged more and earlier. I am frequently asked 'Rob if you could start again, knowing what you know now, what would you do differently?' Leverage more, and get the best people you can find. We could have worked much more on strategy, vision and building the team, freeing time to leverage out most of the boring and difficult jobs to others far better and more qualified than us at the technical aspects. Employing others would have been at a much lower rate of pay than us doing all the work ourselves. We were looking at all the money we thought we could save, not the thousands we cost ourselves or left on the table.

This is shown in how fast many of the students and community members of Progressive Property, one of my property training companies, get results. The proactive ones do well very quickly if they pick up on leverage early, and fast. Many of them are now full-time property investors. Many of them build (multi) million pound property portfolios in nine to eighteen months. Many of them hit net monthly passive income figures of £3000, £5000, £10,000 or £20,000 in similar timeframes. Many are now millionaires. Many quit their old jobs. Many of them are even now training others and respected specialists in the industry, giving back and making an additional income stream. Many of them achieved results quicker, faster, better and with fewer mistakes that we did when we started, because they embraced leverage and learned from the mistakes we made, or at least what we could have done faster, easier and better. But the ones that don't embrace leverage take a lot longer.

Opportunity cost of non-leverage

The results you get and the money you earn aren't as much about what you *are* doing, but what you *are not* doing. If you're selling dinghies you can't sell super yachts. If your prices are low then you're repelling higher paying customers. It's easy to buy into the 'conventional' advice of work harder, work longer and make sacrifices. That's what we did when we started out. We were in so deep we had no view outside. No one was steering the ship but it was going at full steam heading nowhere in particular. Our business couldn't grow because we only had so many hours in the day, no matter how many hours we worked or how hard or even how efficiently we worked. We kept hitting the ceiling. As we got busier, not only was our time taken away from IGTs, but we started making mistakes through fatigue. We were doing the wrong things well, and a lot, and the right things not at all. We kept getting in our own way. The irony was that the whole point of working for ourselves was so we could free up some time to do the things we really loved. But we were too busy. Despite buying around 20 properties in our first year in partnership, and making some fair money, that fair money was getting in the way of big money.

I became a millionaire between the ages of 30 and 31. When my son was nine months old, at the height of my hardest graft, my fiancée sat me down when I arrived home late one night, and said, 'I'm proud of what you've done and the business you've built. But if you keep going at this rate, going to work before Bobby wakes up and coming home after he goes to bed, he will turn 18 and he won't know who his dad is.'

At the time I was defensive about this, because I was working very hard to create a good life for our family. As my ego subsided I saw a parallel vision of two future realities. One where I was working 80 hours a week making a lot of money as perceived by society, wearing my hard work like a badge of honour, but burning myself out, jeopardizing my family, working to live and chasing a never-ending goal. The other was one where I could work from home or anywhere around the world, we could travel on demand, I could spend so much time with my family that they'd end up kicking me out of the house, and with passive income to finance this lifestyle. It was this revelation that set about the leverage, systems, people and processes that became my *Life Leverage* book and philosophy. You just need to make the decision to do the same. Since then it has been easier to make money as a consequence rather than as a goal.

Fast-forward to now, and business for me, and for our companies, is well leveraged. It is not perfect, chaotic sometimes, always disruptive and ever changing, but where we used to manage properties ourselves, we leveraged them to letting agents and then set up our own letting agency with a business partner. Where I used to do all the speaking and training events myself, up to 250 per year, now we have over 100 trainers in our education companies. Where we used to do all the viewings and sourcing of properties ourselves, we now have a buying team. Where we used to buy small single-lets we now buy larger commercial buildings. Where we used to teach locally we now teach globally. Where we once had no staff we now have hundreds in and outsourced. Where we used to make £60 on a weekend, we can now make £600,000. Where we used to do everything ourselves we now have mentors, masterminds and specialists. And so can you – it is a process. There's no way on earth I could have done this on my own or with just plain hard work. Never the finished article, always learning, and I hope I can read this in the future and think what a cute little baby group of companies we had compared to now. It won't happen if I get in the way.

The five vehicles of leverage

There are five vehicles you can leverage:

1 TIME (LIFE)

There's no such thing as 'time management'. You can't manage it because you can't control or change it. You can manage *you*, and how you spend, save, invest and waste time. Time management should be renamed life management. Your aim should be to 'gain' time by 'preserving' time, and minimizing wastage as much as you can. Time is your most valuable yet scarce, ever-decreasing commodity. Because time is a countdown clock that starts the day you are born, the more you invest and the less you waste, the more time you will have to do what you love, with who you love, when you love.

How you perceive time will directly dictate your ability to control and leverage it. Do you see time as the single most precious commodity to preserve at all costs? Do you see time as a gift and to maximize every moment you are graced with? Do you look to multiply and leverage time? Or do you get stuck duplicating it? Do you savour and enjoy every moment? Do you live in the present with gratitude, or do you look back at the past with regret and to the future with fear?

Always value and measure time. Never waste a great opportunity to preserve and leverage time. I once got 'outed' on social media by my business partner for running a meeting while getting my hair cut, but to use his digital thinking back on him: If I get my hair cut twice a month and it takes 30 minutes per haircut, and I save one hour of meetings a month, assuming I live until 97, that is 720 hours leveraged. If I'm worth £10,000 an hour and reinvest the time wisely that's £7.2 million in 60 years.

Many bigger business owners don't work day-to-day, yet they employ thousands of people. They know the value of their time and you often hear them saying, 'It's just not worth my time,' or 'I wouldn't get out of bed for that.' You now know why, and it is wise to take the same attitude and see time as a valuable commodity and investment.

Here are three of the most valuable time-leverage models as they relate to *Money*:

RoTI

Return on Time Invested is a model and *modus operandi* in one. It is a system to follow to analyse how you are using your time. Keep asking yourself, 'Will this give me the best Return on Time Invested?'

This simple question will force you to keep checking that you're using your time well, performing the right tasks and getting maximum leverage. It will force you to earn the maximum amount of money on the minimum amount of time, and to delegate or drop all unleveraged tasks to create the most recurring benefit and income on every potential task.

TOC

Time Opportunity Cost is the cost of the current task or time spent, financial or otherwise. Most people don't know what this is (or can't see it), because all they can see is the benefit or drawback of what they are doing, and not the benefit or drawback of what they *are not* doing or *could be* doing instead. In monetary terms, opportunity cost is simple to measure. If you spend three hours a day on admin that would cost £10 per hour to outsource, that's three hours a day you can't spend selling products that bring in more than £10. If you spend three hours a day doing paperwork for property, that's three hours a day you can't spend finding a new property deal that might make you tens of thousands of pounds. Always consider what you *are not* doing or *could be* doing, instead of just doing. Like RoTI, keep monitoring and measuring two things, 'How am I investing my time, and what else could you I doing with my time?'.

NeTime

Multi-tasking is actually just being distracted trying to do too many things at once, spinning too many plates or task jumping, wasting time and brainpower. NeTime is the way to 'multi-task without multi-tasking'. NeTime stands for *No Extra Time* and enables you to get multiple results for a single unit of time. Here are some NeTime functions:

- > Audio programmes whilst travelling, in the gym, walking, etc.> Calls whilst travelling (train, car)> Watching autobiographical documentaries (enjoy and learn)> Get the train/a driver where possible and create content/work> Gardener, cleaner, cook, dry-cleaning, driver, nanny, maid> Holiday merge with biz plan, vision, speaking engagement or mastermind> Shopping/trips merge with courses/ events> Dinners with mentors/business people> Social events merged with business.
- These are all detailed in the book *Life Leverage* if you need more information on how to leverage NeTime.

2 Money (assets)

You use leverage in income and wealth generation by creating and investing in assets that, once set up, minimize time exchange, under fair exchange. You invest time, capital and resources in assets that produce residual income. You set them up, get them managed by people or systems, then you exclude yourself from the operations. You outsource the ongoing maintenance of the assets, some more intensive and some more passive, and you reinvest the profits into more of them. Here are type of assets you can build, the most relevant of which will be detailed later:

- A business (physical, online, ecommerce)
- Property
- IP (intellectual property: ideas, patents, licences, information, music)
- Investments (stocks, bonds, paper)
- Money lending
- Physical (precious metals, art, watches, wine, classic cars)
- Partnerships (franchise, joint ventures).

Leverage alchemy

Monetary leverage is alchemy from assets. Some examples are fractional reserve banking, a wonder of finance in the opinion of many economists; raising debt for investment properties and other asset classes; options and contracts that control an asset without a deposit, exchange or purchase. Even further leveraged examples are joint ventures where 100 per cent of the funding is provided by another party in exchange for time and management. Or serviced accommodation and sub-letting of standard single-let or multi-let properties. Financial institutions leveraged leverage further by repackaging loans into CDOs (collateralized debt obligations), which are pooled mortgages, bonds and loans into a new credit product. It seems that the only limitation of leverage alchemy is a limitation of implemented imagination and ideas.

Balanced leverage

Before we detail many of the financial levers you can use to make more money with less collateral and time, it's important to address leverage balance. Too much leverage and small (or large) movements in the market can put you in negative equity or you can trigger loan to value covenants with lenders. If you can't cover the deficit you could have your loans recalled and lose your assets. The same can happen to banks if 'reserve requirements' are low (ratio of deposits to loans), there are high volumes of complicated leveraged financial instruments and/or there is a bank run. At the other extreme, being un-leveraged leaves money or assets idle and wasteful. Capital un-leveraged is exposed to inflation. Good debt leverage has the reverse effect, where inflation erodes the real value of debt over time, so you get a double benefit with smart leverage.

Fractional-reserve banking leverage

This is the practice whereby a bank accepts deposits, makes loans or investments, and holds reserves that are a fraction of its deposit liabilities. Reserves are held at the bank as currency, or as deposits in the bank accounts. The Swedish Riksbank was the world's first central bank, created in 1668. Many nations followed suit in the late 1600s to establish central banks, which were given legal power to set the reserve requirement, called the monetary base, which is the ratio of cash to reserves (or cash reserve ratio).

Fractional-reserve banking has critics, but it allows banks to act as financial intermediaries between borrowers and savers, and to provide longer-term loans to borrowers while providing immediate liquidity to depositors. While there is a very small risk of a bank run if depositors wish to withdraw more funds (all at once), than the reserves held by the bank, this is very rare. To mitigate the risk of bank runs and rare widespread crises, governments of most countries regulate and oversee commercial banks. This is achieved by deposit insurance, acting as lender of last resort to commercial banks, reserve requirement regulation that sets the minimum fraction of customer deposits and notes that each commercial bank must hold as reserves (rather than lend out), and interest rate and inflation targets. These regulations keep the system efficient. Any run is more an issue of trust than liquidity, because banks never have enough money in deposits to cover everyone withdrawing at the same time anyway. It only becomes a problem when fear and lack of trust spreads through the media.

Because banks hold reserves that are less than their deposit liabilities, fractional-reserve banking permits the money supply to grow beyond the amount of the underlying base money originally created by the central bank. This is a great display of economic leverage creating growth and increased GDP. Virtually everyone, producers and consumers alike, benefit from the increased money supply through widespread availability of credit in the form of overdrafts, personal loans, mortgages, credit cards and more. It is likely that none of this could be available without this great innovation of leverage. Much can be learned and modelled from this '400-year and still going strong' leverage model for your business and value creation. How could you use a similar concept in your business to increase leveraged money velocity?

Gold standard leverage

To help combat the Great Depression and faced with mounting unemployment and spiralling deflation in the early 1930s, the US government attempted to stimulate the economy. To deter people from cashing in deposits and depleting the gold supply, the US and other governments had to keep interest rates high, but that made it too expensive for people and businesses to borrow. So in 1933, President Franklin D. Roosevelt cut the dollar's ties with gold, allowing the government to pump money into the economy and lower interest rates. 'Most economists now agree 90 per cent of the reason why the US got out of the Great Depression was the break with gold', said Liaquat Ahamed, author of the book *Lords of Finance*.[1] The US continued to allow foreign governments to exchange dollars for gold until 1971, when President Richard Nixon ended the practice to stop dollar-flush foreigners from sapping US gold reserves.

There's a finite supply of gold. In 2011 there was a recorded 165,000 metric tons (or tonnes) of mined gold. Warren Buffett says the total amount of gold in the world above ground could fit into a cube with sides of just 20 meters (67 feet).[2] As restrictive as the existing amount of gold, is the randomness and unpredictability of future discovery. This makes scaling and growth harder. It reduces control over economic policy and diminishes speed to react and recover.

Without coming off the gold standard and creating more money, economic growth would have slowed right down. In the end demand would have outstripped supply and prices risen unsustainably. This tactic also allowed further increased velocity of money and other innovations like crypto-currency to follow suit. This strategic policy was a great example of leverage, and perhaps a move that you could model or at least learn from.

QE LEVERAGE

Quantitative Easing (QE), which is the introduction of new money into the monetary supply by a central bank, is a leveraged concept that also has its critics but has been proven to kick-start and grow economies. QE can increase spending when economies slow down. The theory is that as more money enters the economy, consumers will have more to spend. This will in turn increase company profits and more reinvestment and jobs. This helps to stimulate velocity and confidence. QE can stimulate exports by increasing the monetary base and can stimulate lending which increases the velocity of money, as it tends to lower longer-term interest rates, in turn encouraging borrowing. When banks have more cash they often reduce their lending criteria and pump more lending into the system.

This is a balance, of course. Too much QE can devalue money and central banks can abuse this power. The upside is that any loans you have get devalued too, with inflation paying down the relative amount of your loan. QE is essentially leverage of energy into the economy. While I assume you don't have the power to print money on demand, perhaps you could have your own version of QE leverage by creating additional information, ideas, energy and other currency in your enterprise that can kick-start Your personal GDP and revenues for your business. Can you do that?

CASH (DE) LEVERAGE

Cash in the bank while rates are low is reverse leveraged, as the interest is lower than the rate of inflation. The actual rate of return can be negative. If rates are higher than inflation then you have a tiny margin of leverage. If inflation is 3 per cent and interest rates are 5 per cent, then the leverage is 0.02×, or 2 per cent. There isn't a lot of leverage with cash, until you use it as collateral for leverage.

BANK LEVERAGE

If cash is used as a deposit for a property, the bank will loan against the asset and take a charge. They might loan 50 per cent to 80 per cent of the value of the asset, or more in a boom. If the deposit is 25 per cent and the loan is 75 per cent, then the leverage is 4×, or 400 per cent. Assume £1 million property asset with £250,000 deposit and £750,000 bank loan. The bank does not take any capital growth, so all growth over £1 million is yours. On average, property prices in the UK have doubled every ten years since 1952, according to the Nationwide Building Society. In ten years the property value is £2 million, the loan either £750,000 if on interest only, or up to one-third less if ten years into a 25-year repayment loan, so around £500,000. The equity in the asset has gone from £250,000 to

£1.5 million in ten years, thanks to the leverage on the bank's loan. This has leveraged the initial capital by 6× or 600 per cent.

Assuming the property is rented to a tenant, then the loan has been paid down by the tenant from £750,000 to £500,000, further increasing the leverage. The rent will leave a margin that will be your income, so, in effect, you leverage three ways in owning the asset with the bank's money, paying down the loan with the tenant's money and paying your cashflow with the tenant's money. You can even leverage out the management and maintenance to an agent so you minimize the time input and create a fourth dimension of leverage.

JV leverage

If you could have someone lend you the 25 per cent deposit, or find a way to have a contract or guarantee, then you would create infinite leverage. Provided you play within the rules of the bank, you could get a loan for the deposit from a private lender, and the remaining loan from the bank, to fund 100 per cent of the purchase price of the property asset. Or you could get 100 per cent of the funding of the asset from a joint venture (JV) partner, achieving the same outcome. We bought a commercial property and converted it into 42 units, 100 per cent financed by a private investor who we met through our business and became friends with. He financed the purchase, the bank financed the development, and we own the 42 units jointly and rent them out. We then bought next door and will convert that into another 12 to 20 units, planning dependent. The gross income will be around £363,000 a year, 100 per cent financed by someone else. In this joint venture (JV) the private investor leverages our time, location, knowledge and experience, and we leverage his cash.

Contract leverage

Contracts that gain leverage can be option contracts, where you obtain the legal right to buy the (property) asset or business in a future agreed timeframe. If you gain an option for three years, you can manage the property or business as your own, getting income from a tenant or sales or changing the use to increase the income, without the initial capital outlay to purchase. You then have a grace period to raise the cash, or even some capital value growth to contribute, all while receiving an income stream. Other variations are 'instalment contracts' where you can take an option to purchase the asset and then pay in instalments over an agreed timeframe. This acts as a type of payment plan to pay the purchase price over time, perhaps from the income of the asset you have the contract on in the form of rent, bringing future revenue forward or sweating the asset. This reduces the upfront capital outlay, sometimes to zero.

Smart entrepreneurs are using a variation of a corporate let contract to 'rent-to-rent' properties. Instead of buying them, they rent properties from a landlord in the conventional way, ensuring they are big with many rooms. They then re-let all the rooms to individual tenants, creating a multi-let income. They essentially act as a go-between, paying a good rent to the landlord who is happy that their property is let, and then increasing the income stream by 3× or more. This is highly leveraged because for the cost of one month's deposit and a few fees, a £2000 a month or more gross income can be created from a single-family dwelling, with little upfront capital investment. The downside to 'rent-to-rent' is the lack of capital ownership. The real innovators employ the rent-to-rent strategy, create the income and goodwill from the landlord, and then request option contracts to buy the property in the future to get the capital growth, creating another layer of leverage. These contracts started as a problem, moved into a challenge, then into an idea, worked into a solution, then an agreement, and then turned into money.

3 Systems (processes)

There are three definitions of 'system' relevant to the *Money* philosophy:

1 'A set of things working together as parts of a mechanism or an interconnecting network to make a complex whole.' This could be people and departments in a team, a networked community, social media, online 'to do lists', a group of companies and more. It's many parts creating leverage as a whole entity.

2 'A group of related hardware units or programmes or both, especially when dedicated to a single application.'

Computers, hardware and software, the Internet, apps and other electrical systems that make life faster, easier and better and reduce the need for and cost of complex processes and emotional people.

3 'A set of principles or procedures according to which something is done – an organized scheme or method.' The most efficient way of getting to a desired outcome in a predictable manner. An ordered process or set of values to follow to replicate a result and remove error, inefficiency and wastage.

AUTOMATION

Systems create automation. Automation makes you redundant, not relied upon. Automation of systems removes bottlenecks and dependency on skilled, expensive individuals. Automation creates autonomy and liberation. It disdains duplication and over-reliance on general people, skilled technicians and memory retention. Automation strives for the shortest, simplest and easiest way to maximum productivity and efficiency.

Almost every single action and function in your business and life can be done more efficiently to preserve time. You start with a systems strategy, and then move into the tactics and applications.

Systemize your business

This simple and scalable process will help you systemize your business and sack yourself from the day-to-day operations:

- **Step 1.** Make a note of everything you do that needs you or your knowledge. Note it as you do it (not later) in bullet point form or transfer it to a mind map.
- **Step 2.** Record anything you say on a dictation app or screen record (sales, marketing, scripts, processes, vision) in detail.
- **Step 3.** Send notes and recordings each Tuesday to a virtual or personal assistant to type up and order in a manual with clear page refs, images and indexes.

- **Step 4.** Have your PA or VA send your notes back to you for Friday by 3 pm so you can check them to ensure anyone can understand and follow it. Then send any feedback to the PA/VA to update it over the weekend.
- **Step 5.** Read your manual(s) once a week in parts and once a month in its entirety. Imagine you know nothing about you. Could anyone step in and do your role following this manual? Feedback any tweaks ensuring you keep it organized, in order and succinct.
- **Step 6.** As you grow, instruct your team members to do the same. Have your managers delegate doing the manuals of their teams. For maximum leverage have your PA do yours and make it their responsibility. That's leveraging leverage.

The important key to this that everyone seems to agree with (but rarely does) is *start now*. Not when you are preparing for hiring or sale (as it will take much longer, be much harder, disrupt existing business functions and probably hit sales).

Apps for autonomy

Implementing the following simple systems and apps will give you automation, global mobility and more money and freedom:

- Calendar/diary
- Dropbox (or other file sharing systems like Google drive)
- Social media on all devices
- CRM (customer relations management) system
- Banking (all banking on apps and online)
- ecommerce (Apple Pay, PayPal, iZettle and all credit card apps)
- Audio and eBooks
- Office drive/server (remote access to your central system)
- Password Protection (all passwords in one app)
- Remote AV (home and office automation and security)

- Trello (or other task management network)
- Evernote (or other document creation and sharing app).

Procedures = efficiency

A procedure is the 'best practice' way of implementing a system. Efficiency is performing that system on repeat. It is a checklist, A–Z or 1–15-step process, in the correct order, with constant analysis, iteration and troubleshooting. How can you streamline or shorten the process? How can you make it easier? How can you create leverage or economies of scale?

Consider taking at least one day per month, completely *out* of your business, where you do *no* 'tasks'. Instead collate all the KPIs of your business, management accounts and PnLs and analyse them. More money is hidden in plain sight. Get someone who has a bigger business to be a 'non-exec' of your 'board' and get them to look over them too. Brainstorm ways to reduce costs and increase profit margins and volume.

Decisions

If you want to grow, get out of your own way. I have to confess to finding this one challenging. If much of the knowledge of your business is in your head, and you are central to your business, then you'll hold it back. Not only do you need to leverage and automate, but most importantly, you need to hand over *decisions* to key team members. If you don't let them make key decisions, then they will always have to come back to you; you might as well DIY. Hire great people. Inspire them with your vision. Let them make mistakes. Support and don't control them. Get the hell out of their way!

4 People/skills

Leveraging people isn't about having everyone being your own personal lackey. A character flaw in many entrepreneurs, myself included for many years, is that we wrongly assume that people 'work for us'. We 'pay their wages' and therefore they should 'do what we say'.

That's like expecting your kids to do what they're told just because you're their parent. Ha, good luck with that. If you've ever used the 'I'm your boss' trump card, you've probably lost all the goodwill you may have built and created resentment.

Leveraging people is about alliances, affiliations and relationships, regardless of the payment or employment structure. Look to everyone and anyone as a potential partner or contact. Exchange leverage where you benefit from their skills and roles and they benefit in kind and in payment from you. Leveraging people is about having a clear vision, helping people through your leadership, giving them hope and belief, providing them with incomes and security, and making them feel valued and important. You serve each other, so see it as a partnership and not a hierarchy. The best leverage you have with people's time and skills is the goodwill in the relationship you have.

PAs, VAs, Operations Managers, MDs, CEOs, all other staff, all outsourcers, consultants and specialists are all looking to be 'leveraged' in the form of employment, consultations, contracts and partnerships.

The simple system to leveraging other people's skills and time is this: go back to your IGV (income generating value), and give *any* task on your 'to do' list that would cost *less* than your IGV to outsource to someone else. Pay them, get them on 30-day invoice terms, exchange services – whatever it takes to liberate your time for higher value tasks. Every entrepreneur wrestles with the battles of a small business: 'I can do it better' or 'I can't afford staff' or 'I don't want staff' or 'I have to be seen to be working hard'. Sam Walton did when he started Wal-Mart, which now has more than 2 million staff. The two Steves started in Steve Jobs' garage soldering the motherboards themselves. Apple now lives beyond Steve Jobs' lifetime. In 1954, brothers Dick and Mac opened the first McDonald's. One year later the first franchisee was taken on board. This was Ray Kroc who was the visionary and catalyst to grow McDonald's to employ 1.9 million staff in 2015 and now make about $75 million per day. While you don't have to want to build businesses this big, they all started with a first employee and some concerns about hiring and scaling.

Rewire your brain with two new words

Most people have the default internal question or statement of 'I have to do that' or 'I can't do that' or 'How can I do that?'

The problem with these internal questions is that they are unleveraged. These questions lead to stress, work or time input.

Instead of asking yourself 'How can I do that?' ask 'Who can I get to do that?' Better quality questions create a better quality of life.

Many people think it's OK for all those rich business owners who are in the position to leverage because they have money, but you don't have the resources. You have overheads and kids and mortgages and responsibilities and very little time. Yes, exactly. The longer you leave leverage out of your life, the longer people leverage you. If anyone can do it, you can do it. It is a system and philosophy to follow that every great business has been through.

5 IDEAS AND INFORMATION (LEVERAGE)

Any innovation is based on a creative idea to solve a problem. There was a day when someone didn't have cash but wanted to convert and create value, a solution and a need into money. All money originates from ideas, and so all leverage comes from ideas. The only limit to leverage, therefore, is creativity and resourcefulness, not cash.

Sara Blakely cut off the bottom of her pantyhose and the idea of Spanx was born in 2000. In the first three months, she sold over 50,000 pairs from the back of her apartment. Now her 'crazy idea' has grown to include a full range of products that are sold around the world. She landed on the Forbes World's Billionaires 2012 list, which estimated the company's revenue at just under $250 million.[3] The idea for Pillow Pets dawned on Jennifer Telfer after watching her young sons smash down their soft-toy animals in order to sleep on them like a pillow. The cuddly toy has since exploded, with $300 million in sales in 2010. Joel Glickman, then 50 years old and working in his family's plastics business, started cutting and connecting a bunch of straws together. His creation gave him an idea for K'NEX. After rejections from Hasbro and Mattel, Glickman decided to shut down part of the family's injection moulded plastics business to make his toy himself. In 1993, not long after K'NEX hit the market, Toys R Us founder said it was the best thing he'd seen in years. Four years later sales of the toy had grown to $100 million.

> ## The idea leverage system
>
> 1 Discover and state the *problem*.
> 2 Turn it into *a challenge*.
> 3 Brainstorm and then decide on an *idea*.
> 4 Work the idea into a *solution*.
> 5 Turn the solution into *cash*.
>
> The bigger the problem is in step 1, the bigger the lump of cash will be in step 5. While the rest of the world bemoans the scale of the problem, the innovator who leverages the *Money* philosophy rolls up their sleeves and steps up to the challenge (step 2) in the knowledge that step 5 (cash, result or success) will be proportionately greater.

On 20 March 1991, Eric Clapton's four-year-old son, Conor, fell from a window of a 53rd-floor apartment building in New York City and died. This tragic accident led Clapton to write 'Tears In Heaven' some months later. The song was featured on the soundtrack to the film *Rush*, was on the popular *MTV Unplugged* series, won three GRAMMY Awards in 1993, featured in multiple 'best song' lists, led to Clapton giving up alcohol and drugs, *and* has sold more than seven million copies. He says: 'I almost subconsciously used music for myself as a healing agent, and lo and behold, it worked. I have got a great deal of happiness and a great deal of healing from music.'[4]

INFORMATION MARKETING

As technology has increased the velocity of money, and money has increased the speed of technology, access to information has opened up like never before. You can learn and teach faster and easier than ever, from and to anyone in the world, anywhere in the world, in a fraction of the time. Perhaps the most powerful currency of information is information marketing. Selling information has become one of the biggest innovations and growth industries. This modern industry is worth more than $100 billion worldwide, growing 32.7 per cent from the previous year. Ninety-eight per cent of all information is now digital. Every minute in the digital world 47,000 apps are downloaded, $83,000 in sales are made, 61,141 hours of audio is downloaded, 100,000 new tweets are tweeted, 6 million Facebook pages are viewed, 30 hours of video are uploaded and 1.3 million videos are viewed. All of these you can monetize with maximum leverage and minimal overhead because you hold no stock and there is no limit to the volume you can produce. How you can implement information marketing in your niche will be detailed in Chapter 39.

36

Compounding

A water lily doubles in size every day, and after 30 days will cover the surface of any pond, regardless of its size. Yet after 29 days, it has only covered half the pond. It grows half its size in one-thirtieth of the time.

If you made a £1 bet per hole on a golf course, doubling your bet on each hole, you'd be at £4 on hole 3, £32 on hole 6 and £256 on hole 9. On hole 15, that amount has compounded to £16,384, and on hole 18 the compounded total is £131,072. All from a £1 start. Many of us secretly and naïvely want the last day's lily growth on the first day, or the 18th hole compounded on the first hole. Money and life do not work that way. The last day, or the next day, always have the most inertia and built-up momentum. The maximum leveraged benefit comes rear-loaded nearer the end. A long-term time perspective is mandatory if you want vast and lasting wealth.

Getting off the ground

If you research fuel usage in a space shuttle, you find that the space shuttle uses half its fuel just to get off the ground, and uses 96.2 per cent of its fuel to get one foot into the air, or uses nearly all its fuel in the few seconds immediately after launch. You can see that most of the fuel of a shuttle seems to be used and needed just to get the shuttle off the ground and to get it going. The remaining small amount is used for the entire remainder of the voyage out of the atmosphere, into space, and all the way back again. And so it is with building your wealth. The most energy is required at the start to get your shuttle off the ground. An object that is motionless tends to stay motionless, so you have to work hard enough not to have to work hard. This could be seen as a drawback, or a great benefit, depending on how you view it. Sure, it makes things harder at the start, but it also makes it easier at the end. It requires sweat more than regret to lift off, but that disqualifies most of your would-be competition too.

For each unit of time you are in a niche or enterprise, the inverse relationship between time and money swings the other way. At the start you have to 'work' the hardest for the lowest level, tangible result. It doesn't seem fair, but time isn't fair. Time is not linear or binary, where each unit rewards equally. No two units of time have the same value. Once you have momentum and compounding, ever nearing the 'end', you work the least and earn the most, with ever-reducing friction. And that doesn't seem fair either. But it is the law.

People who think hour-to-hour, earn a wage and spend it. People who think day-to-day are employed, operating functions imposed upon them by managers who can think week-to-week. Higher level managers may plan month-to-month, performing the yearly plan of the highest level managers. The highest level managers are implementing a vision created three to five years into the future by the owners of the enterprise. The enterprise owners take their inspiration from the visionaries who can think and see time in decades. The visionaries take their inspiration from the sages who can see into next generations or lifetimes. The scale and reach of the vision and the financial remuneration is therefore directly related to the length of the time perspective.

Ethereal assets

With every passing day you continue to build momentum and compounding – you build a vast bank of ethereal assets. Because these are intangible, many people give up on their quest for wealth and riches. That's like giving up on a tree before it has grown its roots. It has to grow down to grow up. The greater the scale and spread of the roots, the richer the fruits. These ethereal assets will turn the invisible into the visible and spirit into matter and money.

The intangible assets of reputation, goodwill, brand, networks, mindspace, trust, undeniable proof, volume of customers, followers, fans and referrals, links and comments, reach and visibility, capital, interest on interest, past solutions, faith, inspiration and emotional connections will be wider and deeper and have less friction.

No shortcut to compounding

The flighty, shiny penny, get-rich-unrealistically-quick mindset is a susceptibility to believing the opposite of the law of compounding. It is the naïve belief that somehow somewhere you can have little to none of the front-loaded most-of-the-work-for-none-of-the-money and almost all the most-of-the-money-with-none-of-the-work, at the start. There is an allure for the naïve to something that seems to shortcut the law of compounding, and before they've even given the roots a chance to grow down, they give up, looking for the next thing. They start again and give up and start again and give up and start again. The only things that compound are pain, misery and low self-worth. Then they blame and complain when it all goes wrong. Ironically, it probably wasn't going wrong. The first thing or last thing they started and then stopped would probably have given them wealth and riches if they'd kept at it long enough, even if it wasn't the best thing. Something done at an average level consistently will always make more money, than something shiny done very well for a short time and then given up on.

The cost of change

Imagine a constant heads-up display that you could see in your peripheral vision, like you can get on cars as an optional extra and on computer games. In these you can see 'lives remaining' or 'life force', 'power', 'weapon of choice', 'strengths and weaknesses', 'ammunition remaining' and so on. You have a constant visual measurement in real time of the consequences of your choices and actions. You can see if you are wasting ammo and energy, and you can see your points tally going up or down. Life doesn't give you one of those, but imagine that it did. Imagine that you had a visual feedback mechanism which showed a power bar or battery life gauge of your intangible, ethereal progress and assets. Imagine that you could see the bar go up and down according to the future compounded results and consequences of your actions. Imagine the bar is four-fifths full at the point where it looks like there are few physical results. You'd *never* give up. The *cost of change* would be obvious. You'd know you're almost there.

The cost of change is the cost of resetting compounding to zero again. Imagine Tiger Woods giving up golf at 18 years old because he hadn't won a major yet. That would have reset 16 years of time invested, getting him more than 80 per cent of the way towards multiple major wins and entry into golf's hall of fame. Even a small swing change can have huge long-term costs, as the best golf coaches know, so should be considered very carefully.

Imagine Edison giving up his experiments for the light bulb on his 9998th attempt. There are many stories of people who could have gone on to greatness but stopped just before they allowed compounding to start 'reversing' the most-of-the-work-for-none-of-the-money with the most-of-the-money-with-none-of-the-work.

Most millionaires and billionaires will tell you it takes the longest time and 'hardest work' to make the first million. It took me around four years from starting a 'real' business. Significantly, I made considerably more than a million personally in the next year; more than double the amount of money in less than quarter of the time. It was the 'laziest' or 'easiest' of all the years up to that time, with the least amount of work for the maximum financial results. The next year those results were nearly doubled again. I'm a relative minnow compared to Warren Buffett mostly because he's had an extra 60 years of compounding.

Insta-media

We live in a world of growing instant gratification. We see YouTube videos with 10 million views and get seduced by what seems like overnight successes and celebrities. Pictures of before and after six packs and miracle cures, all tempting our desire for shortcuts. This is an unrealistic fantasy that tempts us because we don't have a clear vision, and therefore get lured by distractions that look easy from the outside. The long-term reality is often poverty and low self-worth, because each time you start again you have to go through the entire seeding, planting and fertilizing process *all* over again. The more this happens, the more you lose confidence in your ability to create compounded wealth, carrying the baggage from one 'opportunity' to the next. You look for further shortcuts to save yourself because you doubt your ability. And so the cycle continues.

Sustained wealth

The deeper the roots, the higher the tree grows, the wider its leaves spread, and the more seeds it produces for future forests (generations). Compounding gives momentum, and works moving forwards or backwards. Ever-growing debt attracts ever-increasing amounts of debt. Ever-growing amounts of money attract ever-increasing amounts of money. In fact, the rich often have a problem with too much money: they can't reinvest it fast enough, because compounding is compounding on compounding, and because they reinvest it, more money comes in. Yes, the rich do get richer. Let compounding work for you, don't keep changing all the time and reverse as quickly as possible the front-loaded most-of-the-work-for-least-money at the start to most-of-the-money-with-least-of-the-work the longer you stay in.

37

The 80/20 Principle

In 1906, Italian economist Vilfredo Pareto created a mathematical formula to describe the unequal distribution of wealth in his country, observing that around 20 per cent of the people owned 80 per cent of the wealth. In the late 1940s, Dr Joseph M Juran attributed the '80/20 rule' to Pareto, calling it the Pareto Principle, which referred to the observation that 80 per cent of Italy's wealth belonged to only 20 per cent of the population. More generally, the Pareto Principle is the observation that most things in life are not distributed evenly; 80/20 became the guideline relative distribution factor or percentage. It can be more extreme such as 90/10, or sometimes in the case of wealth distribution or relative success, 95/5, or 99/1. Here are some examples of 80/20 in action:

- 20 per cent of the input creates 80 per cent of the outcome
- 20 per cent of the workers produce 80 per cent of the work
- 20 per cent of the customers create 80 per cent of the revenue
- 20 per cent of the bugs cause 80 per cent of the crashes
- 20 per cent of the features cause 80 per cent of the usage
- 80 per cent of the value is achieved with 20 per cent of effort
- 80 per cent of the wealth is owned by 20 per cent of people
- 80 per cent of complaints come from 20 per cent of customers
- 80 per cent of sales come from 20 per cent of your products or clients

- 80 per cent of your expenses come from 20 per cent of your overheads.

Later, Richard Koch wrote a book called *The 80/20 Principle: The Secret of Achieving More with Less*. He states that 'The 80/20 principle is one of the great secrets of highly effective people and organizations.' Taking Pareto's Principle into the modern age, studying how to create more with less in an overworked, unproductive era, Koch says:

- A minority of inputs lead to a majority of outputs.
- Focus on the few activities that produce the most satisfaction.
- Most of what we do is low value – eliminate or reduce the 80 per cent of efforts that produce poor results.
- A minority of causes create a majority of effects.
- The critical few – identify and build upon the 20 per cent of efforts that produce 80 per cent of the results.
- In business, focus on the products and customers that make you the most money, and minimize or eliminate the rest.
- A minority of decisions will produce the majority of your results: choice of work, debts, investments, relationships.
- More effort does not equal more reward – focus only on what is crucial, and ignore the rest.[1]

I have found this principle to be uncannily accurate. No two units of time have equal value. In studying wealth distribution, I believe Pareto uncovered a universal law across money, business and general life leverage. You can embrace the principle and achieve maximum wealth with minimum investment of time and money, and maximum results with minimum effort. Most people are on the wrong side experiencing graft not craft, attrition, frustration and painfully slow results. It is two sides of the same coin in that it can work 80/20 or 20/80, and seems to manifest in all areas of our lives. Some other general examples to further show the uncanny accuracy:

- You use 20 per cent of your apps, 80 per cent of the time.
- You wear 80 per cent of your clothes, 20 per cent of the time (ladies, maybe many of them still have the tags on!)

- 80 per cent of your hair is in 20 per cent of the areas (gents, 80 per cent of your baldness is in 20 per cent of the area).
- You get 80 per cent of your happiness from 20 per cent of the things you do (and vice versa).
- 80 per cent of the wear of the carpet is in 20 per cent of the room/surface area.
- 80 per cent of the wear of a car engine is in 20 per cent of the whole engine.
- 80 per cent of the wear on your keyboard is on 20 per cent of the keys.
- 80 per cent of the return on your stock portfolio will be from 20 per cent of the investments.
- You have 80 per cent of your sex in 20 per cent of the available Kama Sutra positions…

80/20 isn't about working harder, it is about working selectively and with ruthless efficiency. Preserve the maximum amount of time, gain the highest hourly rate or value, and leverage wealth and riches. If you combine implementing the laws of 80/20 with compounding, you get huge inertia. In Chapter 27 on the time relationship with money, you calculated your IGV (Income Generating Value) by adding up your total weekly income from all sources and dividing it by your total hours worked. In the example used, where IGV = total income (week) / hours worked (week):

$$£1000 / 55 \text{ hours} = £18.18 \text{ per hour.}$$

When you add 80/20 to this calculation, assuming 80 per cent of your income is earned from 20 per cent of your time (and vice versa), it changes your IGV calculation significantly:

$$20 \text{ per cent IGV} = (\text{total income (week)}) \times 80 \text{ per cent}) / (\text{hours worked (week)}) \times 20 \text{ per cent, } £800 / 11 \text{ hours} = £72.72 \text{ per hour.}$$

This is 4× or 400 per cent more money per hour than a linear time value calculation. But it gets more revealing, when you compare 20/80 against 80/20. Here is the inefficient inverse calculation:

80 per cent IGV = (total income (week)) × 20 per cent / (hours worked (week)) × 80 per cent, £200 / 44 hours = £4.54 per hour.

This is 4× less than the linear time value of £18.18, but a full 16× less than the leveraged 20 per cent £72.72 per hour.

20 per cent of the time, you are likely earning a full 16× more per hour than you are for the remaining 80 per cent of the time. Let's add the effect of compounding onto this calculation. Assuming you were clear on your VVKIK, outsourced all the low value, 80 per cent tasks, and just doubled the amount of 20 per cent tasks you did, here are the results:

- You outsource 60 per cent of all time/work that is in the low value 80 per cent. Assume £10/hr cost. (33 / 55 hours × £10 / hr). Total cost: £330.
- You double, or do twice as much 20 per cent time/work (22/55 hours at £800/11 hours). Total income: £1,600.
- 60 per cent of your time is left free to do as you choose.
- You earn net £1270 in 22 hours as opposed to £1000 in 55 hours.
- That's £270 more for 33 hours less, per week.
- In one year you would earn £14,040 more in 1716 fewer hours.
- In ten years you would earn £140,040 more in 10,716 fewer hours.
- In 50 years you would earn £700,200 more in 53,580 fewer hours.
- 53,580 hours is 6 years and 42 days.

Note that these figures don't take into account inflation, and assume that you follow through with this activity with discipline. I have had critics tell me that this is a clinical way to measure time. I wholeheartedly agree. This is *your* life. Your countdown clock has been going a long time and you may have less time left than you've already consumed. Isn't it worth valuing it with such importance and ruthless efficiency? This is how the rich perceive and invest time to get rich. It is just as easy to do this, as not to do it. Of course there will be some wastage, which is why I did the calculation only doubling the amount of 20 per cent time you reinvest. There will be emotions and temptations when you start. It will need practice to get this moving, but as time is the most valuable commodity we have, it is also the biggest asset we have. If you don't fill your life with high KRAs, IGTs, and more of what you love, it will fill up with others' important tasks, which you won't love. If you don't fill your life with high priorities, life will fill you with low ones.

80/20 summary

80/20 gives insight into why wealth distributes as it does, why it will never equally redistribute, and how you can distribute it unevenly in your favour. Not at the cost of others, but by increasing velocity, YGDP (Your personal GDP) and flow. Focusing your highest KRAs and IGTs and evaluating them at least every six months is the key to ever increasing wealth and riches that compound and compound. You can use 80/20 thinking in all areas related to money and wealth. Who you network with, the places you travel to and how you get there, how you learn a new subject, the books, audios and online learning you consume, the media you follow, marketing, sales, cost saving, how you purchase items, housework leverage, social and work / life merge, managing email, meetings, banking; anything and everything.

38

Selling is serving, solving and caring

The best way to find yourself is to lose yourself in the service of others.

Mahatma Gandhi

There are three things to care about to build and sustain wealth. I call them the 'Trinity of Care':

1 CARE ABOUT HUMANITY

We serve no purpose if we have no value. The way to have unique value to the human race is to serve and solve for (many) others, in our own way. The way you help your species to survive and thrive is to support its evolution, adding value and service to its collaborative progression. The more value you add, the more valuable you become as a part of the greater whole; the more reliant the greater whole is on you for evolution and progression. 'Enlightened self-interest' is the coined phrase for this. The more you serve others, the more problems you solve for others and the bigger the problems you solve for others, the more money, worth and value you bring to your own life too. Bill Gates' vision wasn't 'a personal computer on my desk' and 'eradicate polio for one person', it was vast and global. Elon Musk's vision isn't to colonize Peterborough.

Selling is service to others, giving the buyer what they want under 'fair exchange'. Selling is caring enough about someone to give them something of utility and value, in exchange for money (or other remuneration). Selling is caring enough about someone to discover what is most important to them, and then giving it to them. Earning money is the natural outcome, but also a service to others; being remunerated a share of the overall economy of the transaction, under fair exchange. When they pay you they, in turn, value money and increase their own YGDP.

All acts of service create a greater economy and outlet for others to serve in turn. Acts of service aren't one-way; it's not just the seller that serves the buyer, the employee that serves the employer and the parent who serves the child; it is an interconnected web of service that adds or detracts from economy and progress.

If a footballer serves his team best by scoring goals, saving goals or setting up goals, he will be remunerated accordingly. He doesn't just randomly get paid £350,000 a week. His salary, sponsorship deals and image rights are directly proportional to the service he provides to his team, his manager and the fans. No footballer will ever get that level of salary if he doesn't pass, save, score or set up any goals. His level of service to his team directly impacts the success of his team, and feeds back to his salary. He gets a higher salary than those who add less value and service than him, and a lower salary than those who add more value and service. If he gives no service he loses his place in the team and ultimately loses his contract. If he increases his service other teams want to buy him, and will pay high fees and a higher salary. To this end a footballer is a salesperson, as we all are, because nothing moves until someone sells. The poor, inaccurate perception of 'salespeople' suffocates wealth. It irks me when people moan about footballers' salaries. Whether or not you feel that they make their living diving and rolling around and hounding the referee is beside the point. Footballers earn exactly what they are worth in relation to serving others, in a humanitarian sales transaction. They play the game they are in, as best they can. We all earn exactly what we are worth. No more, and no less. Footballers play within the rules and regulations that are set. The best footballers earn the most. The best footballers entertain the most people, giving the most people passion and purpose and hope and enjoyment. In 2015, 700 million people across the globe tuned in to watch Manchester United play Liverpool. The best footballers inspire the most people to want to play football and be as good as them one day. They are the best sales-people of the game of football, in their own unique way, just like an artist is a salesperson of their own work. I wasn't, which is why a good artist can stay poor. Art is about sales as much as art.

Once the selling and the value exchange stops, is unsustainable, becomes selfish or not under fair exchange, then the balance corrects itself. If a footballer keeps getting injured then the owners of the club negotiate a 'pay per play' contract. If the player doesn't live up to the hype, new salary or play as well as they did in the previous club, they get sold and their value goes down, as does their salary. If they don't maintain a level of performance for the team they get dropped and can even be forced to play with the reserves.

Footballers' salaries are a micro-insight into how the world works regarding selling, serving, solving and remuneration. As footballers get better, they get peripheral deals that earn them more money: sponsorship, endorsements, shares of merchandise and even paid social media posts. In economics these are known as 'marginal services'. The better they get, the more attractive their value is, and the less pushy their selling needs to be. Their level of mastery, linked to how it serves and solves for others, is their service-based sale. This compounds upwards. Cristiano Ronaldo is reportedly paid up to $303,900 per tweet.[1] This is the compounded manifestation of the years of hard work, mastery and level and scale of service to others, in a sales offering that is clear and valuable to the purchaser. They have committed their whole life to their 'art' and, like the entrepreneur, have taken a risk in an uncertain career where most people don't succeed and one injury could ruin their career.

As soon as this value erodes, so does the remuneration. Think what happened to Tiger Woods and Lance Armstrong once things began to unravel. Sponsors cancelled their contracts, media started making demands and the volume of people they served reduced as people changed their views of them and the value they offered.

Serving and solving gives more evidence of the myth of even wealth (re)distribution. As idealistic as socialism and communism are, they don't encourage serving and solving. This is one reason why capitalism is more prevalent in world social systems. Capitalism balances human self-interest (needed to survive and thrive) and the interconnected personal-and-greater-whole benefit of serving and solving. Other 'social' systems discourage self-interest, and can unfairly serve the self-interest of the few people running the system.

You are remunerated in equal balance to the number of people you serve, the scale of the service you provide, the number of problems you solve, and the scale of those problems. That is your 'sales pitch', more so than a wad of brochures and closing techniques.

Here are some examples of people and companies serving and solving in different areas and at different levels:

- Hans Rausing, son of Tetrapak founder Ruben Rausing. Net-worth in excess of $10 billion. Most famous innovation: plastic covered paper milk cartons.
- Post-it Notes generate approximately $1 billion a year in revenue for 3M. The Post-it Note was 'invented' by accident in 1968.
- Ken Modestu receives $23,000 for cutting the hair of the Sultan of Brunei, when expenses from the Dorchester Hotel to South East Asia are added in. Most celebrity hairdressers charge $400 to $1600 per 'cut'.
- Tetris, the simple computer puzzle game, has sold over 100 million copies.
- Eclipse, Roman Abramovich's yacht, is reputed to have cost between $450 million and $1.2 billion to build. It has 70 crew, room for 24 guests, two helipads and a submarine.
- Bill Foege has reputedly helped save 131,000,000 lives by devising the global strategy that led to the eradication of smallpox. He now advises the Bill and Melinda Gates Foundation, with a view to eradicating polio. He was awarded the Presidential Medal of Honor in 2012.

Each of these examples serves and solves in different ways. Here are the ways they serve and solve, and how you can too:

- Solve a small problem for many people.
- Solve a big problem for a few people.
- Solve a small problem multiple times.
- Solve a big problem multiple times.
- Serve charitably.
- Serve materially.
- Serve through entertainment.

The Post-it Note solves a small, simple problem, for many people, many times over. So do the many patents that Tetrapak hold. Roman Abramovich's yacht served one person, once, but with a huge transactional remuneration, and served materially. Bill Foege served charitably, and would be able to monetize his service and recognition. Tetris served through entertainment. Ken Modestu served materially (you could say vanity service), but a perceived service nonetheless.

> If life gets hard for you, help more people and life will help you.
>
> *Rob Moore*

The more money you make for other people, the more money you make for yourself. Increase your focus and scale of serving and solving. Instead of shying away from big problems, attack them and solve them and your value will increase. As your actual IGV increases, so does your self-worth and you naturally move to a higher level of remuneration, service and scale.

2 CARE ABOUT YOURSELF

If you only focus on serving others, without valuing yourself, you will increase your overheads, reduce your margins and have an unsustainable sales proposition. People would value others more if they charged more, because value is a perception related to fair exchange. If both price and value increase, sales increase. Better quality customers are attracted, better referrals are attracted and self-worth is augmented. Invest in yourself. Forgive yourself and others of the perceived wrongs and hurt. Give yourself permission to charge highly and fairly. You will find the high quality customers who value what you do. Constantly work on your self-development, solve bigger problems and be around people who value *your* value. Love yourself for who you are, not who you want to be. Don't delay all value into the future by giving everything away now, just to earn some future credibility and proof. Show the world who you really are and allow others to gain great benefit from your uniqueness.

3 CARE ABOUT MONEY

Give yourself permission to have a love affair with money. Allow yourself to love it, make it, share it; bathe in it if you want to.

Track and measure your net-worth. Keep a close eye on your money, margins, profits (and losses). Have specific financial KPIs for your business. Have your mind on your money and your money on your mind. Release all guilt, shame and fear of being judged around your love affair with money. Money is simply our current mechanism of universal exchange of value. Love what money gives you and others. Use it as a force for good. Learn investing and money management systems to manage it well so it will take care of you. Nurture and improve your knowledge of, and relationship with, money. Teach it to your children and others who know less than you. Ensure you have good systems to chase payments and collect your fees fast and fairly. Do not undersell yourself.

The eight stages of selling

Here are the eight stages of selling that will make sales more effortless and natural for you:

1 Greet or introduce. Introduce yourself with a smile. People form their opinions within the first three to five seconds of meeting you. Your voice, dress, eye contact, manner, caring and confidence are important.

2 Establish rapport. Similarities forge bonds. The quicker you can ask people questions about their lives that lead to common threads between you and them, the easier it is to sell. Let them talk more. Find common ground. Show genuine interest.

3 Identify their need. What's their primary or immediate need? What solution is most important to them? Discover what appears to be missing or problematic in their lives. The number of rejections you receive during the sales process is inversely proportional to how well you've established their need or pain. The deeper and broader their need, the easier it is to make the sale.

4   Confirm and restate their need. Be certain that you've established their real need, beneath the layers. When they've told you what their need or void is, repeat this back to them to gain clarity and a spoken point of reference. Never assume – always make it stated.

5   Create and offer value. Tailor your work as a solution to their issue. Make an offer they can't refuse by giving them what they want. If someone says they can't afford what you're offering, don't have the time or don't want something, all that means is you haven't demonstrated value in their terms. In this case, restate the need and communicate more value. People never have a lack of money, they have a lack of desire and motivation. If you provide the motivation, they'll find the money.

6   Close. Make the sale. Ask for the money. Don't leave it vague or unspoken. Be clear on the terms. Confirm the appointment, get the credit card details and arrange delivery and payment. Do not leave it to them.

7   Provide service, care and value. Deliver the service you promised, then a little more. Call back on the answers to your specific questions, link your services or products to your customers' specific values and your products will sell themselves. Continue the fair exchange process long after the money is in the bank.

8   Ask for referrals and feedback. Once you have incrementally over delivered and you have a raving fan customer, ask them if they know anyone else who could benefit in the same way. Ask for the contact details of three people for every person you ask. Ask for any feedback in a safe environment so they will be honest about what you can improve, and implement relevant iterations.

NO GIMMICKS

If you try to fool people, they'll eventually catch on. If you pressure people, use gimmicky tactics or hard closes, people will give you feedback through buyers' remorse. It will force increased service, support and overheads up. Disgruntled customers will not refer people to you. When you're sincere and speak with integrity from who you are, not who you are trying to be, people will respond most favourably. To sell is not to tell. To sell is to ask, listen and then give.

Sustainable selling is caring, serving and solving. Vast wealth is the scale of this serviced-based selling. Instead of working on pitches, closes and gimmicks, work on serving, solving and caring enough about prospects to discover their values and give them service that is most important to them and their values. Continually improve and develop your offering and the bespoke nature of the solutions and your prices and wealth will rise.

39

Marketing is money

If you have a shop, and the sales are what you sell to the customer in the shop, then marketing is getting them into the shop in the first place. You can't sell anything to no one, therefore marketing is the single most important function of a business. Marketing is money.

The best product no one buys trails behind a mediocre product everyone buys. Of course great products and innovation are important, but I'm going to assume you both desire and create these. Once you've designed, crowd-sourced and iterated your product or service, your marketing gets leads, turns them into customers, then hungry buyers, then ravings and finally referrals. The more the customer already wants what you have and fits within your ideal client demographic, the easier and cheaper your marketing will be. Friction slows down the velocity of money, so poor marketing, or good marketing to the wrong people, slows down your money.

Great marketing embraces both art and science. The art is your intuition of what your market wants, your experience, desirability, beauty and the unknown variables that make it go viral. The science is the data analysis of your marketing KPIs to base investment decisions on. Art and science merge when you have brand, goodwill and experience, but also test, measure and tweak. Merge the art and the science of marketing to get an advantage over your competition.

Scarcity and urgency

If your marketing embraces reducing supply and increasing demand, then your prices will naturally rise. If you have brand goodwill, a large and loyal following who have plenty of money and very limited supply, your prices will be huge. Brands like Nike create scarce, higher priced products (sharks and limited edition Nike Air Jordans) that creates the buying frenzy, that in turn acts as a marketing medium for all the lower priced products like (prints, books and $60 trainers).

Marketing currency

Here is a list of 24 marketing tactics that you can leverage as a form of currency, converting your message through your products and services into money and wealth:

1 Be unique, but be you.
2 Encourage debate and controversy.
3 Start with a deep, narrow niche and go wider later.
4 Always sell something: an idea, action, email opt in or referral.
5 Give value first and ask for money after.
6 Become a known authority in your industry and a celebrity yourself.
7 Keep doing what works until it doesn't (70 per cent of the time), and ...
8 Innovate and test new vehicles and media (30 per cent of the time).
9 Test before you scale.
10 Test and scale pay-per-click advertising (Facebook, Google, Twitter, Instagram, Reddit and new media with high traffic volume).
11 Have presence on all social media platforms with high traffic.
12 Get your followers from one media channel to another (especially from data you don't own to data you do).
13 Balance brand and goodwill with direct response marketing.
14 News-jack media noise, energy and emotion for leverage.
15 Measure LCV (Lifetime Client Value = total sales / total no. of clients). This is not the same as total sales / total products sold.
16 Measure MAC (Maximum Acquisition Cost) per client.
17 Keep reinvesting in marketing by spending a per cent of LCV as a MAC.

18 Measure business specific KPIs like PHR (Per Head Revenue, CPC (Cost Per Click) CPL (Cost Per Lead) CBOM (Cost of 'Bum on Seat') PPC (Purchases Per Client) etc.

19 Repurpose your information into all formats and media for scale.

20 Always ask for a referral after a sale or satisfied customer.

21 If you're not investing in marketing today, you're not getting customers tomorrow.

22 Cut marketing spend *last* in hard times, not first.

23 Never rely on one source of marketing (better one customer from 20 channels than 20 customers from one channel).

24 Ask your customers and demographics what they want, what you should start, stop and keep, and give it to them.

Information and Internet marketing

Four billion people use email, 79 per cent of the population use social media, 51 per cent use blogs, 42 per cent use webinars and 16 per cent use podcasts. This growth shows no sign of slowing down. Print media, TV ads and conventional retail business have been aggressively disrupted. The costs of reaching your exact customer demographic have reduced and your overheads slashed. With a secondhand laptop and a good WiFi signal you can start and scale business faster and easier than ever. A further reduction in overheads and increase in speed is marketing the 'information' related to your business or passion. The demand for information has grown significantly. In 2010 information marketing was a $50 billion industry. By 2013 it was a $62 billion industry, according to the *Wall Street Journal*.[1] Because it is easier than ever to access information, and therefore 'self-teach', the industry has boomed in both free and paid for information. Google currently stores around 15 exabytes of data, which is around 30 million 500-gigabyte personal computers! Because there is virtually no stock-holding, inventory or start-up cost, you can package your knowledge and reach a global customer base with lower friction. You can sell the same or similar piece of low-cost information millions of times and there is no 'download stock limit'. You can repackage and repurpose that information and sell it hosted online, in physical book format, on CD, DVD, eBooks, audiobooks, Kindle, iTunes, Audible, iBooks, newsletters, podcasts, udemy, Facebook groups and pages, iTunes university, on a paid membership site platform, in a seminar room, on a mentorship or mastermind programme, or on a retreat. You can start at £1 and work up to £50,000 or more or similar information, with scale at the lower end and scarcity and personal access to you at the higher end.

When we started Progressive Property, young and unable to grow beards, we had much to say but low inherent brand value. We disrupted by being unique and embracing Internet and information marketing, and we bombarded our industry with valuable information, for free, on forums, e-courses, newsletters, PDFs and at some events. We started to get noticed and build some goodwill, and a few critics, and when I wrote *Property Investing Secrets* (2008) we sold more than we expected. That book, now in its fourth edition, has brought in hundreds of thousands of pounds since 2008. It brought us a new audience, and enough people to hold an event. The first event we ever held, we had 75 or so people turn up. We couldn't believe it. No social media back then, all done via email. That event cost us £97 and brought in £7275 for less than a day's work. Some of the information from that event was taken from our book and expanded upon, with personal experiences and case studies. At that event we invited people to join us for a more indepth, step-by-step Property Investing Masterclass over two days; 25 people bought tickets at £1995 each. That was £49,875. All for information we already had in our heads, from what we'd been doing anyway, and loved to talk about. Information is now not far off a £20 million a year business for us, and we are not the only ones, or the biggest. Dozens of people we've taught have gone on to set up their own information marketing businesses, teaching in their own unique style. There's room for us all, because people are hungry for information in this entrepreneurial revolution.

You can create a product once, like this book, and earn on it many times over. It can generate passive, recurring income for decades to come. It can go viral and get shared and sold by affiliates, resellers and social media addicts. Huge platforms with millions of users like Amazon, Google, Facebook and Udemy do all the legwork of bringing customers to you, for free. Information marketing is quite possibly the most leveraged use of time, giving maximum ROTI.

The pains that people are experiencing in your area of unique genius and experience, you can solve quickly through ever-growing online media outlets. Almost daily there's a new social media platform that you can leverage with access to millions of customers using a free account. You can serve and solve for many people when you honour your value and get it out there. Almost everyone has a book in them; the thing is for most people it is still in them. Serve more people with your unique information, and get paid handsomely (and passively) for it.

40

Entrepreneur, employee or intrapreneur?

There are three main methods of engagement for you to earn or work that are legal and sustainable. These evolve over time, and hybrids emerge. They are: employee; entrepreneur (self-employed); intrapreneur (employed autonomy).

There are upsides and downsides to each. Stereotyped personality types will suit one better than the other two. Some fraternities in the personal development and business world look down on being an employee or intrapreneur, but that is a myopic view. You should take time to consider the type of person you are, your existing knowledge and experience, your risk profile, and make the best of and most money in the one that suits you. Then you can let go of any 'grass is greener on the other side' perceptions, and focus that energy on your life. You could also start in one area, and set a target to move into another, thereby reducing the risks of jacking in a career you took 20 years to build.

Employee

The benefits of being an employee are perceived relative security, consistent covering of overheads, training and support, a clear proven path to grow your career, a team environment to work in, a proven route out of college to earn, a route into retirement, perceived pension provision and some illness, maternity and other personal benefits. If you find a disruptive or huge company to work for you can gain all these benefits, and learn a lot, and get very well paid in the senior positions. You could get shares and earn millions…

…but it could take you decades to work your way up. Job security has also been disrupted in recent times, mostly at the lower pay grades. The last recession saw many people being laid off, and a lot of pension money seems to have disappeared or is now further out of reach. Soon the retirement age will be 137! The upsides of being an employee have reduced in some vocations, but the downsides are still downsides. It's not like wages went up 30 per cent to cover this increased risk. Many people have been forced to look at second streams of income, and in some cases this has been what finally led to them taking the plunge to be an entrepreneur.

Now let's look at how to be a great employee and develop your career in the shortest time with the maximum leverage using the *Money* philosophy.

How to leverage being an employee

Using the *Money* philosophy, stop thinking about what you can get being an employee, and think about balancing self-interest with the interests of your employer. Give to get. You will always get pay rises and promotions if and when you become indispensible to the organization. If they don't appreciate your value, you will get headhunted and someone else will. Here are some very leveragable ways to grow your career fast and make the most money in the shortest time under fair exchange:

- Find out the values of your manager, boss and employer.
- Ask what the highest KRAs (key result areas) you can perform are that give the greatest benefit to the company vision.
- Do the job you want, not the one you have.
- Book in monthly reviews with your manager in which you can show what you've done for the company and receive feedback to grow.
- Bring revenue generating ideas to the company and ask for a remuneration share in them.
- Bring cost-saving ideas to the company and ask for a remuneration share in the saving.
- Ask for clear goals, targets and timeframes to meet your KRAs and your revenue share.
- Over deliver.

- Manage time with hyper-efficiency to make the biggest impact.
- Always care for and serve the customers well.

Entrepreneur (self-employed)

This book is not about the technicalities of accounting so I'm not going to detail the differences between self-employed, sole trader, running a limited company or limited liability partnership. You should get advice from a good accountant for the correct structures, entities and jurisdictions of your business set up and needs. For the purpose of this book, *entrepreneur* means working for yourself. The main downside, as a word of fair warning, is that the risk is higher, which is why the reward is higher. The responsibility is *all* on you, and you can't hide in the middle of a corporate hierarchy. You have to embrace a far wider skillset. You may go many months or longer with little to no income to cover your overheads. It can be a lonely venture at the start when there is just you, the Internet and the four walls of your bedroom. No team, culture or energy to bounce off and no people to support you. No politics to play. You have to manage yourself. There are no personal training and development plans from bosses who have budgets. There are no staff benefits when you are ill or pregnant and no employment system to benefit from. At least sick days will be lower when you're an entrepreneur!

Now that the disclaimer is out of the way, the benefits are actually quite astounding. There are just some of us, maybe you too, who couldn't be anything other than an entrepreneur. I've only been employed twice, and once by my dad, but have been fired three times. What a record! I am absolutely 100 per cent un-em-ploy-able. Thank my lucky stars for entrepreneurship. You might also love the challenge, and not be put off by the downsides because you like the risk. You know that the reward is great too. You like the freedom. You like the buzz of creating something and doing something that matters that you can put your heart into. You like the control. You can't take orders (you have a partner at home for that!). You know you can make a difference. You want to build something lasting.

The entrepreneurial age

There are many compelling reasons why you might want to plan to become an entrepreneur, or if you already are one, keep going and keep growing, despite the challenges you may be having. Some are relatively constant and consistent, and some disruptive. Here are the disruptive ones:

- The growth of ecommerce and Internet sales through fibre optics.
- The speed of growth of future tech such as VR, AI, IoT (Virtual Reality, Artificial Intelligence, the Internet of Things).
- An ever-increasing population to serve, growing at 200,000 a day.
- Time becoming the scarcest of commodities.
- Drones and automation replacing the workforce.
- A stark realization that no government or pension will look after your future.
- The globe being much more (inter) connected.
- Modern mobility, the *Life Leverage* philosophy; you and your phone or laptop (the cloud, apps, WiFi).
- Ever-decreasing start-up costs and overheads.
- Disruptions to finance such as crowdfunding and crypto-currencies.
- Counter cyclical opportunities.

I am excited about the opportunities, vast upsides and mitigated risks of being or becoming an entrepreneur. Never in history has the globe been so connected. But it's not just the disruptions that make being an entrepreneur attractive. Governments need entrepreneurs to have a path open to them for setting up, scaling and creating enterprise, and for protection from the risks. When you run a business you contribute significantly to the state through taxes and employment. Infrastructure, transport, healthcare, fire department, police force and more are greatly subsidized through your enterprise as an entrepreneur. You contribute revenue through taxes levied on that income and capital. In the UK, VAT is charged on almost all purchases, at 20 per cent currently. You pay business rates to run your operation, employer's national insurance (employees that you hire pay national insurance too), corporation tax, personal tax as a director, each employee pays personal tax, capital gains tax on profits and other stealth taxes. Most people who BCDJ do not understand all this revenue and support you generate for your local economy. I'm proud to be an entrepreneur and to help fund our society. Governments and boroughs give you significant tax breaks and protection as an entrepreneur that I, for one, am very grateful for. Here are the consistent, constant benefits of being an entrepreneur:

- Limited liability structures enable you to take risks and limit the risk to your company and not you personally
- Regulations in place to restrict monopolies
- People living longer and longer
- Power to lower interest rates
- Power to print more money
- Progressive tax breaks and grants
- Innovation is encouraged and rewarded
- You are taxed last, after offsetting all costs; employees are taxed first and at source.

These reduce the risk of getting started and protect you so you can profit and produce. They also control you if you get greedy. They create sharing and contribution through your revenue generation and taxation. I truly admire the balance of controls and opportunities that are open to an entrepreneur in the developed world. You need an incentive to want to set up shop, run your enterprise and balance the risk, and so governments offer tax breaks. You can also run many of your affairs as a legitimate business expense, off-setting many capital and income expenses against your income to reduce your declared profit, and therefore your tax bill. Because you pay tax later (PTL) you can earn on the preserved capital, including VAT that isn't yours, and as a legitimate and important function of business get expert advice on how to reduce your tax bill for your company and yourself. Many of your capital purchases, travel, subsistence, education and other expenses can be off-set. By the time you come to pay the tax, in arrears, you could have saved half or more compared to being an employee. If you compound that over a few decades it's likely to be a six- to eight-figure sum.

How to leverage being an entrepreneur

It's actually not as tough as most people think to start your entrepreneurial venture, no matter what your age or experience. You just have to want to do it, be prepared to accept some different upsides and downsides, and *get started*. The Internet gives us all the world's information organized in a way that is easy to find and consume. At the touch of a key you can hack into a free Wi-Fi connection, you can set up online ecommerce accounts such as Amazon or eBay for free, you can sell some old possessions you don't need any more and raise some small start-up capital, to buy and sell some more. You don't need any premises or stock or overheads. You can raise more finance online from peer-to-peer and crowdfunding sites. You can find all your customers online at low cost or free through free social media sites. You can build a brand, reputation and raving fan base for your business or passion that can go viral and global, online, for free, from anywhere in the world. You can set up apps or technology fast and at low cost. You can run your entire business from one device. You can receive money at the speed of light with the flash of a card or a phone. This information is relevant if you already have an enterprise to help you scale or systemize. Here are some ways to help you leverage as an entrepreneur:

- Be clear on the vision, values and purpose of your venture.
- Start now, small or part-time, and set a target date to replace your income and hand in your notice.
- Leverage early by implementing systems as you go, on the go.
- Look to attract the best quality people, early, now.

- Start with outsourcing or work part-time to create the habit.
- Create a great culture that people want to be part of.
- Follow the eight stages of selling.
- Crowdsource your products and services and improve them through feedback (explained in Chapter 42).
- Create clear job descriptions and KRAs for all your team.
- Continue to inspire them through change, growth and disruptions.
- Manage your money well and monitor KPIs closely.
- Draw some profits and reinvest some profits.
- Continually work on your vision and strategy while you hire out for operations and tasks.
- Keep educating yourself, study other successful businesses and people and bring in new ideas from other niches.
- Develop your brand, PR and reputation management.
- Develop and nurture an amazing extended network.
- Get involved in philanthropic ventures.

When leading and managing your team as you grow, one of your very highest KRAs and your greatest management strategy will be beyond rewards and punishments, it will be to inspire. Build a team of a variety of people, personalities and skillsets, but with a similar vision and culture. See the best in people and they will show you their best. Support those who are overly down and challenge those who are overly up. If you want productive employees, give them meaningful work and just a bit more than they think they can do. It's amazing what you can achieve with a great vision and not quite enough time. In turn, they will do more than they ever thought possible.

Merge passion and profession, vocation and vacation and you and your employees will be more integrated, dynamic and inspired. Have a rolling recruitment policy; always be on the scout and look out for talent, so you can find the best people when they are ready and you don't have to hire the worst people when you are ready. If you pay peanuts you get monkeys, but if you pay them more than they're worth, they'll feel guilty about it and distract themselves. Embrace their feedback, get them involved in the strategy and vision, give random gifts and acts of kindness, celebrate births, birthdays and work anniversaries, and care enough to get to know your team personally as well as professionally. Care about them enough to let them vent and air their frustrations without making it about you or your emotions, and they will value you. Help them meet their needs and values and they will stay loyal.

Intrapreneur (employed autonomy)

Very much of the modern entrepreneurial age, the hybrid position is the intrapreneur. This merges the protection and security of an employed position, with the freedom and autonomy of an entrepreneur. Perhaps you have less restrictive working hours or can work from home? You get given projects rather than tasks. You're given autonomy and leadership opportunities. You get options to forge your own breakaway department and are treated and respected like a leader. In *Life Leverage* I shared the story of an employee who 100 per cent outsourced his job, while on the job, and did no work at work. He got fired for that, but now many progressive and innovative companies are embracing the intrapreneur as a way to grow and scale through this disruptive age of business. You have to compete for jobs and attract great talent, and giving intrapreneur opportunities might get you the best people. Many of my team who are technically employees also have ecommerce businesses and invest in property too. If someone comes to me and wants to head up a project or department, or wants more freedom to make a difference, I will rarely get in their way. We can become more like a partnership in that they can use me to pay their bills and I can help them develop their latent entrepreneurial desires. They also get to test if it's really what they want without risking starting from ground zero. Some that you give this freedom to may leave and start up their own business. While at first this was hard to take, knowing we had opened the door for them,

I now see what a great gift we were able to share to have so many successful entrepreneurs who could track back and part credit us in kick-starting their venture.

How to leverage being an intrapreneur

Here are ways to leverage being an intrapreneur to make and give more money. Some are similar to being an employee, and some more akin to being an entrepreneur:

- Find out the values of your manager, boss and employer.
- Ask what the highest KRAs (key result areas) you can perform are that give the greatest benefit to the company vision.
- Lead the project, venture or company as if it were your own.
- Take new opportunities or ventures to your employer and put a proposal to them, with your revenue share.
- Bring cost saving ideas to the company and ask for remuneration.
- Book in monthly reviews with your manager where you can show what you've done for the company and receive feedback to grow.
- Ask for clear goals, targets and timeframes to meet your KRAs and your revenue share.
- Over deliver.
- Learn all the areas of entrepreneurship that make you indispensible such as management, leadership, recruitment and marketing.
- Manage your time with hyper-efficiency to make the biggest impact.
- Work out of hours to earn time off in hours.
- Always care for and serve the customers well.

Never be fearful of sharing ideas, putting proposals together and looking at ways of growing your company. If you fear doing this, maybe you need another employer/partner.

Whichever one of the three methods of engagement you choose for your method of making and giving more money, you can make it serve you. Take time to consider which is the right path for you and your life partner, as often it is good to have balance in the family dynamic, and commit down that road for the long-term. There are many multi-millionaires or successfully balanced people in each of the three areas, but the billionaires are all in the entrepreneur category.

41

Monetizing your passion

Can you merge your passion and profession, vocation and vacation? Can you do what you love, and love what you do? Can you take a hobby and turn it into a fortune? The answer is yes, but not always, and only if you follow models and systems to get there. One thing I am convinced does not work is doing something you dislike, or worse, hate, just to make a living. The more you try to live a dual life of wishing you were at home when you're at work, and dreading going back to work when you're at home, the more disconnected and dissatisfied you will be. Completely separating home life from work life could make you feel bi-polar, enjoying neither and never experiencing the gift of the present moment. According to care2.com, number one on the list of '10 things unhappy people have in common' is that they 'hate their jobs'.[1] It is simply not worth doing something you dislike for decades. I'd encourage you to make a plan to change, based on the 'How to merge your passion and profession' questions below. Most people work to live, but most of the people who make a difference, change the world or live a fulfilling life, live to work, or work and live simultaneously.

Home, family and work life

Too much 'work' and you have unrest at home. Too much home time and you can't make enough money, progress your career or make a dent in the universe. Either way, sacrifice causes inner conflict and resentment on at least one side, and sometimes affects both. But why do they have to be so separate and ring-fenced?

'Balance' is so rarely at the centre. Like the pendulum that swings from one extreme to the other, balance rarely sits perfectly with everything 'just right' and centred. So, to think we can be in a constant state of balancing work and life is, at best, very hard and, at worst, futile. Live work, family and 'life' simultaneously where possible so you don't have to 'balance' and make sacrifices.

I'm not saying be on the emails while you're holding the baby (tried that and you drop the phone or the baby!) But you could be on holiday with the family and have business meetings in the morning while your kids are at Kidzania. You could book a public speaking gig in another country and take your family on a mini-holiday. If your specialized subject interests your family, bring them and they can learn from you. Put your kids in a good private school and drum up some business or raise some cash from the other parents. Take your family away when you book courses and conferences, instead of having to be away from them. Go out for dinner with business owners and wealthy individuals you can learn from. Make some of your nights out a network-building vocation/vacation. Play golf with millionaires. Join the best clubs and gyms for your hobbies and fitness so you can meet great people. View property while you're travelling somewhere new. Find out if there are seminars in the countries you visit. Meet your family at lunchtime. Live in more than one country; summer months in the UK, winter months 'living' in warmer climates for the duration of the school holidays.

Sit down with your family and the important people in your life, and plan evergreen time with *them* – put it in the diary (holidays, date nights, family time, etc.). If something is in the diary and can't be moved, everything else fills time and space around it. If it isn't then it gets superseded, and no space is left for important (but not urgent) things. The further in advance these are booked in, the more the world will move all tasks, gigs and trips around these for you. You will be able to do both with the least amount of sacrifice. I hated holidays, and Gemma hated that I hated holidays. I'd go begrudgingly every five years, feeling like it was a waste of time and that I wasn't progressing. I would end up working all the time (out of choice) while she was horizontal on the beach all day (out of choice). I'd have constant ants in my pants and it drove her mad. Now we merge all work-related events like my speaker courses, book writing bootcamps and high-level masterminds in Monaco, Cayman, Florida, Tenerife and

Dubai with family holidays, so, where possible, work and life become one passion, vocation and vacation. Gemma gets to relax and have multiple holidays, we take the kids, they are involved in my 'work' life and I am heavily involved in their growing up.

It can be done. It doesn't have to be ten weeks of hard graft and then one weekend with your family. Your family are not worth sacrificing for some extra cash. You just have to make the plan, and follow the six questions coming up.

Because everyone in your family has different values, it's not always easy to keep everyone in your family happy. I believe you absolutely must learn the values of your family members. Ask your partner and your kids: 'What's the most important thing to you in your life?' a few times over, without projecting that it should involve you. Listen, and you will have a blueprint of how to love them, serve them, live with them and also how to influence them when you particularly want something that's important to you. You will have access to knowledge most people don't have of those they love. You can build a life for your family that meets all your needs and values. This is what happened when we merged 'work' trips with holidays; all of our family got their values met. I have had hundreds of people share with me that this single action has made the biggest difference in their entire life across all areas.

In addition to your family, look to learn the values of your business partner, best friends, boss, MD or main team members – anyone important who assists you closely in your vision and is a big part of your life. A sustainable relationship is where both parties are having their individual values honoured. Get your family and key partners involved in your business planning, goal setting and vision. Have a family vision meeting every year where each family member contributes to the overall family values and vision. Set goals with your kids from a young age so they are able to achieve a worthy aim, feel good, and you get to teach them skills that will stand them in good stead for life. Again, you can do this on a work–play holiday.

The less you separate work and life, and the more ways you find to compartmentalize time, merging passion with profession and vocation with vacation, the longer you will stay in the business and the bigger a legacy you will leave. You'll have a great relationship with your kids and might get laid every now and again too?

How to merge your passion and profession

Ask yourself these six questions now, as you start, and at least once a year, to check in as you evolve. Ask and answer them in conjunction with each other:

1 DO I LOVE IT NOW?

If you have a keen interest and are inspired by your fledgling or existing business, whether passion or profession or both, you will do the initial graft required to get it off the ground. You will endure the challenges and time lag that are part and parcel of starting out or scaling up. This is a great place to start, and will ensure you have passion and not just a desire to make money. While you might get started, you won't necessarily stay the course. You really can make money from virtually anything as long as you follow the 'Formula for Wealth' and solve meaningful problems.

2 WILL I LIKELY LOVE IT IN TEN YEARS?

I loved art. I loved property. I loved being my own boss as landlord of a pub. But I have a personality type that could love mostly anything when it is new and exciting, but often blindly naïve when it comes to the reality of scaling and sustaining it. My passion for art diminished over time as I struggled to monetize it. The pressures of overheads and the business side of art that I didn't embrace tested the love for my passion/profession. My passion for being a landlord never actually existed beyond the initial excitement of being my own boss and it was in a dying industry. My passion for property wasn't in viewings, negotiations, tenant management or dealing with brokers and solicitors. Hindsight is a wonderful thing, but the experience gained from these niches I started-then-stopped would be to consider if this current niche is an area I could see myself in ten years from now. Writing, teaching with the simultaneous benefit of learning about business, self-development and money has become that lifelong passion. It took me a few years and niches to learn this. And that's OK. You earn or you learn, and everything can be seen as a test. There's no harm in using one niche as a bridge or stepping-stone to a greater passion-profession merge in the future, much like you'd move up a career ladder. This long-time horizon thought process should negate all susceptibility to get rich quick, overwhelm, confusion and procrastination.

3 WILL I STILL LOVE IT WHEN IT GETS HARD?

It is easy when it is easy. But nothing ever meaningful and enduring came without challenge to force you to grow and gain wisdom. If you can say you will enjoy the challenges that your niche brings, or at least you'll be prepared to roll up your sleeves, get stuck in and influence others to support you, you have an ideal niche or model suited to your vision and values.

4 DO I HAVE SKILLS AND EXPERIENCE IN IT (OR A DESIRE TO LEARN)?

If you do something you love because you love it, but you have no skills or experience in it, you have a hobby not a business. As well as interest, skills and experience will be required. Of course we all start somewhere, and experience can be gained over time. Best to look at what you're good at *as well as* what you enjoy. It is common that you are good at what you like doing, but not a given.

5 IS THERE A REAL MARKET FOR IT?

A great idea without a market is only an idea. Value and fair exchange without scale limits your business, which diminishes its sustainability. Just because you like it and find it useful, doesn't mean the rest of the world does. Watch a few episodes of *Dragons' Den* to see how people can be blinkered around their idea that solves a universal problem for all six of their friends. There are quick and easy searches that can be done on Google: word tracker, the Google search keyword tool, observing the number of searches when you search, checking groups and responses on social media, running some test pay per click ads to check for volume and responsiveness, asking on Reddit, and searching for existing books on Amazon and Audible. Within a day you could have completed this down and dirty research to start testing.

6 CAN I MAKE CONSISTENT PROFITS FROM IT?

Some markets are cyclical, opportunist or time sensitive. Pop-up shops pop up in shopping centres around Christmas, with short leases, and then disappear in the New Year. Some products are very seasonal. Some markets get disrupted frequently. Some markets are mature and hard to infiltrate. If you can choose a niche that is consistently scalable, has longevity and utility, you can leverage compounding more effectively. It takes a lot of energy to start again, again and again.

The more of these you can say a decisive, proven 'Yes' to, the better the business model or niche you have, and the more vast and lasting wealth you will create and generate. If you have passion (1, 2 and 3) but no experience or market, you have a hobby. If you have experience and a market (4, 5 and 6) but no passion, you have a job you hate. If you have all six, you have the potential to live your passion, profession, vocation and mission, and maybe make mountains of money. Excellent!

42

A licence to print money

The following is a simple four-step (4S) model that is as much a licence to print money as any model I've seen. It is a scalable and repeatable system, not an opportunistic smash and grab:

1 SURVEY

Crowdsource the ideas, systems and solutions from your target market. Survey your would-be demographic and existing customer base and ask them specifically what they want and don't want. Use the three-step question formula of: 1 Start; 2 Stop; and 3 Keep:

1 What would you like us to *start* doing that we are not doing?
2 What would like us to *stop* doing that we are doing (wrong)?
3 What would you like us to *keep* doing that we are doing (well)?

Then dig for their biggest pains. What do they want solving? How do they want serving? What would make their lives faster, easier, better, longer, more entertaining and happier? What saves them time, makes them money and gives them freedom? It is such a risk and potentially very expensive to jump into a new business, model or niche without some testing first. In 1983, Atari infamously buried a rumoured 700,000 cartridges of the game ET after a failed launch, in a landfill site in Mexico. Don't be Atari and ET. The best way to negate this risk is to know what the customer wants in advance of making nearly one million units of them.

The fastest and cheapest testing is to survey people who will be and already are your customers. You are formulating a blueprint that you know in advance will have hungry buyers ready and waiting to consume. The magic in crowdsourcing is that it can become part of the marketing process. If you had been involved at the development stage in a product or service then you have awareness of it before it is launched. It will nag away at you like when you hear of a release date for the new album of your favourite band. If the producer embraces your desires and launches something you want, you have bought into and been a part of creating it. You part own it in your mind. It is no effort or risk at all to buy what you know you already want. You will tell others to buy it too.

The title and subtitle of this book was crowdsourced through our online communities. I get an idea, likely inspired by the community. I ask, test, tweak, take on feedback, merge, ask again. Then we have a title and subtitle that many people are aware of and have bought into. I don't even have to like it myself. We just have to get it past the publishers then! You can even test preferred learning formats such as physical version, Kindle, audio or ebook.

2 SOLVE

Commit to solving the answers to your questions and the problems of your customers. The solutions can be products, services, systems, processes, apps, ideas, information, IP, licences, franchises, consultancies, cures and more. Crowdsource the formats of the solution such as online, video, manual, book, DVD, personal service, live stream, webinar, apps, cloud, braille, transcription, translated, face-to-face and so on. The customer not only gets the products and services they desire but in their favoured format too.

3 SERVE

Create, test, iterate and scale your product or service. Go to market with an MVP (minimum viable product) and test to a smaller segment of your customer base. Give discounts for early adopters to test your product and give you feedback for version 2.0. Get perfect later; start now but de-risk. Ask your beta testers to be honest with feedback and ask them what you would need to do for them to recommend it to their friends. Your version 3.0 or 7.0 may be an iterated evolution through each version, improving steadily, or a full-scale revolution due to market feedback or change. Continue to engage with your customers beyond the launch of version 1.0, and care far beyond them giving you the money.

Google's initial search engine sold appliances to businesses and its own search technology to other search engines, and it was a disaster. Google radically changed course, the company launched its AdWords programme, which allowed businesses to advertise to people searching for things on Google.com. Almost overnight, Google took the leap from 'popular search tool' to 'advertising juggernaut'. In 2008, Google reported to the SEC that it had generated $21 billion in advertising-driven revenue alone.

4 Scale

Once you have a robust product with unbiased feedback and test launch data, it's time to scale. Not before, but not never. Each time you launch a new product or version, you carry all the goodwill from previous good launches. You can now safely and easily create better solutions, new products and spin-offs and more durable systems and processes to deal with a higher volume.

With this system and licence to print money you can grow through challenges, move closer to your vision, create ever-growing wealth while mitigating the risk of burying all your stock that you don't sell in a landfill! This model applies to every product, service or idea I've ever researched. There is the very rare visionary who seems to believe and have proven that they know what their customers want. Henry Ford famously said, 'If I had asked people what they wanted, they would have said faster horses,' but these people are rare and even the best companies have failures like Atari did.

43

Pricing and value

Pricing and value can be a chicken-and-egg quandary for many. If you have low self-worth, your prices will likely be too low. If your prices are too high, sales will drop, as could your self-worth. If you increase value you could reduce margin. If you increase price, you could reduce perceived value and you could lose the few customers you have. What to do?

Start with yourself

Work on yourself and you'll work on your money. Forgive yourself for your guilt and shame of the past that's still unresolved. Forgive others who've wronged you or you hold angst towards and stop blaming them; they did the best they could with what they knew.

Stop fearing the future that hasn't happened yet. Remove self-imposed limitations and illusions or those imposed through religion, society, family, media and geography. Continue to invest time and budget in your network and your net-worth knowledge.

Price elasticity and testing

There is a simple model for pricing in relation to value and fair exchange. Price elasticity is a measure of the effect of a price change or a change in the quantity supplied on the demand for a product or service. So there is a sweet spot in pricing between volume and margin, where you get an optimum price without reducing scale. For every product and service, that is an unknown and ever-moving variable. There is a minimum, maximum and mean in your pricing, and you find these ranges through price split testing.

Be sure to look at all price test variables in your business model. Test the prices of the products at the front-end to find the sweet spot between margin and volume. Then increase or reduce as you add further offerings onto the back-end to increase LCV revenue and profit. Some prices will be more fixed, others more variable and some will seem to have little or no price ceiling.

Increase your prices

Your prices must be sustainable by covering all overheads and leaving a fair margin of profit. That margin could be 40 per cent on low volume, 20 per cent on medium volume and 5 per cent on huge volume and scale. You must keep a close eye on all your KPIs to know your gross and net profit margins, because you could be scaling a problem and compounding a loss. You need profit to serve your self-interest of building a capitalist profit-making entity otherwise you're a charity or hobby. You need profit to be able to offer and deliver a great service that people value. The market and your customers will soon tell you when you get greedy and you will be drawn back into balance through feedback, reputational damage and associated costs. You will be forced to increase service and value or give money back. Price testing will help you balance self-interest with humanitarian interest. Even without this testing you could increase your prices now, with no extra value proposition, and with little risk to your business. I strongly recommend you raise your prices now between 5 per cent and 20 per cent. Five per cent will just about cover inflation, 10 per cent will make a little bit and 20 per cent will enable you to reinvest part of the increased profit in a better service, and part to make a fairer margin for yourself and your shareholders. The earlier and smaller the business, and the more disruptive the market, the easier this is to do.

10 PER CENT EASY, 20 PER CENT ADVISABLE

A 10 per cent rise or decline in any price is palatable to most people. If you had a stock portfolio and it went up 10 per cent you wouldn't go manic and jump with joy. You wouldn't go into a deep depression if it dropped 10 per cent either. You'd mostly accept without any strong emotion a 10 per cent swing in prices, profits and losses. So put your prices up 10 per cent *now*, because your customers will feel the same way towards a 10 per cent move in price.

INCREASE VALUE PROPOSITION

Perhaps a fear of losing your customers, or complaints and perceptions of others could be stopping you increasing your prices? This is quite a common concern, otherwise everyone would simply increase their prices, right? (Well done Rob for stating the obvious!) Rolex have no problem raising their prices. They are just about to increase prices by a reported 11 per cent. In addition to that they have brought out some higher-level models like the Sky Dweller, and moved the positioning of one of their flagship watches, the Daytona, much higher. When I bought my first Rolex Daytona in 2008, I paid just over £5000 for a three-year-old all-steel model. The new price of the equivalent new model Daytona is around £10,200, just eight years later.

If you still have perceived fear of raising your prices then do some elasticity testing. Or creep up the prices using a price escalation model. Bump them up gently and incrementally as you build confidence and proof. If you are still fighting with yourself to raise your prices, which I hope you have overcome, then increase the value proposition. Give more to get more. Analyse your model, products and services and look how you can:

- Give a better service. It is said that you don't get anything for nothing, so to force your prices up, give more first. Be careful not to give so much that you reduce or reverse your margin and fair exchange. Give 10 per cent more value with 2–5 per cent more costs and you can easily sustain a 10 per cent increase or more in prices with little to no attrition.

- Make delivery faster, easier and/or better. People pay good money to relieve pain. The bigger, faster and easier the solution or cure, the more they will pay. Improve speed, reduce friction and improve efficiency, and your prices will reflect this with an upward trajectory.
- Increase perceived value by giving highly perceived benefits that have little to no extra overhead cost to you. There are likely many things you can add to your product or service that have little to no cost to you, but increase perceived value to your customer. You might recall when hotels started putting little chocolates on your pillow, car manufacturers gave you free mats with car purchases and waitresses signed their name and wrote 'thank you' on the receipt near the part where you write in your tip. You could offer different formats of your products that are hosted online and have virtually no overheads. You could do limited editions of products. Audemars Piguet make limited editions of their Royal Oak Offshore watches, and the price can be 50 per cent more for a small variation on the same watch. You could create higher priced, more bespoke versions to individualize your offerings like Overfinch do with Range Rovers and Vertu do with phones. Brainstorm all the ways you could increase the perceived benefit to your clients, and then go through each one and look at how you can do that using creativity rather than cost.
- Repackage or 'sex up' what you already have. When you get an Apple product, the packaging is almost as worthy of pride of place as the product itself. It's like you're opening a beautifully wrapped Christmas present that you hope is the one you always wished for. The packaging of any product or service gives an impression that increases the perception and value to the customer. Many blind tests have proven this with wine and food. So discover ways you can repackage what you have to give it a more elevated status, and then elevate your prices to match. Look to make your products and services unique and individual where possible, as people hold value to things that are different.

- Move the 'free line'. The easier, faster and higher the volume of information we can all access for free, the more *you* have to give for free, to receive. You never get something for nothing. The more you give first, the more you get later. Moving the free line means giving more value up front than you did previously, to earn the right and build the trust for your first purchase. Is there anything you can give as a product or as information, up front and for free, that will build trust, prior usage and proof into your offer? This can build goodwill that will extend lifetime client value (LCV). A well used but simple version is the free fudge you get in Cambridge, opposite Kings College, that draws you into the shop. There is a fruit seller in my hometown that gives out free big red juicy strawberries and you end up buying a punnet you never came out for. In the world of Internet and information marketing, giving valuable PDF eBooks and reports, audios and YouTube videos all build trust and goodwill for less friction of future purchases. You want your new client to think, 'If the free stuff is this good, the paid stuff must be great'. My podcast 'The Disruptive Entrepreneur', free, with no ads or pitches, has attracted hundreds of thousands of pounds of business my way almost by accident, but as a consequence of the upfront value. Come up with ways you can do your own versions of these in your enterprise.

Imagine if you implemented all five of these examples of ways to increase perceived value. Just a 4 per cent incremental improvement in each area and you can increase your prices by 20 per cent. So what's stopping you?

Low prices repel higher fees

Most people look at the customers, business and money they may lose if they increase their prices, but fail to see the opposite truth. Your pricing is the main gateway to attract the type of customer and business that you want. They say, 'If you pay peanuts you get monkeys' and so it can be with your pricing.

Your fees attract the type of clients who pay what you price up at, and repel all others. If your fees are low you are repelling higher paying clients. It is delusional to have low prices and wish for higher paying customers. You have to send them the right message. If your fees are high, the high price repels those who can't afford or justify the higher prices. This is a great pre-qualifier and time saver for you. You repel the window shoppers, timewasters and people who want a tenner for a fiver. You attract those who can easily afford what you have. They are easier to please, value your service more, and are more discerning. They have a great network that could become your referred clients. Increase your fees, create higher-level brands, attract higher-paying clients and more wealth, riches and margins will come your way. So what's stopping you?

Commodity pricing and market 'ceilings'

Many people resist increasing prices, citing that their market has a price ceiling. They feel *their* niche has a clear price ceiling that can't be exceeded, that *their* market is mature, saturated or commoditized, where prices are standardized. People make their outside world an internal reality, but who says an industry can't be disrupted? You have three clear choices if you feel your niche is commoditized, and that is to:

DISRUPT YOUR NICHE AND FORCE PRICES AND SERVICE UPWARDS

Do you remember the days when your phone was for making calls? Then text messaging came along and crept the innovation forward. Then the iPhone came along, disrupted the niche, gave more value and changed the perception of how to use a phone. Music, apps and all things imaginable. The floodgates opened up for ever-increasing prices. It is said that if you give £500 to a rich person they could turn it into a million one day, and if you give £500 to a poor person they will turn it into an iPhone. Apple completely changed the game. They broke the pattern and removed the perceived price ceiling.

Do you also remember the day when you bought a cheap, practical vacuum cleaner that looked a bit like a Dalek but did its job? Then Dyson came along. I recall very clearly going to see a good friend of mine who is a successful senior manager in the banking world. He invited me to his new house and I was excited to see both him and his new home. As he opened the door to invite us in, the first thing he did was to direct me into his store cupboard and show me his new digital bagless Dyson vacuum cleaner, like it was his newborn son. I don't ever recall him giving such pride of place to his 1980s Hoover.

You can't get away with gimmicks or charging too much. Feedback from customers and the wider market will redress this balance. Do not be concerned if you perceive others not giving fair exchange, they will have their challenges and you should focus your energy in serving your customers, followers and fans. In the instances of Apple and Dyson, increased perceived and actual value was created. Life was made easier, faster and better, and time was preserved. Ergonomics and elegance were introduced into otherwise standard-looking products. Care was taken to give people exactly what they wanted, and to be able to leverage the product as an accessory to increase self-importance. The next risk to Apple's dominance will be if they can continue to innovate at the rate that Steve Jobs did, and how much they rely on past goodwill for future sales. If their new products are too expensive or aren't progressive enough, things may change for the most capitalized company in the world.

CREATE A BREAKAWAY, HIGHER PRICED BRAND

To de-risk pricing mistakes, create extra income streams and test price elasticity, preserve your existing models or prices by creating new ones. Attract higher quality, paying customers.

GET INTO A NEW NICHE

You have been given many options to increasing your fees. If you are strongly resisting increasing your prices after all these potential solutions, then you have the freedom of choice to move into a new niche. If you want more money and you want to make more of a difference, perhaps you need to consider changing your market. There are likely markets that are harder, more competitive and more mature than others, so pick wisely. But know that you do have a choice and that you are in control.

You rate vs the market rate

There is a market rate, which can be more commoditized or standardized, like air travel and insurance, and there is a 'You rate'. Having already addressed that even commoditized markets can be disrupted and price ceilings broken through, as Apple and Dyson did, 'You rate' has no ceiling at all. Nowhere on earth is there a maximum hourly rate, maximum net-worth ceiling or maximum value any one person can charge or be worth. There is literally no ceiling other than your self-imposed limitations of belief, self-worth and value. Ensure you add a maximum fair exchange 'You rate' into your market rate to achieve leveraged value on your time, experience and uniqueness. When a highly regarded watchmaker like Gerald Genta designs for a watch brand, it can elevate the status and value of the brand. Genta designed for IWC, Patek Philippe and, famously, the Royal Oak design for Audemars Piguet, which are highly sought after and now very expensive (and addictive, I might add). Arnold Schwarzenegger, Shaquille O'Neill, Leo Messi and Michael Schumacher have all endorsed a model or range of Audemars Piguet. When Stella McCartney designed for H&M and Adidas she elevated their brands, as did Jasper Conran when designing for, and endorsing, Debenhams. You can aim to have the same effect on your business and the brands you are behind.

Work on yourself and increase your 'You rate'. Not only will your prices continue to rise, but you will disrupt and innovate entire markets. You will set new pricing standards and perceptions that never existed before. You can consider joint ventures with others who can increase the value perception of your brand, like Arnold Schwarzenegger with Audemars Piguet and Rory McIlroy with Bose and Rolex.

Your financial ceiling

How would Trump or a tramp feel about having $1 million in the bank? A tramp might feel like they'd won the lottery and Trump might panic that he is hours from going into his overdraft! Your perception of what 'a lot of money' is will become your financial ceiling.

£1000 or £100,000 is not a lot of money. £1 million or £10 million or £100 million is not a lot of money. There are trillions flowing with great velocity around the world hundreds and thousands of times. Twenty per cent of people are controlling the velocity of 80 per cent of it. Remove your personal ceilings by turning scarcity thinking into an abundant mindset. There is more than enough. You are more than enough. There is no niche or commoditized marketplace or economic cycle or low-paying customer that can define *your* value or *your* economy. Each time you hear yourself say, 'That's a lot of money,' check in and correct yourself. The future you (or a billionaire) will think it is chump change. Just as you would increase weights at the gym, increase your personally limited financial ceiling continually and progressively.

Self-fulfilling pricing

As you operate under fair exchange, you increase your self-worth because you feel adequately remunerated for your time and work. This in turn helps you increase your prices and value. Your gratitude will be reflected in your service, and the gratitude of the customer will be reflected in more purchases and referrals. You are able to make a fair profit, which means you can increase the scale of your service and reinvest into quality and value. Furthermore as you increase your prices and value, you attract a better quality of customer who values what you offer, and is willing to pay more. As better quality people pay more and more, you can give and serve more, creating a virtuous cycle of growth and contribution, increasing the velocity of money and pushing your prices and value up again and again and again.

> Find something you have a burning passion for, find a way to improve people's lives with it, then write huge invoices with a warm smile on your face.
>
> *Rob Moore*

44

Models for making money (now and in the future)

Where most people feel it is hard to make money, I feel there are so many genuine opportunities out there that often the more challenging decisions are what to say 'No' to. This chapter is not about the latest money making fad that will be a distant memory not long after this book is published. A genuine model or business opportunity should have longevity to sustain and gain momentum and compounding, and follow the *Money* philosophy.

Adding *you* as the variable to the model

There are models that make money that you wouldn't love to do. There are models that you'd love to do that don't make any money. And then there are models that you'd love to do that make money. Start from this position, and not just because there seems to be money in it, or just because you love it. Brian Tracy, a Canadian-born American motivational speaker and self-development author of over 70 books, tells me that one minute spent planning saves five minutes or more doing (or wasting). If you love it but there's no money in it, you will be forced to stop, and start again. If it is just about the money, you will not endure the challenges because the enjoyment will disappear fast, and you'll start again, again. A business model must serve you, and not the other way around. Ask yourself:

1 WHAT COULD I BE GREAT AT OR EVEN THE BEST AT?

Being the best pays a disproportionately high amount of money. If you make money, you can just as easily lose it, but once you have learned something of value, you can't unlearn it. Applied knowledge is power. Those who know the most or are the best in any niche usually get remunerated disproportionately.

The average boxer's salary is $75,760. The tenth-highest earning boxer of all time for a *single fight*, Miguel Cotto, earned $8 million. That's 106 times more for *one fight* than the average yearly salary of the average boxer. One of the highest earning boxers of all time for a single fight, Oscar de la Hoya, earned $56 million for one fight: seven times more than the tenth-highest fight earnings.[1] Everything is not equal. If you question this as 'skill' or 'talent' rather than knowledge (though skill is 'applied knowledge'), then look at lawyers' salaries. Lawyers earned an average annual salary of $131,990 in 2013, yet the tenth-highest earning lawyer, Ana Quincoces, has a net-worth of $8 million. The highest earning lawyer in the world, according to 'The Richest', has a net-worth of $1.7 billion: 212.5× the tenth-highest earning lawyer. It is likely that the highest earning lawyer has more knowledge than the tenth-highest earning lawyer, but nowhere near 10 × as much.[2]

If you invest time and learning to get to the very top of your profession, and don't keep chopping and changing, you are likely to earn a disproportionate, inordinate amount of money, control and freedom. You can leverage this process even further, by choosing a profession that has a disproportionate, inordinate amount of money, control and freedom compared to other professions or vocations.

2 What's a passion that i'd never call work?

What do you love to do? Suspend disbelief about your inability to earn, and search through what you've always loved to do. A common trait in the titans of wealth and the happiest people is that they do what they love, most of the time, and more than others. People will buy and pay for your passion, because it's attractive. People will support your cause and purpose, because living your purpose on purpose supports humanity.

3 What would i do if money were no object?

What would you do if your vocation was your vacation and money was no object? What doesn't feel like work? What do you do where time seems to stand still for you? What brings out the best in you? What do you do that others feel inspired by when you bring it to life? What are you known for? Take time to consider and answer these questions when starting or scaling a new or next model.

4 WHAT WOULD HAPPEN IF I ACCEPTED THE HARDEST CHALLENGES?

There are some niches that not only would you endure the challenges, you might even enjoy them. Imagine a coder or scientist who loves a big problem to solve. They don't give up at the first hurdle; they endure and rise to the challenge. There will always be challenge and this is often the Litmus test that you are in the right vocation. Can you stand the heat? Do you love the heat? Those who can deal with and stand up to the world's biggest problems have the world's biggest bank accounts.

5 IN WHAT AREAS WOULD I ENJOY SERVING AND SOLVING FOR OTHERS?

In what niches could you see yourself loving to serve and help others? You could have something you love to do, but don't enjoy helping others in, and vice versa. Consider these questions, and the authentic model for your next level of business, wealth and money will become clear to you.

An authentic model for business

Imagine if there were no risks to starting again or scaling up. Imagine if you were guaranteed all the help you needed along the way to do what you love and love what you do. Imagine if you could create your ideal work–life balance. Well you can, now. Here's how:

- Choose a vocation with a path of least resistance and limitless *upside* that *you* control. This is the *real* definition of security. If your current career or vocation is limiting you, then you're in the wrong place. In the 'If you could start again with no risk' scenario, you'd probably choose a vocation where the earning potential was limitless, the roles/positions/career path were limitless, the number of customers was limitless, your ability to make money and make a difference was limitless, your reach was limitless, freedom and creativity and enterprise were limitless, and your ability to grow was limitless. What's stopping you from making this choice now?

Choose a vocation that's also a vacation and profession that's also a passion. You have nothing to run away from, take time off from or 'holiday' from if you do what you love and love what you do. Why does it have to be that you spend most of your waking life doing something you hate in order to buy a bit of time and earn a bit of money to do what you love with the remnants of what's left? It doesn't have to be that way. You can choose to merge your passion and profession, or find the roles within your profession that you're best at and you love (most of the time), and outsource the rest.

- Study what the most successful people whom you admire or idolize do, and copy (the best parts of) it. Your idols are likely to have created a life you want, and therefore have learned, as perceived by you, to merge passion and profession. They probably make a ridiculous amount of money too. If they can do it, you can do it too. Most of them are self-created, and most of them idolized someone before you idolized them. One of the easiest, safest and quickest ways to create your ideal life is to study them, leverage their journey to fast-track yours and model what they've done to be where they are. This concept is so simple you'd think everybody would do it. The problem is that people think it's too hard, that they can't do it, that their idols had it easy, or they are just envious and resentful of successful people. But the reality is that most of us start quite equal, and the successful find systems and strategies that get them to where they want to be.

The wealth of the richest 1 per cent in the world amounts to $110 trillion, or 65 times as much as the poorest half of the world. So which *Money* 'strategy' are you going to learn? The 1 per cent way or the 99 per cent way? If one person can become self-created, you can too. Model their best strategies and own the traits of the greats. Know what to keep going at, and what to give up on. In the general whoop-whoop-rah-rah world of personal development, giving up is seen as a weakness. But giving up is only a weakness if you give up on something of high-value, high return or importance. Giving up is actually the smartest, strongest and most courageous thing to do if what you are doing is of low-value or low return on time or money. Don't keep going at something for months or years, like I did with my architecture degree, just because 'giving up' is seen as a weakness. I could have saved myself two years and 11 months if I'd trusted my intuition and not worried about what people I hardly knew thought of me. Millions could be made if that time were given back to me. If you pick your models wisely then you will know what you need to keep going at and what you need to drop to move forward. Steve Jobs famously did this when he went back to Apple, getting the company to drop most of their A.N. Other products to liberate time to focus on the few that could make the biggest difference. Know what to do, and do what you know. Don't get sucked in by someone else's plans for you or unsolicited advice about your work and life. Don't follow the walking dead crowd. Live life your way, on your terms, on purpose with the goal of making more, growing more and giving more.

Models that have been proven over decades or centuries

When you study the titans of wealth, you notice that those who've created vast wealth have many similarities in their business models, despite being in different niches. The main similarity is the 'network concept'. The network concept is a new or existing, but leveragable, network that provides vast reach, quickly. It could be new and disruptive, or it can be in existence, but you leverage or build upon the existing network. Here are the some of the most significant examples in the last two centuries:

- Rail (mail, passengers)
- Steel (to create rail networks)
- Electricity
- Oil
- Cars (freight)
- Air travel (mail, passengers)
- Telecommunications (radio, TV, phone)
- Fibre optics (silicon)
- Tarmac (roads)
- Computing (semi-conductors, micro-chips)
- Internet (computing, peer-to-peer, ecommerce, search engines, social media, apps, big data, crypto currency, VR, AI).

We can learn so much about the future of our business by looking at the past. While it isn't likely there will be another steel or gold rush, and much of the oil has been extracted, there will be the new version of the old concept: the new network concept phenomenon. There will be new disruptive and sustainable ways to provide basic human needs such as green and renewable energies, further travel to distant planets, and even information exchange through QE (Quantum Entanglement). More on these in a moment.

Asset-backed models

Asset-backed business models have a capital as well as an income element. If businesses grow for long enough, they will likely build a capital value by having premises, stock, capital items on the balance sheet and shareholder or saleable value. But for many small businesses this never comes, takes decades or is just a dream. There are business models that you can leverage that have capital as well as income value and leverage. Capital value often creates a more residual income stream and can reduce overheads, which, in turn, increases income. For example, if you had premises with no mortgage on, your overheads would be much lower and therefore your margin would be higher. Here are the types of asset-backed models you can leverage, or at least work towards, or even hybridize and add in to your own business:

A general business with capital elements

There are multiple ways to add capital elements to your business that will make it more robust, reduce overheads, and increase capital buffers and saleable value. You could invest in premises rather than renting them, and have a capital repayment element to the loan on the building. You could add assets to the balance sheet that don't heavily depreciate. You could leave some retained profits in the business to keep a capital buffer. You could sell shares in the business in exchange for capital, contacts and advisors on the board. You could create capital-based additional products and services like IP and franchise models.

Property

According to Forbes, of the ten fastest growing small businesses, five are in the property, building, real estate, contractor industry.[3] This is both surprising and not suprising. It is not surprising in that property has been a consistently growing asset for centuries. Since records for taxation purposes began in 1088, property has risen around 10 per cent per year ever since, with some temporary fluctuations of higher and slower growth. Yet it is the maturity of property which makes it suprising that many of the fastest growing sectors are property related. There is a significant shortage of housing in many cities due to influxes in immigration, increases in population and a lack of development from local councils and governments. This has spurred growth in construction and development, and has been a factor in increasing prices, especially in major cities like London.

This is not a property or real estate book. If that is your desired area of interest, my business partner, Mark Homer, and I have written three books on this subject, should you choose to research it. Property was our foundation to building wealth. We were initially far more interested in property investing, then developing, than in general business. You discover as you grow that property becomes a business, and is a great counterfoil to have and leverage with income-generating non-asset-backed businesses such as education, lettings and estate agency. It is great to have a property business as one or more of your multiple income streams, because it covers the capital element of a business and produces a significant residual income stream if managed and leveraged well. Property is much less prone to liquidation, has greater utility than many business models and is the single and, often, only asset that a bank will use as security to lend money to you and your business.

IP (ideas, patents, licences, franchise, information, music)

Intellectual property has a capital value. It can be an asset that pays residual income like an album for a band, a licence that has an income stream attached, a patent that is sold and/or has a royalty income stream, or information that can be sold in many formats. Rights or ownership of the capital element of IP can be fully sold, leased, rented or held as an asset for the income stream.

A franchise can be replicated and scaled so that one initial piece of capital such as the information, system and manual can then be leveraged and scaled nationally or globally. McDonald's operates 36,525 franchised restaurants across the globe, employing 420,000 people. These franchises can be sold for a significant capital sum, the rights and ownership of the IP retained, and then a share of the profits taken as income.

A music album, song, book, game, online course or other form of IP can be created once and then sold hundreds, thousands or millions of times for years or decades. These forms of IP can then be repurposed into other formats such as online, apps, live events, retreats, limited editions and more, and the income streams increased. Brand value can then be compounded as IP can be leveraged in the form of merchandise, sponsorships and endorsements. Look at ways you can create IP around your business models to add these capital and income elements to your existing niche.

Investments (stocks, bonds, paper, etc.)

There will be more detail about investing in Chapter 46. I have a property business that has an investment element to it where we purchase and hold properties for long-term income and capital growth. We also own our own buildings and training facilities. Warren Buffett's business is investing for himself and external investors through Berkshire Hathaway. IFAs advise on investments and are paid fees and commissions to do so. There are regulated and unregulated investments sold in many areas such as the stock market, physical metals, art, renewable and green energy and more. This isn't a book about how to do that. A great book on this subject is *Uncommon Sense* by Mark Homer.[4] Having a business that invests on behalf of you and others isn't for everyone, but Warren Buffett became the richest man in the world doing it. There may be opportunities for you too, if it is a good fit.

Money lending

A natural progression from making lots of money is to lend it out. Banks do it. Central banks do it. Money attracts money, and hoarding money does not. Over time money lenders have made significant wealth and riches. In some fraternities money lenders are looked upon with disdain, and in some religions lending money for interest is forbidden. If you can see through these and view lending money as a way to increase GDP, and offer a valuable service to fill demand, then you could add this element to your business model. Consumers lend to producers. Economies become much larger with money lending. Micro loans are kick-starting economies in the Third World. There are of course risks, but there are with any and all models. When you have built more wealth and have more income streams, it is likely you will, at some point, consider lending money.

Physical (precious metals, art, watches, wine, classic cars)

Physical assets and models have retained capital value. If your business is selling assets, not only do you have a profit margin, you have a capital asset. You may have appreciating value stored in your stock, where other business models have reducing capital value in stock. Many classic Porsches have gone up significantly in recent years. Art and watch dealers may buy some art and watches for themselves in times of strong price growth. If you are extremely capital intensive that can raise its own challenges, so it is smart to balance capital and income (discussed in Chapter 46).

Models that matter and make a difference

Models that matter and make a real difference to humanity are likely to scale and sustain. These can be in disruptive technologies like renewable and sustainable energy, technology, pharmaceuticals, exploration and so on, or in time-tested and mature markets like health care, insurance, food, security and shelter. As long as people are people, there are human needs that will always have to be met and that will transcend any changing or disruptive technologies. According to Maslow's hierarchy of needs, there are five levels of human needs. Four of the levels are known as deficiency needs, where motivation will kick in if these are unmet, growing stronger the longer they are unmet. The fifth level includes 'growth' needs. The first four levels must be met to move to the fifth growth level, and each level must be sufficient to move up to and meet the next level. As the species has evolved and lower basic needs are taken for granted in the Third World, the fifth level has become more relevant, important and exaggerated. It is not a given that everyone will meet the higher-level growth needs, known as self-actualization or self-fulfillment. Here are the five levels:

1 Physiological (food, water, warmth, rest)
2 Safety (security, safety)
3 Belongingness and love (intimate relationship, friends)
4 Esteem (prestige and accomplishment)
5 Self-actualization (achieving full potential, creativity)

Any business model that fulfils these will scale. Business models that scale serving basic physiological needs will survive, thrive and sustain, but may be more mature and competitive, and harder to get into. Walmart started providing food, and is now the world's third largest employer with over 2.1 million staff. Only two public sector companies are larger, and one is the United States Department of Defense, which meets the second need of safety. It could be argued that if the second need of security isn't met it will jeopardize the most basic of human needs. Insurance is a huge industry because it serves the need of security and safety. Many water, electricity, gas and oil companies are vast, scaled and have sustained for decades and even centuries. If you are ever short of employment you can always become a midwife, funeral director or tax collector!

As you move up through the hierarchy of needs, you solve different problems. Dating sites, wedding planners and social media communities exist and scale because of our desire for love, belongingness and friendship. These are strong emotions and if you can connect people you can create a meaningful business. The Huffington Post states that online dating is a \$2.2 billion industry.[5] New disruptive sites like Tinder have emerged and scaled fast. If you can leverage multiple models such as the Internet with social media and belongingness, you will increase the speed and scale.

Levels four and five on Maslow's hierarchy of needs are the 'feeling of accomplishment and fulfilling of self'. People will pay significant money to feel significant, important and prestigious, and to be viewed as such by others. Call it ego, call it vanity. For some it is a need. People will pay vast sums to restructure their look, hide their flaws, be accepted by others and have elevated status. The evidence is everywhere from plastic surgery to paying to jump queues to first class travel to £50k watches (cough) to diamonds to huge weddings to handbag dogs. Many of these kinds of business models leverage emotions, and this can make the sales process have much less friction. As long as you offer great value and service, and people want what you've got, then models that leverage and serve esteem and self-actualization can help you know more, make more and give more money.

People are also interested in better health, living longer, being happier, being at peace, having more freedom, saving and preserving time, achieving balance and increasing confidence. Beyond that, they may have addictions that need feeding, which is why the tobacco, coffee, sugar, pharmaceutical and even illegal drugs models are so scaled. (Please note before you write to me that I am not advising setting up an illegal drugs ring, though the model is very cash intensive!)

Entertainment

Over centuries people have paid to be entertained. The court jester, or fool, during the medieval and Renaissance eras, was often a member of the household of a nobleman or a monarch employed to entertain him and his guests. A jester was also a performer who entertained common folk at fairs and markets. We have a strong desire to be entertained as much as we do to be informed and educated. The seventh largest customer base company in the US is Nintendo with the Wii, with 39.4 million customers on that one console alone. The X Box 360 from Microsoft has sold 33.8 million units and the PS3 from Sony has sold 21 million units. Families saw the Wii as a product their kids could enjoy, and extra hardware like the Wii fit has helped with the console's longevity.[6] Video gaming is the sixth-largest growth area. Lego is the 86th most valuable brand in the world according to Forbes 2016, with a $7.1 billion brand value. Disney is at 72 on the Forbes list of 'world's biggest companies' with a market capitalization of $169.3 billion.[7] All for products we have no need or real utility for. Jerry Seinfeld, the famous US entertainer, had a ten-year combined income of over $900 million between 2006 and 2016 and, according to Forbes, in 2016 Kevin Hart made $87.5 million in his latest tax year.[8]

Models that can scale

It's all very well having great business models from one or more of those already covered, but if they can't scale then you reduce your wealth. Some models scale better than others. Models that leverage the network concept scale very quickly, and are always a great place to start. WhatsApp would not have sold for $19 billion in five years by building its vast user base via pigeon communication. 98 per cent of all information is now digital. Every minute 204 million emails are sent (4 billion people use email), 47,000 apps are downloaded, $83,000 in sales are made, 61,141 hours of audio is downloaded, 3,000 photos are uploaded, 20 million photos are viewed, 100,000 new tweets are tweeted (79 per cent of the population use social media), ten new Wikipedia articles are published, 6 million Facebook pages are viewed, 2 million Google searches are made, 30 hours of video are uploaded and 1.3 million videos are viewed.[9]

Any model that sells information is very scalable because you leverage the speed of fibre optics, the scale of the globe and you have very low overheads. 'Information marketing' – the selling of information, is a modern industry worth more than $100 billion worldwide, growing 32.7 per cent from the previous year. There has been significant growth in online media sales in the last two decades. Audible has over 200,000 audio books in 'stock'. iTunes exceeded 25 billion songs sold in 2013. Apple don't release the numbers of podcast downloads, but Lisbyn, just one podcast hosting company had 3 billion downloads in 2012. This is a growth area because, depending on sources, between 16 per cent and 20 per cent of the US use podcasts, whereas at least 80 per cent use email. According to Omny Studio, the hosting company of my podcast, 'The Disruptive Entrepreneur' uses 2.5 terabytes of data per month through the volume of downloads, which is the same as 300 HD movies or 800,000 songs. Who'd have thought my mouth would have taken up so much bandwidth?! No need to message me and answer that, either!

There are many high-volume webinar and online course platforms like GoToMeeting and Udemy that leverage content across the globe. There are virtually zero fixed costs to online or electronic information and courses, and the cost is only in the upfront creation. You can sell your music from a home computer studio. You can even sell your rants and tweets. You can sell through free social media channels that reach billions of people in a fraction of a second. You can set up an online presence or 'shop front' for next to nothing, exchange money on portals like PayPal, and you have a business ready to trade. Your information business is about as low-risk as a business can be. There is no stockholding, inventory or overheads. You can run your business from home without premises from anywhere in the world, anytime with a global customer base.

You can sell the same/similar piece of low-cost information millions of times; there is no 'download stock limit'. You can repackage and repurpose that information and sell it hosted online, in physical book format, on CD, DVD, audiobook, Kindle, iTunes, Audible, iBooks, iTunes university, on a paid membership site platform, in a seminar room, on a mentorship or mastermind programme, or on a retreat.

You create and set up your product once, like this book, and you can earn on it many times over. Once the product is created, it can generate residual, passive, recurring income for years or decades to come. It can go viral and get shared and sold by affiliates and resellers and social media addicts. Information and ideas marketing are quite possibly the most leveraged use of time, giving maximum return with minimum wastage. There is virtually no duplication of time and everything you create is a genuine asset if leveraged effectively.

You have unique talents, skills and expertise. In at least one specific area, you are better than most people on the planet. The pains that people are experiencing in this area you can solve quickly through the above outlets and media. You can serve and solve many people, you just didn't know you could or didn't know your value. Until now, that is.

Partnerships and joint ventures

A partnership, joint venture (JV) or affiliation can grow a model, reach and brand for both parties more than they could alone. There have been many high profile successful JVs like Sony–Ericsson, Virgin–MBNA, Conran–Debenhams, Nike–Jordan and Land Rover–Jaguar. Of course they don't always work out, so make sure your vision and values are aligned but your skillsets and reach are different. Sponsorships and endorsements are a kind of JV, with the celebrity or company investing money to support the partner and piggyback off their reach.

Models that innovate (without undue risk)

Any model that innovates and progresses mankind will be a model worth researching to move into. Innovation can happen too early, so be careful not to be too disruptive or ahead of your time. SixDegrees.

com was the original online social network, based on the game 'Six degrees of Kevin Bacon'. It had high growth from its start in 1997, but disappeared. Could it have been Facebook if the timing was right? Ask Jeeves was a few years too early and even helped Google become so huge. Remember Tivo the TV recording device?

How can you improve what already exists? Steve Jobs cut a deal to use the mouse that was owned by Xerox, lying dormant in a test facility. It is reputed he copied their user interface too. Apple were not the first company to use touch technology in their phones, HTC used it before them, combined with a toggle that Jobs hated. He simply improved the usability. Music does the same where genres inspire new genres and bands disrupt by merging or innovating them. Rage Against The Machine had a rock, metal and rap merge that was part of a scene that changed music. It is said that hip-hop originated or was inspired by Muhammad Ali's rhythmic poetry, used to taunt his opponents. Richard Branson is famous for disrupting niches that he thinks have become lazy or monopolistic where service needs to improve. Because growth serves humanity, anything in business that encourages improvement will be rewarded with wealth and riches.

Cyclical and counter-cyclical models

Some models perform well going with the cycle and some against it. In property, as prices decrease rents tend to increase, and as you go through leaner times letting agents and rentals tend to strengthen. Many non-essential or higher-end retail businesses struggle in leaner times, but you may notice that many 'cash for gold' shops pop up everywhere. Aldi, Lidl and other lower-end supermarkets boomed in the recession of post-2007, as did most discount retailers. It is said the 'sin industry', such as tobacco, alcohol and gambling, often thrives in a recession. Chocolate sales often increase too. There are models that are more 'recession proof' than others. In an article in Insidermonkey. com it is claimed that in addition to the models above, tattoo artists, fast- or candy-food stores and pet pampering salons are recession-proof businesses, as well as healthcare, online security, dating, repairs, funerals and education (being an educator).[10]

Arbitrage

George Soros made $1 billion in a single day shorting the pound when he sold over $10 billion worth of British pounds in September 1992. After the pound fell 10 per cent in value, he made profits exceeding $1 billion and was referred to as 'the man who broke the Bank of England'. The trade idea was simple: sell pounds when they are at a higher price, buy them back when the price drops. In finance this is known as a 'short', in which one stands to make money when the price falls. In 2016 the pound weakened considerably post-Brexit, and this presented some opportunities to arbitrage currency and commodities. Arbitrage is the simultaneous buying and selling of securities, currency or commodities in different markets or in derivative forms in order to take advantage of differing prices for the same asset. I should disclaim that I am not giving financial advice, but hoping to awaken you to counter-cyclical models and for you to have the vision to see it in the future. In 2016 watch prices were very high. As the pound was weak watch prices in the US were even higher compared to the UK. Gold watches in particular had gone up significantly. There are no capital gains taxes on watches, so opportunities have arisen to trade across currencies, being mindful of any import duties. An unusually low pound offered shorting opportunities not seen for many years. This can, of course, be done in reverse when the pound is strong.

I am often asked what assets I hold and what percentage of my overall net-worth each one takes. The answer depends on the climate, cycle, opportunities, interest rates, inflation and so on. More detail on asset allocation will come in the next chapter. If interest rates are very low, it makes no sense to hold much cash. If they are high, it does. If rates are high you may borrow or leverage less. If currency is very weak, you may hold more physical assets. You may look to offload some assets if you feel prices have been strong for a long time, or you might buy in if they have been weak, or you feel the class is somewhere near the bottom of the cycle. You can't predict when this will happen, but you can use history and your experience as a guide, and you can 'pound cost average' the investing by buying in and selling out at different points, and with differing amounts, to reduce risk.

There are *always* opportunities. Most people think there are only opportunities in a boom, but there are often more and bigger ones in a bust, because you are investing against the tide with less competition and money velocity is changing *en masse*. Microsoft was built on and after a recession, and in the global recession of 2007 and 2008 many of our competitors went under. We emerged as one of the biggest entities in our niche by default and virtue of being one of the few left. We would not have experienced this leveraged opportunity if we had started in the boom when some competitors were 100 times bigger than us.

The bigger your asset base, the more you can arbitrage and leverage counter-cyclical opportunities by simply reallocating. When in bust, scale up for the boom before the masses, and when in boom, plan and prepare for the busts before the masses.

Multiple streams of income (leveraged)

The average millionaire has three streams of income. Many companies have even more. Apple have iPhones, iPads, Macs, iTunes, Apple TV, app store, iCloud and more. Millionaires and billionaires may earn their main living though one income stream, but then will diversify profits and models to grow and then protect their wealth. You might re-invest profits into ISAs, property, stocks, buying shares in other businesses, public speaking and information products around your knowledge, and more.

It is a risk to your long-term wealth and riches to only have one source or stream of income. If that gets disrupted, so do you. If you have a career change of heart or mid-life crisis, you have no options. Income streams compound because you can re-invest ever-growing profits into existing streams to grow them, or into new streams. The challenge of building multiple streams of income is how and when. In my book *Multiple Streams of Property Income*,[11] I share a 70–20–10 model to reliably and sustainably build multiple income streams. If you only have one model or product, you only have one stream. If you try to build five models or streams simultaneously, you get overwhelmed and can't focus on any for long enough to build any income streams. It is wise to keep your main thing your main thing, but with a smaller amount of your time on additional streams. The 70–20–10 model suggests you spend 70 per cent of your time and resource on your main income stream, 20 per cent of your time and resource on your secondary income stream, and 10 per cent of your time and resource on your tertiary or future income stream. As you increase your main 70 per cent income stream, systemize it, hand-over the management of it, then you can bring your previous 20 per cent to be your new 70 per cent, your previous 10 per cent to be your new 20 per cent, and a new stream to be your new 10 per cent. You've now gone from one main and two small income streams, to one fully systemized stream giving residual income, one main income stream and two smaller ones. You repeat the process moving up to five, with two systemized, one main and two smaller streams. Only bring in a new income stream when you have systemized an existing one so that you don't get overwhelmed and spread too thin. A band doesn't write five albums at once. One album at a time to progressively build a catalogue, then go on tour, have merchandise deals and so on. If you follow this model, over time you will build a vast and lasting flow of money and riches.

Cross-stream leverage

You can increase the speed and ease of creating multiple streams of income by leveraging your existing streams. If you have a property portfolio and an estate agent manages them all, you get 'cross-stream leverage' by setting up a letting agency. You leverage the existing portfolio, knowledge, experience and contacts you already have, to build the new income stream quicker than if you started again. There is talk of Airbnb going into concierge where they can provide add-on services such as taxis, filling your fridge and so on, 'luxe' where they offer luxury level accommodation, and even into real estate selling houses. If you brainstormed you could think of many extra cross-stream opportunities for Airbnb. They could have Airbnb miles like in the airline industry. There are likely latent cross-stream revenue and income opportunities dormant in your business right now that you could scale up to make more money in less time.

A peer into the future

In Chapter 6, we explored some future monetary disruptions. It won't be long before people are experiencing a parallel world in Virtual Reality. House viewings, holidays, social media, dating and more will be experienced through a headset that will get more and more sophisticated, engaging more of our senses and becoming more and more lifelike. There are already online currencies, cities and worlds that VR could plug into. Who knows, in the future this could become the real-life Matrix? There will be sponsorship and marketing opportunities on this platform, especially if a free or 'freemium' model is used. VR leverages the network concept and connects people across the globe. Think of all the leverage the iPhone created. The phone opened the floodgates for music, iTunes, Apple Pay, apps, GPS and maps, data sharing, fitness, health and even bio-hacking. All of these and more will be leverageable on VR. It might not be your immediate business model, but could you embrace it or spend 10 per cent of your time looking into disruptions to your industry by bringing this technology in? You may not want to be first, but you will want to be fast.

45

How to raise money

Think carefully before you sell half your company for a few hundred grand. Money always has a cost attached that exceeds the interest you pay. Ideas create income, so look to leverage ideas as much as you look to raise capital. Be clear on why you want to raise capital:

- To grow faster than you could on your own
- To develop products you couldn't on your own
- To get experienced investors on your board
- To invest in property and other assets you couldn't on your own
- To get yourself out of a sticky situation.

If you feel capital will help one or more of the above for you, here are some ways to raise capital, starting with the areas that give away the least collateral and should be the quickest. All areas of raising finance will have balanced downsides, so be clear what cost you are prepared to pay. Keep an open mind and you'll likely access more cash when you need it. And we all need it.

Gift from family

There are some inheritance tax breaks if you get a capital gift from your parents, that reduce the longer you've had the gift while they are alive. If your family will pass on a financial legacy and inheritance to you, you could look to get that earlier than their death. You could do a deal so they benefit while they're alive, like an advance of your inheritance. If you propose a venture rather than expect a handout your family may be open-minded. Get good tax advice.

Loan from friends or family

These 'investors' are not professional lenders or partners. They may never have loaned money before. The upside is you could get a better rate than a bank (as long as your friends actually like you!). They may need more persuasion and education on investing first. The trust should already be there, but you may have more to lose if it goes wrong. Then again they will likely be more forgiving than a bank. This may be a good place to raise finance to get started, or out of a hole, but not for bigger projects.

Personal loan from a bank

The unsecured amount of borrowing you can get is going up. You can access this cash fast as long as you have good credit. When rates are low this can be good value. For smaller amounts it is fast and liquid, but will be costly on bigger and longer-term amounts. Some people are able to access multiple loans. Be careful not to take a rate too high just because you need the money. Nowadays, you can have the cash almost there and then if you apply through your app, and some people apply for many at once.

Equity restructure from an existing asset

If you have an existing property or other asset that can be used as security, you could restructure your finance and draw that equity to invest. When rates are low, cost of long-term finance like mortgages can be very low too. It can be a good way to create money you didn't have to earn and leverage to grow other assets or businesses. If you have access to commercial lenders and you have a portfolio already, a restructure can save you thousands of pounds in interest. 'Floating' charges across multiple assets can enable access to funds without having to refinance multiple assets.

Mortgage or finance secured on an asset

As above, by raising finance on an asset that is unencumbered (no debt or borrowing secured against it). This could be a family home or investment. When you offer security it is much easier to access long-term finance at competitive rates. Get a good broker to give you options and a full range of lenders. Cash stuck in a property is unleveraged and could be utilized better. It's not that hard to turn equity in one property into three to five investment properties while still keeping the initial property.

Selling shares in your business

Selling shares or equity in your business can raise capital to invest into it for new products, research and development, staff, marketing and more. You can also retain some profit for yourself. You'll likely need to show some profits over a consistent timeframe, or be good at selling a vision. You can be a start-up and raise capital at angel investing events like London (or local) Business Angels and Angels Den. Get your vision clear, your pitch concise and sexy and get feedback from experienced business owners and investors. In the short-term the money feels cheap, or free, as you have no interest to pay or personal collateral to give, but over time you will be giving away control and ongoing profits. If you can get angels or investors with experience and contacts that may make the deal worth doing.

Loan from private investors or angels

Private finance is somewhere between friends and family and banks. You borrow from any individual with money. They range from non-experienced investors with cash gaining no interest through to angels, dragons and 'vultures'. Any non-institutional private investor could lend with a loan agreement, buy equity or do a joint venture. Any contact you make could be a future private investor, so treat everyone you meet like you could work together in the future.

If you keep every contact you make at Business Angel events then you build your own black book of very well-financed and networked investors and 'whales'. Every meeting has future possibilities.

Bridging loan

An expensive but fast method of 'bridging' a finance gap. If you are short of cash to finish a project, or in very urgent need, bridging is very quick, but very expensive. If it can get you over the line or be hybrid-ized with another method of finance, then it could serve you well. Best only for very short-term as it can cost 2 per cent, 3 per cent or more per month.

Crowdfunding

Using crowdfunding sites like Zopa and Funding Circle give you access to private finance, pooled together, with a regulated platform connecting lenders and borrowers. You can choose your risk level, and often borrow smaller amounts without giving security. Platforms and apps make the application process simple, and more niched crowd-funding platforms, like ones specifically for property, have emerged.

Kickstarter

Kickstarter is a crowdfunding platform with a twist. It circumvents traditional investment avenues. Project creators choose a deadline and minimum funding goal and if the goal is not met by the deadline, no funds are collected, as a kind of assurance contract. The platform is open to backers from anywhere in the world and has reportedly received more than $1.9 billion in pledges from 9.4 million backers to fund 257,000 creative projects. People who back Kickstarter projects are offered tangible rewards and one-of-a-kind experiences in exchange for their pledges, rather than cash or equity.

Joint venture (JV)

A JV can be where one party (you?) does the work running the business or asset, sourcing, managing and maintaining it, and the other party invests the money. It can also be where you go into partnership or business together, both working in the business or asset class with split roles and responsibilities. Perhaps you divide the financial investment either 50/50 or according to an agreed shareholding. I have partnerships that are 50/50, 50/25/25 where I am a 25 per cent shareholder or a 33.3/33.3/33.3 (recurring) where I have one third shareholding. You have flexibility to apportion roles, shares, who puts how much (or how little) cash in, and you can have complementary and opposing skillsets with shareholders or partners for the benefit of having all bases covered in your enterprise.

Because virtually everyone runs out of cash at one point, no matter how rich, JVs are a common and efficient way to keep businesses and assets growing cost effectively. Many finance raising methods merge into JVs and most good businesses have partnerships.

Credit cards

Fast, liquid, but expensive. Some people juggle the 0 per cent time offers, though interest can build up if you miss those timelines. You can rack up quite a spending limit if you get a few cards, but be careful to use credit as a last resort, for personal investment or emergencies, and pay it off fast and in full. Many people who earn well keep upping their limits and getting new cards not just to spend on, but to have as a back-up plan and to earn points on. In 2015, a Chinese billionaire bought $170 million painting with his credit card so he could use the points for free airfare.

Sell all your shit on eBay!

If all else fails, clear out your basement, attic and wardrobe and sell as much as you can. While this statement is slightly flippant, I sold a Roland electric drum kit that my fiancée wanted rid of, and plenty of hi-fi and electronic gear back in 2008, and raised enough cash for a deposit for a small investment property. If for nothing else, do it for the law of vacuum prosperity. It got me started and built momentum. Small things lead to big things. If you're rich you probably have far too many possessions you don't use or need, so clear them out and get leverage on the cash.

Building your cash pipeline

Here are smart and strategic ways to get good contacts, access to capital and manage JVs with the least amount of friction and therefore lowest cost:

1 START BUILDING THE RELATIONSHIPS/LOOKING FOR PARTNERS BEFORE YOU NEED THE CASH

If you need the cash it's easier to sense the need or desperation. No one wants to work with or lend money to anyone who's desperate. People don't loan you money or do JVs for you, they do it for their own motives. Take a long-term view and start looking before you need the money so that when you do, the relationship is already established. Be great at what you do. Keep learning, growing and giving. Remember anyone could be a future lender or JV partner so treat everyone well and keep doors open.

2 GET NOTICED WITHOUT SAYING 'LOOK AT ME, LOOK AT ME'

Be seen helping others on and offline. Network a lot. One event per week and you will have 52 events under your belt. You'll get noticed. Merge passion and profession with social business events. Share what you know. Help people. Let people watch you safely from afar and they will decide for themselves before you ask them for money. Don't just be seen or pitch when you are in need of cash.

3 FOLLOW UP WITH EVERYONE

Have a semi-script and add some personal notes and things you noticed and liked about the person you met. Follow up with everyone, then move on to point 4.

4 THREE TO TEN 'TOUCH POINTS'

Most people will consider working with you on or around the fifth meeting or contact point. A few will take less. Many will take seven to ten. I've surveyed thousands of people to get this data. Be smart and start timing when you 'ask for the money', or start talking business. Be clear on what you do and don't do and communicate clearly so people understand you. Even if any business isn't done initially they will keep you in mind for the future.

5 BE AN AMBI-VERT

An ambi-vert is between an introvert and an extrovert. If any extreme is better then be an extrovert, but the best balance is ambi-vert. Be seen, help, share, keep learning and stay (relatively) humble. Make a good impression.

6 LEARN THE VALUES OF YOUR POTENTIAL PARTNER

Have an elevator pitch that is conversational, gentle, short, elegant yet compelling, and focused on your potential partner and what they get. Knowing their values enables you to create seemingly bespoke pitches that scratch the itches. Always leave people having learned something from you and with more than you took.

7 AGREEMENT

Once you have a relationship and it is time to get into the details of the JV, create a heads of terms (a non-binding document that outlines the main issues relevant to a tentative partnership or other agreement). At the very least gain clarity on roles, shares and responsibilities. Ensure you get a legal agreement such as a JV, partnership or shareholders contract and have legal representation. Having an agreement not only protects both parties' interests, but forces you to go through the necessary details of roles, money flow and security, negotiating each point and answering the harder questions upfront, for easier and better business down the line.

Once you find one wealthy partner, they open doors for more and more and more. They will keep using and reusing you to lend to and partner with, and reduce the friction and distrust by introducing you to their well-financed and connected contacts. You could meet a potential JV or business partner in the most unlikely places. I met Mark at the very first property networking event I went to in

Peterborough. He was the last person I spoke to. I exchanged cards with everyone, and followed up. Within four weeks he'd helped me get a job at a property investing company. Within three months we were buying our first property together. By the end of that year we had 20 or so together. Eleven years on and our partnership is still going strong. Don't get ready, be ready. People are watching you now. Money is very close…

46

Money management and mastery

You can work hard for your money, or your money can work hard for you. You can exchange time for money, or you can build assets that create passive income and preserve your valuable time. It is possible for anyone to build a plan and follow a system to become wealthy. It doesn't matter where you start, it matters *that* you start. It seems that many people know the price of everything but the value of nothing. People don't know the value of their time, of each task, of the depreciation of items they buy or the value of assets that go up. The media is full of programmes and ideas on how to save a few quid but not much on how to manage and earn more. People are happy to share how much they saved buying an item, but it is taboo to talk about how much people earn. You won't get more money until you learn to manage what you already have. What you appreciate, appreciates, and you get what you expect, not what you deserve. So a focus on managing and appreciating money, respecting the laws that govern it, and then following and sticking to money management systems will create more wealth. The more you do it, the easier it gets, the more you build new habits and the more you get leverage and compounding working for you.

You can't master what you don't measure

For many people money has become harder to manage because we don't touch and feel it as much as we used to. Previously you'd get a weekly cash wage packet; you'd hold and carry it. You had a physical, tangible measure of your week's work. Today most money is transferred and exchanged electronically, much faster, with tax and national insurance already deducted and bills all going out with much less left or felt through your hands. Easy come easy go. People value money more the harder it is to earn and the more tangible it is. Old habits can die hard. This outlook needs to change and a new view and management of money needs to be set up and implemented. So let's begin.

A five-step money management system

1 *You* must manage your money

No one is responsible for managing your money but *you*. No parent or guardian, no IFA or wealth manager or agent, no one but you. I once walked into Barclays bank to make a transaction. They'd just refurbished the bank and there were new personal desks where you could sit with an advisor. It was a simple transaction I wanted to make, but someone asked me to sit down as they could process it there and I could jump the queue. I wasn't a millionaire at this stage, but money was good and there was some capital in my account. The advisor was maybe 20 years old, his uniform was a little big for him and his name badge wasn't quite straight. He punched in my account numbers and accessed my accounts and his eyes popped out of his head like a cartoon character. He got visibly excited. The amount in my bank was not outrageously high. He went into a scripted pitch about how I could be using the money better and that he could advise me on better ways to invest it. I guess at the time he was on a salary of about £14,000. I politely declined; he pushed back, I politely declined again and life carried on as normal. As I walked out and played what had just happened over in my mind it started to grate on me. The lad was doing nothing wrong. He was starting a career, and fair play to him for giving me the pitch. But the system in the bank of someone pitching to manage my money who had no experience or money of his own is all wrong, and very dangerous. I vowed there and then to commit my life to continually learning about money, and 100 per cent managing my own. And I suggest to you that you should too.

This will not be a rant of all the schemes and scams. Everyone has the right to sell their wares. This is a pledge to you to manage, protect and master one of the most important aspects of your life. Commit to continual learning and growth. You wouldn't outsource the raising of your kids, though perhaps from time to time you might feel like doing so. Yes I'm all for leverage, but some things should never be leveraged. A friend of mine lost a large capital sum and said to his advisor, 'Is all my money really gone?' He replied, 'No of course not, it's just with someone else!' No IFA or money manager or agent will ever care as much about your money as you do. No piece of software or financial instrument cares about how you feel about your money. Learn from everyone, but control your wealth yourself. Managing and mastering your own money is an area of great return on both time and money. It is a personal, high-level KRA. It is merging passion and profession. Plan your wealth, measure and monitor your wealth, allocate and re-allocate your wealth, track and count your wealth and enjoy your wealth. When you lose some of your wealth you have no one else to blame, but you get to learn and get better at it, and make more.

2 You must have a future financial plan

Now that you take full responsibility for your wealth, you need a specific plan to make, and then give, more money. You'd be wise to have short-term and long-term plans. You can start with a plan to get out of debt, daily budgets, weekly to monthly plans, then six-month, one-year, three-year, five-, ten- and then 50-year plans, if you have enough life in you, of course. Then you plan beyond your lifetime for your legacy. People with a longer time horizon and ability to plan further into the future are those who change the world, make a lasting difference and create vast wealth and riches.

GET OUT OF DEBT

What leads most people into debt? Trying to catch up with people who are already there. According to CreditLoan.com, the average American will now pay more than $600,000 in interest over the course of a lifetime.[1] If you are in debt, you are not alone, but you can see just how much it will cost you. Your first financial goal should be to get out of bad debt fast, especially if you have debt on liabilities.

From now on *never spend more than you earn.* Set up direct debits each month and pay off the maximum you can, on the day your pay comes in so the temptation to spend it is circumvented. Load up on the highest debt first, paying a higher percentage of the most expensive debt, so that you repay the least amount of interest. Consolidate debt where possible and necessary, especially when interest rates are low. Do what you can if you are in a financial rut by negotiating payment holidays or taking longer loans with smaller repayments. Set a target date to be clear of all debt, and put in as much disposable income as you can to get rid of it quickly. Debt compounds, so you need to take control now and make some short-term sacrifices for long-term wealth. Review your outgoings every six months and adjust your spending and DDs as they creep up. Change providers, negotiate new deals, consolidate and get rid of all wastage.

DAILY BUDGETS

While paying off debt, work out a daily spend or budget you can live on that leaves money for savings, then investment and speculation. Teach yourself the discipline of managing a smaller amount of money. You can save $112,000 over a lifetime by bringing your lunch to work.[2] Manage the small costs and larger amounts will take care of themselves. Until you can do that you won't get a larger sum of money. Reduce non-essential spending and start building your savings – one of the foundations of wealth building. Target spending under your budget so you can have one day a week when you can afford to spend a little more as a reward. Even as you gain wealth, practise living on humble means in some areas to stay in control of your spending.

WEEKLY AND MONTHLY PLANS

Now that you are managing budgets more effectively, your horizon of time can and will expand. You can start to make weekly and monthly budgets and financial plans. You may do both, or you may do one or the other depending on whether you get paid weekly or monthly. Set up a monthly direct debit to pay into an SANT account (Save And Never Touch) on the first day of the month after payday.

Reduce some direct debits and personal overheads. Create a part-time or second income stream if you see fit. Create a personal profit margin, which will be explained later in this chapter.

ONE- AND THREE-YEAR PLANS

Project forward an increase in earnings. Increase your SANT DD every 6 to 12 months. Calculate the increased margins and set them as targets. Target a maintenance or very small rise in personal overhead, far lower than the increase in earnings, and target a percentage of overheads to income. Start to see a significant upward trend and trajectory. Add in target amounts to invest and speculate with, and start giving some away to causes that matter to you. Start saving significant sums for future events like your kids' school fees, second homes and other perceived personal assets and targets.

FIVE- AND TEN-YEAR PLANS

With this level of vision and forward planning, you can build huge companies and vast personal and professional wealth. You could target between 100 per cent and 200 per cent year-on-year growth, depending on your existing size. It's easier to grow quickly early in your business and personal career. If you sustained a 50 per cent year-on-year growth for a decade or more you'd be in the league of Progressive Property and Microsoft, so you'd be doing well. You can make very ambitious plans and goals, and move into areas you know you want to, but don't know how yet, just as President Kennedy did in 1961 with the goal of sending an American safely to the moon before the end of the decade. This was very ambitious, but forged a path and set a deadline that was achieved and progressed the whole of mankind. You can plan new ventures you know you want to move into but are not yet in the position to, or BHAGs as they are often called: Big Hairy Audacious Goals. These can be motivating because they're exciting, possibly scary, but there's no immediate pressure to hit them and no naïvety that you can reach them in an unrealistically short time. Plan your pension, the inheritance for your children if relevant, school fees even if your kids aren't born yet and a foundation or charitable cause.

50-YEAR AND LEGACY PLANS

People and companies with this scale of vision change the world. Japanese organizations often plan 25 and 50 years into the future using the spirit of 'Kaizen'. Toyota plan decades into the future. The Meiji restoration of Japan was a 100-year plan. Many of the greatest visionaries and billionaires make plans that go beyond their lifetime. Many people overestimate what they can achieve in a short time but underestimate what they can achieve in a lifetime. Start planning so far ahead that the goals and visions can be vast and inspiring, without any pressure for instant achievement. You can be guided and make smart strategic decisions, say 'No' to distractions and be as patient as you like. Interestingly the longer term planning really helps you make and achieve the short-term plans and goals. You can plan your overall net-worth, or placement on the rich list, or inhabiting Mars, like Elon Musk, with this length of planning.

3 Four financial stepping-stones

There are four financial 'stepping-stones' that can take you through the levels of financial control to opulence. It will be wise to fill in your current situation and then target amounts that will guide you through the levels as 'stepping-stones' to wealth and riches:

LEVEL 1: STABILITY

At level 1, you are out of bad debt, and have basic living costs covered by income from assets. You can survive, but not yet thrive. This should be your first 'stepping-stone' to target. Calculate what basic living costs you'd need to house, feed and clothe yourself and your family, with amenities such as water, heating and essential items covered, but no more. When stripped down, it is often surprising how little you need to survive and, as such, this target does not seem insurmountable.

LEVEL 2: SECURITY

At level 2, you have a humble lifestyle covered by income from assets. In addition to level 1, you may have some travel, a car, a holiday, TV, Internet and a little spending money. You could certainly get by and have a fair living on this amount, but you can't enjoy the fruits of your work too much, and still have to watch your money closely. Add around 50 per cent of your level 1 stability income to arrive at your level 2 security figure, give or take 15 per cent or what works for you.

LEVEL 3: FREEDOM

At level 3, you are able to live your ideal lifestyle with income from assets. You can travel, put your kids through a good school, have some luxury items and you no longer have any money worries. You can become a 'Lifestyle Entrepreneur' running a 'Lifestyle Business', but you aren't yet at vast scale and wealth. Add 100 per cent to 150 per cent of your level 2 security figure, or what works for you but isn't the lifestyle of a billionaire.

LEVEL 4: OPULENCE

At level 4, you are able to do absolutely anything, anytime, anywhere with anyone, covered by income from assets. Even better is you still can't spend it all and it seems to grow and compound each month. You can live an opulent lifestyle with life's great luxuries, give and contribute handsomely and still see your wealth get ever more vast.

Add 500 per cent to your level 3 freedom figure, or an amount that seems so huge that you couldn't spend it.

These four levels are coined 'stepping-stones' because they give incremental checkpoints going from debt to basic overheads covered and up through to opulence. You give yourself a great sense of progress each time you get close to, hit and surpass a level, which becomes a self-fulfilling prophecy. I strongly recommend that you set yourself these four levels of targets in your six-monthly goals and your net-worth statement. Review them regularly. Allow yourself small celebrations and rewards for incremental gains and bigger ones when you transition from stone-to-stone.

4 The seven layers of money

There are seven layers of using money. They can form a wealth hierarchy, if ordered and leveraged correctly, and in the right order:

LAYER 1: SPENDING (WANT AND NEED)

Spending on necessities comes first for your basic survival. Many people are in debt so can't even afford to cater for their basic needs without getting further into debt. This might be a lack of knowledge on the management of money, which is easy to fix, a current inability to earn enough, trying to keep up with the Jones's or some emotional or deeper belief issues around money, covered in Section 4. Yet most people can actually live on a lot less than they think or have become accustomed and addicted to. 'Need' spending is often confused with 'want' spending. You need less than you think you need. Budget the amount you need for basic amenities for you and your family, and set it as your level 1 stepping-stone of financial stability.

'Want' spending is what keeps most people poor, or turns them broke. It is spending on liabilities or perishables that decay in value and produce no capital or income residual. Wealthy people are susceptible to this too, especially people new into money. According to Scottish Widows, 9 million people in the UK have no savings at all.[3] That is around 15 per cent of the population. According to a More study, 33 per cent of UK residents have less than £500 savings to their name. Only 12 per cent of UK residents have £50,000 or more in savings/investments (only two years' humble living expenses for a couple). Twenty-one per cent of Americans don't even have a savings account, and 62 per cent have less than $1,000 dollars in savings.[4]

The biggest difference between the rich and poor is that the sustainably rich 'spend' (invest) money on assets that produce (passive) income, and preserve their capital. They then spend income that is residual and gets replaced by the asset, on liabilities and perishables. They preserve the time and capital, and money that recurs is used for spending, allowing the capital to grow. Set your 'need' spending level, then minimize your 'want' spending until you have savings and assets that produce buffers and income.

Buy (liabilities) low

Anything that goes down in value will erode capital. Capital should be preserved at all costs. Many of your non-essential items can be bought secondhand, at sample sales, on eBay, in the sales, at certain times of the year like Black Friday, at outlet villages and shopping centres, from friends, and when the items are no longer the newest model. If you take one year's worth of all these items, the compounded savings can be significant. Be careful not to get into diminishing law of returns and spend so long saving a small amount of money but wasting so much time that it costs you more money.

Turn spending habits into investing habits

If you can turn much of your spending habits into investing habits, you will make 80/20 compounding work for you, save and make possibly hundreds of thousands or even millions, *and* have a valuable life skill most don't have. Think of every material item you buy as a liability-cash-drain, and apply an investor mentality to each purchase. Think:

Step 1. Can I get by without it?
Step 2. Can I buy it secondhand at the bottom of the depreciation curve?
Step 3. Can I turn it into an asset?
Step 4. Can I sell or exchange it before it drops in value further?
Step 5. What's the lowest cost method of finance?

You can use the above five steps for almost any material, non-perishable item such as cars, watches, handbags, jewellery, clothing, furniture, AV equipment, and even holidays and travel.

Cost of capital and 15-year implication

All spent or invested capital has a potential 'opportunity cost' of being spent, in that it could have produced a better return elsewhere. Many people consider cost of capital when investing, but not when spending. You will see in a moment how dramatic and significant saved capital can compound, so consider the cost of future earnings when spending money. If you take that one step further and look at the 15-year cost of capital implication, then the numbers get so big that even small savings will look worthwhile.

LAYER 2: SAVING

The first stage of mastering money management. Sounds obvious but most people's results prove it isn't. Saving is the foundation of building wealth. It builds a capital base to build from and the roots that bear the fruits. It also teaches fundamentals that build wealth such as delaying gratification, discipline, long-time horizon thinking and learning to manage well what you have so you can attract more. But, despite the power of compounding, saving alone will not create vast wealth and serve your life's vision; hence this is level 2 of 7. The problem with saving alone is that it rear-loads all the benefits.

Here's an example of the power but also the limitation of saving alone, and not moving through to levels 3 to 7. A live scenario posted in one of my online communities was a question from Matthew Watson in its original unedited form: 'Rob, with the law of compounding and for example if I want to save £300 per month that's £3600 a year the interest is low how will the law of compounding make so much of difference.' Here is my answer: 'Matthew, yes it's only £3600 a year. Let's assume you could beat inflation by net 2 per cent:

- End of year 1: £3672
- End of year 2: £7414.44 (interest worked out earned on full 12 months)
- End of year 3: £11,237.78
- End of year 4: £15,135.54
- End of year 5: £19,109.23
- End of year 10: £40,207.37
- End of year 15: £63,501.42
- End of year 25: £120,842.01
- End of year 35: £187,513.12
- End of year 50: £325,858.77

It took 15 years to get to £63,501, but the last 15 years gave over £138,000.

If you make it just 3 per cent net, here are the figures:

- Year 1: £3782.16
- Year 3: £11,690.27
- Year 5: £20,080
- Year 10: £43,358.22
- Year 25: £137,894.71
- Year 50: £438,585.50

On the one hand, you can see how compounding builds momentum, and the longer you give it to grow, the more powerful it is. You can also see that small amounts at the start, in this case just 1 per cent net, return more and can have a big difference at the end. But it takes years and years to build its power. Even at year 50, saving £300 pcm and getting a 3 per cent net return on it only gives £438,585.50. At 5 per cent net yearly passive income from that capital sum, after 50 years of saving you have £21,929 a year to live on. But in 50 years, that would have been eroded by inflation and as such would not hold as much value. According to Nationwide house price data, the average price of property in the UK 50 years ago was £3465. That buys an average secondhand car now. So what will a small yearly salary 'buy' in 50 years' time? Maybe a week's food shopping or basic living?

Here are some ways in which you can increase your savings and saving power, and some simple strategies to 'game' yourself to make it easier than you think to save. Over the last decade some smart mentors who are worth millions, even billions, have taught me some great little games around saving money:

PYF (PAY YOURSELF FIRST)

Possibly the most important concept in saving, earning and money. Most people get paid *last*. They get their pay packet and tax, national insurance and student loan contributions have already been deducted. Then almost as soon at that net amount hits their bank account, which can be as little as half their gross pay, mortgage or rent, council tax, heating, water, Internet, Sky and other TV subscriptions, car, home, medical, life and pet insurance, mobile phone, charity and gym all get taken out and before you get to touch and feel *any* of your salary. And then who gets paid last? You. This needs to change. People mistakenly assume they can't pay themselves first because they can't afford to, but they can't afford to because they are paying themselves last. So start by setting up a standing order for money to go into two different accounts on payday: (1) your savings account and (2) your spending account. It doesn't matter how much you start with, just do it. The rest will get covered. Even if you are a little short you still can get resourceful and find a way to earn a little on the side to make the difference. Resourcefulness is a much under-utilized skill every human possesses, so PYF, save plenty and leverage your innate ability to get creative.

CASH PRESERVATION (OR REGULAR SHOCK ANTICIPATION)

You will need a level of savings to move into investing; not just for investment, but to cover you for 'irregular shocks'. According to the Federal Reserve, 52 per cent of Americans would not be able to cover an emergency of $400, and would need to sell or borrow to cover the cost.[5] You will only get hurt by big expenses if you don't have capital reserves to cover them, so build those capital reserves first. Have a target amount, then use that as your new imagined zero. Build on that with capital to invest, and never dip into your reserves, letting them grow larger and larger.

Money bucketing

Having 'buckets' that you set up as direct debits or targets to apportion gives you a system to grow your wealth. Below are the buckets you could set up, even with different bank accounts. The percentages are suggested starting points, and as you grow your wealth the expenses bucket will reduce and the others will grow.

- **Bucket 1.** SANT 5 per cent (Save And Never Touch)
- **Bucket 2.** Irregular shock savings 5 per cent
- **Bucket 3.** Bucket list 10 per cent (future opulent spending/ life goals)

- **Bucket 4.** You asset 10 per cent (investing in your education and mentorship)
- **Bucket 5.** Investments 10 per cent
- **Bucket 6.** Give back 5 per cent
- **Bucket 7.** Expenses 55 per cent (living and taxes)

If your expenses are higher than 55 per cent, adjust the percentages accordingly. You might restructure your buckets like this:

- **Bucket 1.** SANT 3 per cent (Save And Never Touch)
- **Bucket 2.** Irregular shock savings 5 per cent
- **Bucket 3.** Bucket list 2 per cent (future opulent spending/ life goals)
- **Bucket 4.** You asset 5 per cent (investing in your education and mentorship)
- **Bucket 5.** Investments 3 per cent
- **Bucket 6.** Give back 2 per cent
- **Bucket 7.** Expenses 80 per cent (living and taxes)

As you grow your wealth you might target a bucket system like this:

- **Bucket 1.** SANT 5 per cent (Save And Never Touch)
- **Bucket 2.** Irregular shock savings 0 per cent (achieved)
- **Bucket 3.** Bucket list 10 per cent (future opulent spending/ life goals)
- **Bucket 4.** You asset 15 per cent (investing in your education and mentorship)
- **Bucket 5.** Investments 35 per cent
- **Bucket 6.** Give back 10 per cent
- **Bucket 7.** Expenses 25 per cent (living, taxes, freedom and opulence)

BANK ACCOUNT MANAGEMENT

It is easier than ever to manage all your money online, from one app folder on your phone. Ensure all your bank accounts are both online and on app. Then set up payees of yourself between all accounts so that you can pay any money across accounts anytime anywhere without more rigorous checks or blocks from your banks. Have one main bank account for all your expenses, and one main account for your property portfolio or income from other assets and associated DDs like mortgages and insurances out, and rents in. If you have JV partners, set up a new account that you can both access for each partner, as joint signatories. Have a savings account for each current account, and ensure you keep less than the bank's insured limit it guarantees in each account. Save all your account details in a secure password app for easy access. Set up your bucket DDs as above, and now you have an automated and real-time bank account management system that can save and invest for you and manage and move money in real time, globally. Have all your business bank accounts accessible to you online and in app so at any time you can spot-check cashflow and your multiple business accounts. As you make more and more money you will need more bank accounts, and there will be much more money flow. This system will manage even a vast network of accounts.

SAVE ALL COINS

If you save each coin that you get to a different savings pot, you'll be surprised how quickly they can grow. I use ones, twos, fives and tens for saving for my kids to invest when they grow up. Twenties get used as a reward for my son to win when he putts (although that soon moved up to higher amounts as he got the taste for it). Fifties, one pound and two pound coins all get saved and then converted into Krugerrands to save and store.

BREAK NOTES INTO COINS WHERE YOU CAN AFFORD TO

I also save £5 notes to convert to Krugerrands and spend ten pounds, twenty pounds and fifty pound notes. I like to break big notes to have more small notes and coins to save. This can amount to many thousands of pounds a year. My business partner and I have coin-operated dryers in many of our properties, and we do the same thing with those coins. We have a coin counting machine that whizzes through them and bags them up. Despite being a relatively small amount of money it brings a great deal of (childish) joy! It's also a great discipline and strategy to share with and teach your kids. The reason I detailed the compounding nature of savings earlier was to illustrate that the longer you do this the more powerful it becomes. You can now get piggy banks with no means to get the money out and small coin safes that you can set a future date to open to help with your discipline. While small and simple, I know many deca- and centi-millionaires who follow and strangely enjoy these disciplines and apparently small measures. I think it goes back to your ability to manage small amounts of money to attract and allow in larger amounts of money. And maybe a love for money too?

However, interest rates barely keep up with inflation, and as more money gets put into the monetary system it devalues the existing money. Money today is worth more than money tomorrow. So once you've saved a good capital base you need to move to layer 3 as quickly as possible to beat inflation and opportunity cost.

LAYER 3: BORROWING

Once you've mastered saving and money bucketing, then you start leveraging good debt for investments. You can raise mortgages against property investments or finance against a business. It is wise to use good collateral and safe gearing when investing. When the banks are bearish they will ensure safety for you with their more strict lending criteria. As they become bullish and loan to values increase, they take on more risk and lend to unworthy borrowers at rates they can't repay and at increasing leverage that exposes them to small market changes.

Pre-2007, people were using remortgaged money from properties that had gone up in value to live on. Every two years, sometimes less, they would refinance onto a higher loan to value, or cash out some of the growth, increasing the loan size. This is unsustainable, and was part of the undoing of many of the banks and private speculators. If some of the refinance money had been saved and most of the rest reinvested into lower-risk investments, many who went bust in the crash-cum-recession of 2008 may have survived and then thrived as great buying opportunities emerged. With increased potential reward comes increased risk, so take borrowing seriously and don't see it as free money, like many homeowners did in the early to mid-2000s. Yet without leverage and borrowing, results and vast wealth will be much slower, so borrow wisely with low rates of return and safe loan to values, build long-term proven relationships with banks and leverage this to move to layers 4 and 5.

LAYER 4: INVESTING

Saving comes before investing, because investing has more risks. If you lose your investment (which can happen) and have no savings supporting it, you lose everything. Once you have a foundational savings pot to cover irregular shocks and a buffer on top, say 6 to 12 months living expenses, then you can start using some of the money you were putting away as savings, to invest. You'll want to do this as soon as possible to protect your cash from inflation and whimsical spending.

When you start investing, you should look for relatively low-risk investments with a relatively low knowledge barrier to entry. Start with cash by deciding how much you'd love to make in a day, and simply start carrying that amount in your wallet or pocket. Don't spend this money. It's purely a psychological cushion, so put it in a separate section of your wallet, away from your spending money. To have no money in your pocket is like driving on empty. I was told to do this by one of my early mentors and have been doing it for 11 years now – I can't quite explain how and why it works to drive more money, but it has worked for me. It also means if you are ever very exposed, isolated or in trouble, you have cash to help you out.

Above this level, invest in stocks, property or a business venture you have knowledge or experience in, as this is the next lowest risk and probably the lowest resistance from a standing start. Only add to your investment portfolio when you have gained some good returns or have saved more to invest, and look to both gently increase risk and gently de-risk. You de-risk by investing in very low risk but low return assets like physical gold and bonds. You gently increase risk by moving into slightly higher risk investments to you like new classes that are quite safe but you don't know well. You move to slightly more risk like specific stocks you pick out, more expensive properties or add-on investments like adding a lettings arm to a property port-folio or business.

LAYER 5: SPECULATING

Many people speculate thinking they are investing. Speculation is higher-risk investing, with greater potential for reward, and with money that you can afford to lose. If you speculate before you invest, like investing in a start-up business you know little about, you risk losing both your investment and your savings. You should only move up to speculation once you've gained investment knowledge and skill and your investments are multi-layered, with varying levels of risk and thus de-risked and protected from losses. Speculation might be investments you have little knowledge in but are keen to move into. It might be more volatile or cyclical investments or models, or new models with less proven data for success such as new technology. War-ren Buffett didn't get involved in investing in tech companies in the Nasdaq for this very reason, and in the end it proved to be wise. Very niche models and classes with specific technical knowledge required to make good returns, like watches, wine or art, can also be specula-tive until you've proven the track. Trying to time markets that are hard to time could turn investing into speculating. Once you have a full cycle or two of knowledge then you reduce the risks. My friend Andreas Panayiotou, billionaire property tycoon, said to me that he just felt that things were 'too good' in the boom preceding the global 2007 recession, and felt that things could go badly wrong. So he sold 6000 buy-to-let rental properties. His timing turned out to be per-fect but he had two full cycles of experience to make that call. Even then he said there was an element of luck involved. Sometimes you use your intuition and take a bit of a calculated gamble. Some people convince themselves that punts are investments. They are not. There's a time and a place for speculation, once all the layers below are built. Speculation requires a lot of self-honesty and good control of your emotions.

Layer 6: Insuring

This is a nice problem. Once you have wealth, the world tries to take some of it off you, to teach you to grow. Once you get to a level of riches, you need to insure against loss or attack as much as you need to make more. You explore insurance through diversification, tax reduction and mitigation, adjustments for inflation, self-insurance and protection strategies.

As your wealth increases so do your tax levels. As you gain more material items, maintenance and insurance costs go up and your risk of theft or damage goes up. There are fees and taxes and commissions and tolls and hidden costs that eat into purchases and investments that you need to watch out for. A 0.75 per cent difference in investment fees can mean losing $30,000 over 20 years in a $100,000 portfolio, according to the SEC. Small percentages of big amounts are still big amounts. As you have more money, more people, companies and charities want you to give it away to them.

You insure your wealth by diversifying your investments, having multiple layers of wealth and assets, low-risk foundational wealth protectors, stored capital, cyclical assets or businesses and assets that people don't know about. You'll need to insure against risk, theft and loss. Self-insure by stashing away capital and liquid assets that can cover loss, damage or theft, instead of paying into multiple insurance policies. Instead of flaunting it you start to protect and hide it. Protection becomes more important than creation.

Layer 7: Giving

Once you have moved up through the previous six layers, you can then give back more frequently. Of course you can continually give back via donating a percentage of your income in your money bucketing system, or better, donating your time and experience into something that means something to you. Wealth built through the six layers buys/frees/leverages time to do more and more of this. Poor people with poor money beliefs often give too much away too early because they have guilt, fear and shame around money. They feel they are alleviating pain or shame by giving it away, yet can't afford to and thus stay poor and get subsidised by the wealthy. Then there are others who never give any away and are too self-centred, where society finds a way of gaining balance back and taking money away.

The further up the levels you go, the more your knowledge, experience and expertise become more valuable than your money, to make more money. You gain insights and experience into 'no money down' investing, or at least 'none of your money' investing, and people investing their money into you. You leverage, forge joint venture partnerships, utilize compounding, brand and reputation and have multiple streams of income. The more you have the more you can afford and the more you desire to give away, and in turn the more the world perceives you as a giver. The world always gives more to a giver.

5 Assets and liabilities

An asset is something that pays a residual income return, whereas a liability is one that takes income to sustain, or depreciates. Simply put, an asset pays money out and a liability costs money. Simple enough, right? Well in reality, not clear-cut. Some may see their own home as an asset, because the capital appreciation and low cost of finance mean you make more than it costs to live in, yet others would see it as a liability because it doesn't produce an income stream. In truth, most asset classes can be assets if managed well, and liabilities if not understood. And then it depends if you are investing for capital gains or income streams. If you give a muppet a solid property investment it will become a liability quickly. If you gave Richard Branson a good business idea it could become a capital and income asset very quickly. The strength and viability of an asset depends on the class, knowledge and experience of the investor, the market trends and timing and cycle, interest rates, currency conditions and more. There are universally recognized assets like property and stocks, but that doesn't make them a sure thing. Follow these guidelines:

BE CLEAR ON STRATEGY AND CLASS: CAPITAL OR INCOME, EARNED OR PASSIVE

If you're buying an investment property, not to live in, it needs to produce income. If you are buying gold as a currency hedge or a store of value, you are preserving capital. If you are building a business you might work in it for some years, merging your passion and profession and doing meaningful work. If you put some cash in a mutual fund you don't expect to be involved in the management and allocation of the money. So, be clear if you are investing for capital, income, aggressively or defensively, putting your time in to build something vast or hands-off and as passive as possible. As you build your layers and scale of wealth, it's likely you'll have multiple asset classes and multiple income streams, active and passive, capital and income. Don't be naïve. Don't get emotional. Have a plan and execute it, building up on layers and levels of risk.

DON'T ASSUME 'GOOD' INVESTMENTS ARE GOOD AND 'BAD' ONES ARE BAD

Good investments go bad with bad execution. Unknown or un-sexy investments can perform well with smarts and experience. Filter media hype or the daily publications that have little to no experience in the assets and businesses they comment on. Some of the best and consistently appreciating watches are the ones that look non-descript. Some of the best yielding properties are standard lower-end basic accommodation. Some very expensive art isn't necessarily the most technically skilled work. It is often best to observe the masses and then ignore them. Time, experience and learning from the best will give you the best investments with the best returns and likely the ones others overlook.

ASPIRE TO LEARN DEEPLY ABOUT THE CLASS YOU INVEST IN

Linked to the previous section, most of the returns and the money follow the very small percentage of investors and business owners who know the most. It is disproportionate. It is wise to have a main area of expertise, that you do long and deep and don't stop, and focus 70 per cent to 80 per cent or your time and investment in that niche, and then one or two secondary areas that you have passion in but aren't your day-to-day. If you have a partner you can leverage them and they can leverage you. I take stock recommendations from my business partner and he takes watch recommendations from me. He buys most of our property assets and I drive most of the strategy for our business-related assets. Our main niche is property, with education and lettings as our subsidiary niches and interests. There are dozens of models and classes we like the look of from the outside, but know when we're self-honest that they're beyond the scope of our time and experience. Stick to what you know and keep improving at it for 80 per cent of your time, and test and play and diversify only in the remaining 20 per cent (guide only, tweak percentages if desired).

COMPARE RETURNS AND BENEFITS AGAINST OTHER CLASSES AND OPPORTUNITIES

No asset classes are absolutely and definitely better or worse than others, all the time. Sure, some have the most history and sustainability, but all asset classes go through cycles. Some come and go. All go through peaks and troughs and cycles. Lending criteria, interest rates, currency fluctuations and regulations will all impact classes to varying degrees at differing times. Some people shorted the pound with Brexit, others made market bets on the US presidential candidacy, some bought into banks and higher-end supermarkets post-recession, some arbitraged currency when the pound weakened, but all of these strategies were short-term plays. Always look at an asset or investment class in relation to the other opportunities and opportunity costs out there. Factor in variables such as interest rates, fees, bank margins and your time as a cost. In 2016 watch prices got ridiculously high in my view. I had no selling plans for my entire life, but couldn't turn down some sales and trades as the profits were significant and I felt there may not be another chance for a decade or more. In 2016 the pound was so historically weak against the dollar that it aroused my interest in some investing areas I wouldn't normally entertain. Conversely in 2016 we were loaded with cash and ready to buy many commercial properties, but the stock just wasn't there. Leaving significant cash in the bank for a year can have a serious cost, so some of that capital got moved into other investments.

ALLOCATE AND RE-ALLOCATE ASSETS STRATEGICALLY

Again linked to the previous section, manage the allocation of your assets wisely. Too much liquidity when rates are low can cost you with both inflation and opportunity cost. Not enough cash when prices are low and you could miss some great buying opportunities.

Don't have all your capital or assets in one class as you could be over exposed. Don't have your asset allocation too thin that you lose out on leverage and compounding. When your portfolio of assets and businesses gets large enough, re-allocation or consolidation can have huge results. If you have a loan of £100 million at 4 per cent a year you're paying £4 million a year in interest. Get that down by just 1 per cent and you save £1 million a year in interest alone! That might be a better use of and return on time than getting £1 million of extra income or equity. Check in at least once a year that your asset allocation is weighted correctly for your strategy, vision and the current opportunities. If not review your portfolio and re- or de-leverage, focus more on capital or income, physical or non-physical, UK or overseas, short-term or long-term.

MERGE PASSION AND PROFESSION, HOBBY AND INVESTMENT

Are there any areas of investing you could see as a hobby and would enjoy doing? I have a good friend who enjoys Lego, and as such makes him well suited to invest in it. I have a passion for watches. My fiancée has a passion for handbags. Two out of those three have proven good investments to merge passion and profession! As I am interested in watches my knowledge will naturally increase as I enjoy the research, buying, valuing and exchanging. I enjoy the interaction with dealers and passionate collectors and tracking the prices back over time. I enjoy learning about the history of the brands and the heritage of the movements and technologies. I enjoy interviewing the CEOs of the world's best watchmakers for my podcast. If I just kept doing it as a hobby I'd have to be an idiot not to spot some common opportunities. What areas of business, investing and money could you see that you have a passion for? Art? Watches? Diamonds? Gold? Property? Stocks? Buying businesses? Jewellery? Antiques? Classic cars? Lego? It doesn't really matter, as long as you enjoy it, because you will find your way to the best knowledge and margins, even if it didn't pay.

TEST NEW INVESTMENTS AND INCOME STREAMS BEFORE SCALING

It is a mistake to go all in on one strategy before you have gained some experience and data, and overcome some challenges. *Be wary* of stories like Elon Musk's and Richard Dyson's who got down to their last pennies, or even got into debt to the tune of millions, and then succeeded big. This may be a glorified story, simplified for media, and for every one big success story where a superstar risked everything, there are likely hundreds who lost everything. *Do not* base your investing and business strategy on a one in a million chance. *Do not* scale up into newer, riskier speculations until you've gained some results and experience. *Do not* bet the house on a gamble. Test, tweak, review, redo, repeat. No one ever went bust risking money they could afford to lose.

More money management concepts

What is it that makes someone susceptible to schemes, scams and unrealistic get-rich-quick programmes? How can you spot the difference between genuine, secure passive income and the selling of a dream that can become a nightmare? In observing and serving more than 400,000 people in property and business development, the common threads of susceptibility to get rich quick schemes are:

1. **Being a newbie:** We all start somewhere. 'Every master was once a disaster' as one of my mentors used to tell me. Set a timeframe to just learn, learn, learn. Don't make any rash or important decisions for a few weeks or months. Just learn and watch and research and get a foundational level of knowledge. Pick out the go-to experts in the niche and follow their work. We are all the same when we start.

2. **Being naïve:** Sometimes people are too positive or optimistic and don't have the ability to take a sceptical view. Sometimes people have had an easier or more sheltered

357

upbringing, or have just done very well. Follow step one and look at the risks and downsides before you make any big decisions. Strive for balance of optimism and scepticism.

3. **Being desperate:** We are weaker, more vulnerable and susceptible to schemes and scams when we are desperate. We can become myopic and only look at the upsides. Take a step back, stay patient, get good counsel from smart and experienced people and cool your emotions or desperation before you enter or move into new niches and models.

4. **Lacking vision and values clarity:** If you are not clear on your vision and values, you will randomly take opportunities that come your way with no system or logic. You will follow and be a slave to your emotions and other's ability to persuade you. If you haven't already, follow the values and vision exercises in this book and in more detail in *Life Leverage*.

5. **Being greedy:** Be patient. Don't try to take too much, too soon. Balance realism and optimism. Don't look for progress at the expense of others.

6. **Comparing yourself to others:** It's easy to get distracted by what we perceive others are achieving. We often don't see the reality, much like a graceful swan who's legs are kicking wildly under the surface of the water. *People only compare themselves to others when they don't know who they are.* Do not make strategic decisions because of what you think others are doing or achieving. *Compare yourself to where you were in the past and where you want to be, for inspiration and motivation.*

Cashflow vs profit

Cashflow and profit are obviously not the same. Many start-ups and grown up businesses act like they don't know the difference, and that's dangerous for wealth building.

Cashflow is the net amount of cash and cash-equivalents moving in and out of a business. It can be positive or negative. Cashflow is a liquid asset that enables a company or person to settle debts, reinvest in its business, return money to shareholders, pay expenses and provide a buffer against future financial challenges. It includes retained profits not yet drawn down. Net cashflow includes accounts receivable and other items for which payment has not yet been received. Cashflow benchmarks the quality of a company's income and how liquid it is, indicating the solvency of a company.

Profit is how much money a business is making deducting all expenses. These expenses can be fixed and/or variable costs. Fixed costs remain the same for the short-term such as rent, fixed salaries, insurances and depreciation. Variable costs change month to month such as cost of sales, heating and marketing spend. Even a profitable business can fail if the business has an unbalanced cashflow.

A business or person may be profitable on paper, but have inadequate cash to pay immediate expenses. A company can be profitable yet insolvent. This can happen because most businesses allow a grace period between when goods or services are delivered and when they are paid. Some big, immediate and unexpected expenses, legal battles, debtors going bust or not paying, too much cash held in stock that doesn't sell and other unplanned cash events, can result in a company running out of cash.

Credit and Business Finance '(a 'mono line'' credit insurance broker, specializing in protecting companies against bad debts) identifies poor cashflow management as the main reason small businesses fail. Ensure you set up a cashflow forecast that will indicate where and when cash is coming in and when cash needs to be paid out. I receive a weekly statement produced within my businesses with a 'cash in bank' figure, creditors, debtors and retained profit amounts. There is a gross actual current 'cash in bank' figure and a net after reconciled amounts. We don't hold much stock but if we did I might request that be included. If we were 10× the size, held a lot of stock and had lower margins I might request this figure more frequently. This can be compared to previous years as a measure of progress and stability.

Evaluate payment terms to ensure there is not too much grace period or time lag between delivery and payment. Bringing payment forward can improve your cashflow. Having better systems, ensuring customers are paying on time and are good quality, using collections if necessary, and evaluating the profitability of customers and products, will all improve your cash position. Target cash flows as well as profits and watch your cash closely. For long-term products and delivery, monitor profitability closely. You could have good cashflow with big upfront fees that could be creating a loss down the line. Driving turnover that doesn't have a good profit margin can hide or delay solvency issues. In this regard not all money is profit.

Saving money or wasting time?

There's nothing wrong with making a living, as long as it isn't getting in the way of making a fortune. ROTI (return on time invested) is as important a metric as ROI (return on investment). All time has a financial measure (or ROI) in your business and life. No two units of time have the same value. If you are earning £50/hr it could be costing you £100/hr elsewhere. Time as well as money has an opportunity cost. You could get into diminishing law of returns where you end up spending a lot of time in an area that has diminishing monetary value to you. Technical, fearful or analytical people can get sucked into this. If you want free time, someone else has to manage your business affairs, and their time has a cost that you would have to invest to liberate you. Continue to measure your IGV (income generating value) every three or six months. Continually ask yourself hour-by-hour and day-by-day 'Is this the very best use of my time, right now, that could make the biggest difference to me in my life'? Delegate, delay or delete everything else.

47

Net-worth (measure and increase)

The ultimate, most accurate and absolute measurement of your money is your net-worth. You are paid exactly what you are worth. Where focus goes, energy flows and results show, yet most people don't measure their personal net-worth. The rich do, so that should tell you something about wealth. You can wait until you have money to measure, or you can start measuring your money now. The latter will drive the former.

I used to think about money much more when I was poor, constantly worrying about it and my lack of it. Because what you appreciate appreciates, my debt, worries and financial scarcity appreciated the more I thought about them. It consumed me. It affected my relationships. I remember having a girlfriend that had to pay for us to go out. I felt shamed and embarrassed by that, so much so that when I made some money, and after we had split up, I sent her a cheque and paid it all back. It upset her but she still cashed the cheque! I relied on my parents for work and housing into my mid-20s. There wasn't a day when I didn't worry about money. If I had put all those debt-ridden thoughts into planning and measuring my worth, over the eight years I lost my way financially, that could have amounted to 600 or more hours of time that could have been put to good use. Changing your focus from worrying about money and debt to measuring, targeting and scaling net-worth will have profoundly positive impacts across mindset and materials, emotions and outcomes. Your personal net-worth is measured as:

Total assets – total expenses

Total assets are all physical, cash, IP and saleable entities with equity. And total expenses are all debt and liabilities after depreciation.

Net-worth of your companies or properties might be:

Total market value capital – (total debt - liquidation costs)

Total market value capital is cash in bank, stock, other assets or total valuation of business, including any property values. Total debt is all mortgages, loans, depreciation and cost of liquidation of assets.

Personally, I do not add the value of my companies to my net-worth, because I don't have a sale strategy. Valuations can vary wildly and money is only money when it's in the bank. If I were to add the value of our companies to my personal net-worth statement, I may work out a valuation measurement that is accepted in our industry, for example EBITDA, then a multiplier of the measurement that seems realistic, and then take 20 per cent off as a contingency, and apportion the value according to my percentage shareholding. If you wanted to apportion your company value to your net-worth statement I recommend doing it at a realistically low valuation, and ring-fence it from the rest of your metrics.

Here are some net-worth exercises, routines and KPIs you will want to start and review every six months:

1 TOTAL NET-WORTH

Start with where you are now, even if it is low or even negative. Target an increased net-worth to a specific number every six months. I personally target every year, in the November before the year ahead, read at least weekly and then review every six months. I've created a vision and goals document to help you do this clearly: http://tiny.cc/RMgoals

Add all your assets and capital items with retained value (depreciated), and create a total. Subtract all your debt and liabilities.

2 CAPITAL TO ASSETS RATIO (LOAN TO VALUE)

Capital to assets ratio, or loan to value, is the amount of capital you have as a percentage of your overall assets. Banks are regulated by a similar metric known as CAR (Capital Adequacy Ratio) or CRAR (Capital to Risk Assets Ratio), which protects against low capital reserves. Your capital to assets ratio is your metric to measure leverage, exposure and debt ratios. You might start at 25 per cent capital to assets value. Target an increase to 35 per cent. Then 50 per cent. Once you get to 50 per cent, you might reduce your target if you have a plan to grow and re-invest in assets.

3 Monthly spend vs income percentage

The lower your monthly spend as a percentage of income, the more free you are financially. You have more room for growth, re-investment, opulence or protection from Irregular Shocks. Start where you are, and for some that will be more than 100 per cent. Target 90 per cent, 80 per cent, down to 50 per cent and then lower.

4 Living costs covered (LCC) timeframe (months)

Living costs covered (months) is the amount of months you could live without earning any extra money, active or passive. If your living expenses were £5,000 and you had £5,000 savings, your LCC is one month. Target an increase in LCC every six months to measure how financially free you are and how covered your pension and retirement is. When you have an LCC that will last a lifetime, provided you die next Tuesday, you know you are from Peterborough! Seriously though, when you hit an LCC that is longer than your lifetime, you know you have built a solid lifetime legacy to continue beyond you. If some tough financial events occurred, you and your family would be safe and sustained for life.

Exercises and affirmations

To increase your net-worth, here are some simple exercises and habits you can easily work into your routine. As it is wise to honour both the spiritual and material, some visual and affirmation practices will fit hand in hand with your net-worth planning and targeting. I recommend you do the following:

Personal affirmations

For 11 years I've been affirming ten words that link to the lifestyle, vision and person I want to become. I must confess to being a little skeptical at first, perhaps through lack of experience and my imagined stereotype of the kind of people who do affirmations. I am grateful to my former self that I decided to reserve judgment and test.

Affirmation originally meant 'to make steady, solid assurance, assertion that something is true, strengthen, and confirm'..You are not chanting or incanting like a hippy-maniac like me on my exercise bike or walking down Park Road, you are creating a solid foundation for, and asserting your goals to bring them to life.

Go over your values and the things you most want to attain, and who you want to become, and condense them into five to ten words. Words such as wealth, success, strength, happiness, gratitude, service, and so on could be useful to you. Once you have created these words, note them down in the goals and vision document I shared with you. Have them on your screensaver too. Perhaps laminate the list by your bed. Every night when you go to sleep, incant these a few times in your mind, visualizing an image to go with the words. Feel it in your body as well as saying it in your mind. Once you've done this for a few days or weeks, the words will be memorized forever, and your subconscious super-computer mind will go to work bringing them into material reality in your life. You could do these affirmations in the morning too, or when you want to get yourself in a good state or zone, or when you meditate, if that is part of your daily routine. Attraction without action is just a distraction, so you can't just sit in the house and expect these things to all come through the letterbox, but this is the ethereal to the material that you will set about in your day-to-day activities. I am still amazed to this day how few people set clear goals. Goal-setting is a commonality of successful people from athletes to entrepreneurs. Everybody knows how to set goals, yet most people don't do it. To know and not to do is not to know. So fill in, in full, the goals and vision document I've provided for you, and make this section a daily habit to turn your goals and vision into physical reality.

Create a vision board

To further affirm (make firm) your goals, create visual cues and 'primers' that can remind, guide and re-inspire your goals and vision daily. Creating a 'pride of place' space that displays what you want for your life and it will bring it to life. When you create a vision board and place it in a space where you see it often like on a wall, on your screensaver or on your phone, you essentially end up doing short visualization exercises throughout the day, often through your unconscious mind without even knowing it. It has been reported that the brain patterns activated when a weightlifter lifts heavy weights are also similarly activated when the lifter has simply imagined (visualized) lifting the weights.[1] Create a vision board and put pictures and quotes up that inspire you and are a visual form of your goals, vision and values. Science suggests it is important that the vision board makes you feel something, as we often forget things we see and hear, but rarely forget how they make us feel. This is yours, so add anything that inspires and motivates you and choose images that bring everything on it to life in your chosen areas of relationships, career and finances, home, travel, personal growth and health.

Prime your mind

When I was young, my dad used to say I was always good at finding money on the floor of the pub. He said I'd spot money anywhere, before anyone else. He said it so much that I believed it, and it became a reinforced reality. I truly believed it. But when I got into debt, I did the opposite, continually focusing on debt and worry. I reinforced it unknowingly, it became my reality, and I believed it. I didn't know then that this was 'priming'.

Priming is a memory effect in which exposure to one stimulus influences the response to another stimulus. The seminal experiments of Meyer and Schvaneveldt in the early 1970s and work which Cialdini has progressed further in his book *Pre-suasion*, explore how priming can influence the resulting behaviour or action.[2]

The Reticular Activating system (RAS) is the part of your brain that acts as a filter between your conscious and subconscious mind. At every given moment our nervous system is bombarded with information. We take in eight million bits of information at any one time, and the vast majority of that information we simply don't need or couldn't consciously handle. Your RAS takes it all in, but filters most of this out of your conscious attention. With priming, visualization and affirmation, you can literally programme your RAS, which works in pictures, not words. By following the steps in this section, you are feeding the RAS images to look out for, and it will start filtering images accordingly, paying attention to the things you have visually focused on, that previously would have been filtered out as irrelevant. The RAS will believe any message you give it, but the message will be much stronger if it is consistent and congruent with your self-image. When a stimulus is experienced, it is also primed. This means that the brain will process later experiences of the stimulus more quickly. So your vision board that evokes images and feelings of your vision and desired life, repeatedly in your conscious and unconscious mind through repetition on walls, pictures and devices, will be brought to life. The more you think about and act upon monetary ideas, decision and actions, the more it is primed. You bypass your conscious mind, and therefore the conscious critical thought processes like skepticism (not knowing the 'how' yet), excuses and limiting beliefs, and go straight to the unconscious super-computer that has more power than we humans can comprehend. Listening to audio, especially on 1.5× or 2× speed, has the same effect. If you don't have this book on audio yet, get it now. Programme your unconscious with audio books and podcasts and record your goals and affirmations on audio and listen back to them regularly. Bombard your RAS with money and wealth images, and it will unconsciously filter and focus on them for you. Mix this with consistent action, iteration and improvement, and there will be virtually no ceiling to your wealth, success and money.

How to be a multi-millionaire artist

When I was trying to forge a career as an artist, I couldn't get over my inner conflict that money and art didn't mix. Maybe you have your own vocational equivalent of art. The revelation that you can merge your passion and profession, and monetize a creative vocation while truly and freely expressing yourself, came late to me. It was a positive shock to learn that my self-worth was holding back my net-worth.

If I were to go back and start again as an artist, knowing all that I know now, and implementing the lessons from *Money*, here's how I might do art a little differently:

1 **Wealth while live/alive:** I give myself permission to make a handsome living and profit out of art. I am commited to fair exchange and valuing myself in my work. I will ignore all preconceived ideas that arty types don't or shouldn't make money, and you only make real money in art when you're dead. I see it as my duty to build wealth around my art to serve myself and others and live my legacy as a great artist to be remembered.

2 **Self-worth:** I'm worthy of wealth and riches. All my life's work brought me to be an artist. That has value that people will pay for. My worth must be reflected in my prices and service. My chosen profession that I love is an amazing way to express my unique value and talent.

3 **Marketing is money:** The world isn't going to hand me a living. I have to share my message with the world. I have to be proud without being cocky, and relentlessly promote my work while caring for others. Being the best artist is only part of the business of art. I need to communicate my value, uniqueness and what I stand for and against. I won't be scared of ruffling feathers as long as it is authentic to who I am. I need to balance scale and scarcity, always retaining my perceived value. Embrace all leveraged and networked media to get my work seen and my brand built. Be open to changing technology, don't just paint all day alone in my dark studio listening to Rammstein when I don't sell my work.

4 **Serve, solve and care:** I need to care about myself to let my passion overpower my fears, and care about others to give them work they want to pay fair and big money for. My commissions should be just what my clients want, having listened very carefully to their exact needs, and I should care about the small bespoke details and personalizations. I will overdeliver and then ask for referrals. I will listen to the problems my clients have and solve them through my work, knowing that this is *my* economy and it negates busts in *the* economy.

5 Fair exchange: I will give my clients a little more value than they pay for. I will choose a niche and customer type specifically, ideally with no price ceiling. I must continually grow and increase my value and prices. I must always do the right thing, solve customer issues and trust that the money will come in abundance. I will make sure I reinvest fair profits into marketing, growth and to my important charitable causes.

6 Leverage: I must value my time to the maximum and look to reduce my time for money exchange. I should consider print runs not just originals. Could I leverage others to paint my work? Could I produce digital art that has networked scale? Could I set up an artist training business or academy? I need to have systems and scalability and not be the typical one-man band artist. Can I find the best agents and gallery owners and not just sell my work alone, and give them a healthy share of the price. Get out of Peterborough and network with my best buyers and wealthy collectors, and get introductions to their friends and affluent contacts. Embrace all (social) media, brands and new innovations. Partnerships are vital; I should find a Mark Homer type business partner if I can, and look to have life-long agent friends like Jorge Mendes. Perhaps Damien Hirst might be my mentor?

7 Ignore the haters: There will always be critics and haters and I must know the difference. I will listen to those who give me feedback and look to consistently improve. I must be gracious with all critique and politely move on. I will not let critique affect my mood, vision or living legacy. I must follow my own path clearly and not get dragged down other people's. I must be grateful for all that I have: the good and the challenging.

8 Compounding: Keep on keeping on. I must keep my main thing my main thing and must not keep starting and stopping. I must be patient. Have faith, work hard *and* smart. Do my mantras and visioning daily, balance realistic and optimistic goals and targets, and allow compounding to build great momentum. More work is at the start and more money at the end. Then pass on my gift to others. Set up an art school or foundation. Enable those less fortunate to have a creative outlet, funded by capitalism. Teach my students the business of art like Warhol understood, and not just art.

There is nothing was wrong with art, and nothing was wrong with me, other than what I'd allowed myself to believe. I wasn't broken, and everything I wanted to be, do and have was latent within me, ready to be liberated and unleashed.

This is *you*. Be authentic. Be yourself. Don't be like I was as an artist. Unleash your latent hunger for what you love. Share it with the world with care and service but shameless persistence. Create your own story and psychology of money to know more, make more and give more.

48

So what are Ferrari drivers really like?

The 2005 Rob needed to pop out late at night. He turned off his German death metal, put on his hoodie and got on his bike to ride to the petrol station to get a £497 (inflation) loaf of bread. He was pretty depressed about life. As he 'parked' up he saw a red Ferrari 458 Spider pull in to fill up. The future Rob (let's call him Robert) got out and picked out the VPower fuel and filled up the red beast. It took about 15 minutes and £4744 to fill. As this was happening the 2005 Rob felt torn. He loved Italian supercars and had done since he was a young boy. He'd always dreamed of having one. This was his favourite model and colour, but this guy driving it *must* be a twat. Look at his suit. He must have nicked the car, rented it for the day or used drug money to buy it.

Should he talk to him, or go back and paint more? Just as this was going through his head, the future Rob looked over and smiled. 'Alright?' he said. 2005 Rob sheepishly walked over and said, 'Nice car mate'. Robert (future Rob) humbly replied 'Thank you'. They got talking. They both had boyhood passions for cars, both had dreamed about having the new Ferrari, but only one of them had crashed one. Rob was looking at getting into property, and Robert had just moved into a new house that he was revamping and wanted some bespoke art. As the fuel nozzle clicked, Robert asked Rob for a card. They shook hands and Rob went to get his loaf of bread. As he went to pay for his bread, Rob thought to himself, 'That guy wasn't as big a twat as I thought. And even if he is, if he buys a load of my art I am sure I can like him. Maybe he has some rich mates too?' Robert paid at the pump, drove off and crashed his Ferrari right into the News International building.

Who knows where this encounter leads? Perhaps Robert commissions Rob for some bespoke pieces of art. Perhaps Robert gets

Rob into property, becomes his mentor and changes the course of his life? Perhaps Rob becomes wealthy, keeps art as a hobby and sets up schools and foundations to help other young, aspiring artists and entrepreneurs? Perhaps the 2005 Rob even becomes the future Robert?

How do you define someone who is rich? Can you judge or stereotype them? Is it the car they drive? Is it if they have made a million? Or are a net-worth millionaire? Perhaps being a millionaire in future inflation-adjusted years isn't rich anymore? Perhaps billionaire is the new millionaire? Every person I know whom others would define as rich, I'd define as wealthy. Every one of them honours their unique abilities. Every one of them has wrestled with and overcome their fears and the challenges that now drive them. Every one of them is a producer. Every one of them serves vast numbers of people. Every one of them has a healthy respect for money. Every one of them supports philanthropic causes.

But almost everything else is different: age, sex, geography, upbringing, niche, model, media, ethos, values and personality type. No two wealthy people are the same, which means there's space for us all. If one person can be wealthy, anyone can be wealthy, and you can be wealthy.

So what are Ferrari drivers like? They are like all wealthy people: unique individuals. There are flash ones and subtle ones, loud ones and humble ones, rich ones and can-only-just-afford-them ones, enthusiastic ones, boyhood dream achiever ones, and ones who can't drive them at all well. You can't define Ferrari drivers. You can't define the rich. But you can define you.

Why not learn from them? Education saved my life, when I got out of my own way and let go of most of my poor judgments. The world needs better education, and much more of it. There are many people who don't have easy access to good education, but you do. The monetary systems have good intentions in redistributing money, but it isn't just money that is needed. In fact, money given to poor knowledge can make a situation worse. It is for this reason that many of the titans of wealth have founded and funded universities, libraries and foundations. It is for this reason that Bill and Melinda Gates set up their foundation, and Warren Buffett backed it with billions. It is my personal vision to create smart financial education and wealth across the globe. Contact me if you'd like to help or contribute to create more financial independence and education across the globe.

Money is the force and universal exchange for all good in the world. It fuels and finances all growth and evolution. It is a measure of merit and a mechanism and measure of value. Money converts creativity and individual expression into production. Money is care and service connecting communities and societies. It funds and accelerates all innovation and solves the world's biggest problems. Money balances selfish and selfless interests and could be one of the greatest inventions of man.

Money was created in the image of mankind and how you manage and master money will be in the image of you and will remain in your immortal legacy. Value your life's work like Picasso did. Merge your art and your business like Warhol and Hirst did. You now know the story and psychology of money. You now know more. Now it's up to you to make more and give more like the titans of wealth did.

What are you going to do now?

The two most important laws of money have been saved right to the very end. The laws of:

1 GOYA (get off your arse (or ass))
2 JFDI (just F'in do it!)

When all is said and done, more is said than done and to know and not to do is not to know, so just go.

Go and make tonnes of money. Go and serve others at a much bigger level. Go and create your ideal vision, and live your values using money as leverage. Go and make a difference on this planet. Go and use money as a force for and the root of all good. Go and create something meaningful that lives beyond you.

This is the beginning of a very exciting road. The rest is up to you. I'm grateful to be a small part in your road to riches, I am here for you in my online communities, podcasts and anywhere else you can find me. You can follow and contact me here, send me a message, write a review on Amazon, pose me a question or have a good rant: www.facebook.com/robmooreprogressive

You can also add me on twitter @robprogressive

I believe in you, my friend. I hope that we will talk in the future and you will be telling me your stories of action, leverage and wealth.

I have faith that you are one of the doers and not the talkers. Get perfect later. Just keep moving forward, persist in taking action towards your goal and you will achieve great things in your life despite setbacks. Think big, start small. Start now.

'It's easy to do, but also easy not to do.'

I hope you choose the easy part ;-)

I promised gifts at the start of this book. One of them is shared twice in the book, just in case you came right to the end to get it first ;-) Here they all are:

- The goals and vision document:
  http://tiny.cc/RMGoals
- 'The Disruptive Entrepreneur' podcast:
  http://bit.ly/disentpodcast
- The most beneficial/leveraged apps I use:
  http://tiny.cc/RobsApp
- My favourite biographies/documentaries:
  http://tiny.cc/Robdocs

If you think this book could help people you care about, please recommend it to them. Share the gift of knowing, making and giving more money to those you care about. Someone cared about me enough in 2005, and recommended a book to me that changed my life completely. I wasn't really a reader back in 2005, and Mike Wildman who owned a gallery that hung some of my art, persisted to get me to read *Think and Grow Rich* by Napoleon Hill.

Wow. That book shook me but inspired me. Thank you, Mike. I will always remember that moment. Please share that gift with others so together we can make a difference.

Notes

Chapter 6

1 Sam Parr, 'The fastest self-made billionaires', The Hustle, 24 November 2015, accessed at: https://thehustle.co/fastest-self-made-billionaires

2 Amy Loddington, 'Payment phobia more common than fear of spiders', Financial Reporter, 5 June 2013, accessed at: http://www.financialreporter.co.uk/finance-news/payment-phobia-more-common-than-fear-of-spiders.html

3 'Brits reluctant to use contactless credit cards', MoneyExpert, 19 May 2011, accessed at: https://www.moneyexpert.com/news/brits-reluctant-use-contactless-credit-cards-800549506/

4 Jeff Desiardins, 'The shift to a cashless society is snowballing', Visual Capitalist, 17 May 2016, accessed at: http://www.visualcapitalist.com/shift-cashless-society-snowballing/

5 Simon Champ, 'Banks should be afraid, the disruption of financial services has only just begun', The Telegraph, 22 August 2015, accessed at: http://www.telegraph.co.uk/finance/newsbysector/banksandfinance/11818325/Banks-should-be-afraid-the-disruption-of-financial-services-has-only-just-begun.html

6 Kevin Kelly, The Inevitable (Viking Press, 2016)

7 You can find the interview with Kevin Kelly on 'The Disruptive Entrepreneur' podcast, episode 52: http://bit.ly/disentpodast

Chapter 7

1 From 'Money can buy happiness', *The Economist*, 2 May 2013, accessed at: https://www.economist.com/blogs/graphicdetail/2013/05/daily-chart-0

Chapter 8

1 Kevin Murphy, 'Powerball winners live modestly, give back to hometown,' Reuters, 23 February 2013, accessed at: http://www.reuters.com/article/us-usa-lottery-missouri-idUSBRE91M0CB20130223

2 Thomas Piketty, *Capital* (Harvard University Press, 2013)

Chapter 9

1 Mervyn King, *The End of Alchemy: Money, Banking and the Future of the Global Economy* (Little, Brown, 2016)

2 Data taken from https://coinmarketcap.com/currencies/

Chapter 11

1 Emmie Martin and Tanza Loudenback, 'The 20 most generous people in the world', Business Insider, 12 October 2015, accessed at: http://uk.businessinsider.com/most-generous-people-in-the-world-2015-10

Chapter 12

1 Definitions from http://www.etymonline.com/ and dictionary.com

Chapter 13

1 Ann Saphir, 'Fed survey highlights widening US wealth, income gap', Reuters, 4 September 2014, accessed at: http://uk.reuters.com/article/us-usa-fed-consumers-idUKKBN0GZ2DU20140904

Chapter 14

1 Smriti Bhagat, Moira Burke, Carlos Diuk, Ismail Onur Filz, Sergey Edunov, 'Three and a half degrees of separation', Facebook Research, 4 February 2016, accessed at: https://research.fb.com/three-and-a-half-degrees-of-separation/

Chapter 15

1 George Silverman, *The Secrets of Word-of-Mouth Marketing: How to Trigger Exponential Sales Through Runaway Word of Mouth* (Amacom, 2011)

Chapter 16

1 John Demartini, *The Riches Within: Your Seven Secret Treasures* (Hay House, 2008)

Chapter 17

1 Quote from 'Capitalism: An A–Z of businesss quotations', *The Economist*, 6 July 2012, accessed at: https://www.economist.com/blogs/schumpeter/2012/07/z-business-quotations
2 Mervyn King, *The End of Alchemy: Money, Banking and the Future of the Global Economy* (Little, Brown, 2016)

Chapter 21

1 Catherine Clifford '62 per cent of American billionaires are self-made' 4 January 2016, accessed at: https://www.entrepreneur.com/article/269593

2 Thomas J. Stanley, 'America: Where Millionaires are Self-Made' 6 May 2014, accessed at: http://www.thomasjstanley.com/2014/05/america-where-millionaires-are-self-made/

3 David J. Lieberman, *The Science of Happiness: How to Stop the Struggle and Start Your Life* (Gildan Media, 2013)

Chapter 22

1 'Financial stress may cause heart attack, back pain and migraines' Sify News, 9 April 2012, accessed at: http://www.sify.com/news/financial-stress-may-cause-heart-attack-back-pain-and-migraines-news-health-me3lOgjhadhsi.html

2 *Ibid.*

3 David Mielach, 'How Worrying About Money Affects Your Health', Business News Daily, 25 April 2012, accessed at: http://www.businessnewsdaily.com/2419-money-worry-health.html

4 'A dozen shocking personal finance statistics', Business Insider, 22 June 2011, accessed at: http://www.businessinsider.com/a-dozen-shocking-personal-finance-statistics-2011-5?IR=T

5 J.R. Thorpe, 'Why do we envy others? Things to know about the psychology of feeling green', 22 July 2016, accessed at: https://www.bustle.com/articles/174232-why-do-we-envy-others-7-things-to-know-about-the-psychology-of-feeling-green

6 From Gregory L. Morris, *Investing with the Trend: A Rules-Based Approach to Money Management* (Bloomberg Press, 2014)

7 Cyril Chern, *The Commercial Mediator's Handbook* (Routledge, 2015)

Chapter 24

1 Accessed at: http://tim.blog/2007/09/18/real-mind-control-the-21-day-no-complaint-experiment/

Chapter 25

1 Rob Moore, *Life Leverage* (Progressive Property Ltd, 2016)

Chapter 27

1 Data from: http://www.bowker.com/products/servbusi_default.shtm

Chapter 28

1 Richard Branson, posted on LinkedIn, 24 February 2014, accessed at: https://www.linkedin.com/pulse/20140224234637-204068115-best-advice-protect-the-downside

2 Quoted in Kathleen Elkins, '11 things to give up if you want to be a millionaire', CNBC, 11 May 2017, accessed at: http://www.cnbc.com/2017/05/11/things-to-give-up-if-you-want-to-be-a-millionaire.html

3 Drake Baer, '9 books billionaire Warren Buffet thinks everyone should read', Business Insider, 2 September 2014, accessed at: http://uk.businessinsider.com/warren-buffett-favorite-business-books-2014-8?r=US&IR=T

4 Libby Kane, 'What rich people have next to their beds', Business Insider, 17 June 2014, accessed at: http://uk.businessinsider.com/rich-people-read-self-improvement-books-2014-6

5 Tom Corley, 'How many books does the average self-made millionaire read?' RichHabits.net, accessed at: http://richhabits.net/how-many-books-does-the-average-self-made-millionaire-read/

6   From Marguerite Ward, '7 Habits of highlight success-
    ful people, from a man who spent 5 years studying them',
    CNBC, 29 November 2016, accessed at: http://www.cnbc.
    com/2016/11/29/7-habits-of-highly-successful-people-
    from-a-man-who-spent-5-years-studying-them.html?view
    =story&%24DEVICE%24=native-android-mobile

7   From Richard Feloni, 'After interviewing more than 50 of
    Wall Street's best investors, Tony Robbins found the best
    investing advice for average people is remarkably sim-
    ple', Business Insider, 2 March 2017, accessed at: http://
    uk.businessinsider.com/tony-robbins-investing-advice-
    warren-buffett-jack-bogle-2017-3?r=US&IR=T

8   From Kathleen Elkins, '13 habits of self-made millionaires,
    from a man who spent 5 years studying rich people',
    Business Insider, 17 March 2016, accessed at: http://uk.
    businessinsider.com/habits-of-self-made-millionaires-
    2016-3?r=US&IR=T

9   Catherine Clifford, '62 per cent of American billionaires are
    self-made' 4 January 2016, accessed at: https://www.entre-
    preneur. com/article/269593

10 Nathan McAlone, 'Here's how much tech giants like Apple
    and Google make per employee', Business Insider, 6 Octo-
    ber 2016, accessed at: http://uk.businessinsider.com/
    top-tech-companies-revenue-per-employee-2015-10

Chapter 35

1   From 'Why did the US abandon the Gold Standard?' Mental
    Floss, 5 October 2012, accessed at: http://mentalfloss.com/
    article/12715/why-did-us-abandon-gold-standard

2   Ed Prior, 'How much gold is there in the world?', BBC
    News, 1 April 2013, accessed at: http://www.bbc.co.uk/
    news/magazine-21969100

3   Data from 'Forbes World's Billionaires 2012', 7 May 2012,
    accessed at: https://www.forbes.com/sites/luisakroll/2012/
    03/07/forbes-worlds-billionaires-2012/#719403f32c9d

Chapter 36

1 From http://ultimateclassicrock.com/eric-clapton-tears-in-heaven/

Chapter 37

1 Richard Koch, *The 80/20 Principle: The Secret of Achieving More with Less* (Nicholas Brealey Publishing, 1997)

Chapter 38

1 Kevin Palmer, 'How Cristiano Ronaldo can earn more than to €230,000 per tweet', *Irish Independent*, 13 July 2017, accessed at: http://www.independent.ie/sport/soccer/other-soccer/how-cristiano-ronaldo-can-earn-more-than-230000-per-tweet-31502936.html

Chapter 39

1 Elizabeth Dwoskin, 'Study: Digital Marketing Industry worth $62 billion', *The Wall Street Journal*, 14 October 2013, accessed at: https://blogs.wsj.com/digits/2013/10/14/study-digital-marketing-industry-worth-62-billion/

Chapter 41

1 From care2.com, '10 things unhappy people have in common', 7 July 2013, accessed at: http://www.care2.com/greenliving/10-things-unhappy-people-have-in-common-2.html

Chapter 44

1 Data from https://www.bls.gov/oes/2012/may/oes272021. htmand http://work.chron.com/salaries-pro-boxers-30165. html

2 Data from: https://one-400.com/5-of-the-richest-lawyers-in-america/

3 Mary Ellen Biery, 'The 10 fastest-growing industries in small business 2015', Forbes, 14 June 2105, accessed at: https://www.forbes.com/sites/sageworks/2015/06/14/the-10-fastest-growing-industries-in-small-business/#13a30f2141fd

4 Mark Homer, *Uncommon Sense: The Popular Misconceptions of Business, Investing and Finance and How to Profit by Going Against the Tide* (John Murray Learning, 2017)

5 Martha T.S. Laham 2016, '7 unromantic facts about online dating', The Huffington Post, 21 November 2015, accessed at: http://www.huffingtonpost.com/martha-ts-laham-/onine-dating-tips_b_8568126.html

6 'American companies with the most customers', *The Wall Street Journal*, 30 April 2012, accessed at: http://247wallst.com/special-report/2012/04/30/american-companies-with-the-most-customers/2/

7 Data from: https://www.forbes.com/forbes/welcome/?to URL=https://www.forbes.com/companies/lego-group/&refURL=https://www.google.co.uk/&referrer=https://www.google.co.uk/

8 Madeline Berg, 'The highest-paid comedians 2016: Kevin Hart dethrones Jerry Seinfeld as cash king of comedy with $87.5 million payday', Forbes, 26 September 2016, accessed at: https://www.forbes.com/sites/maddieberg/2016/09/27/the-highest-paid-comedians-2016-kevin-hart-out-jokes-jerry-seinfeld-with-87-5-million-payday/

9 Data from: http://www.nexogy.com/blog/so-what-happens-in-an-internet-minute and http://archive.jsonline.com/business/wireless-technology-forums-aim-to-go-beyond-jargon-b99266272z1-259664851.html/

10 '11 Recession-proof businesses you can start now', Insider Monkey, 4 June 2015, accessed at: http://www.insider-monkey.com/blog/11-recession-proof-businesses-you-can-start-now-351593

11 Rob Moore, *Multiple Streams of Property Income* (Progressive Property Ltd, 2013)

Chapter 46

1 Roger Connell, 'Downsizing? Ditch these items', The Apopka Voice, 23 October 2016, accessed at: http://theapopkavoice.com/downsizing-ditch-these-items/

2 'Financial statistics that will shock you', Financial One, 112 December 2016, accessed at: http://financialonecreditunion.blogspot.co.uk/2016/12/

3 'The gap between savers and non-savers is widening', Scottish Widows, accessed at: http://www.scottishwidows.co.uk/knowledge-centre/savings/saver-nonsaver-gap-widens.html

4 Belinda Robinson, 'At least 9m people don't have any savings, and those that do are feeling the impact of low rates on their nest egg', This is Money, 6 March 2014, accessed at: http://www.thisismoney.co.uk/money/saving/article-2574646/At-9m-people-not-savings-feeling-impact-low-rates-nest-egg.html

5 Neal Gabler, 'The secret shame of middle-class Americans', The Atlantic, May 2016, accessed at: https://www.theatlantic.com/magazine/archive/2016/05/my-secret-shame/476415/,

Chapter 47

1 Zack Miller, 'Goal setting and expectations: strategies for setting and achieving your goals', LivePlan, 26 October 2016, accessed at: https://www.liveplan.com/blog/2016/10/goal-setting-expectations-strategies-setting-achieving-goals/

2 Robert Cialdini, *Pre-Suasion: A Revolutionary Way to Influence and Persuade* (Simon & Schuster, 2016)

Index

Enjoy Money? Then try

THE MONEY PODCAST

You read this book, so you're clearly looking for more from life. The Money Podcast will dive into how to make, manage and master money. Rob will call upon his contacts and interview millionaires, billionaires, economists and money masters from all walks of life.

The Money Podcast is for anyone who wants to make more money in a job, profession or passion, for money masters and money disasters. They say money doesn't make you happy, Rob says "It does!".

Subscribe today.

Featured episodes:

#2 Reasons you owe it to yourself to be rich

#9 The easiest way to teach your kids about money

#11 Is being materialistic really that bad?

#12 How to get a (significant) pay rise

Find out more at <u>www.stitcher.com/podcast/progressiveproperty/the-money-podcast</u>

Also available from Rob Moore

You are just one small step away from the life you know you deserve.
It's time to leverage your life.

Life Leverage means taking control of your life, easily balancing your work and free time, making the most money with the minimum time input & wastage, and living a happier and more successful life. Using Rob Moore's remarkable Life Leverage model, you'll quickly banish & outsource all your confusion, frustration and stress & live your ideal, globally mobile life, doing more of what you love on your own terms.

Paperback: 9781473640283
Ebook: 9781473640290

For more information, please visit
www.hodder.co.uk